THE ASTONISHED MUSE

The astonished Muse finds thousands at her side

RALPH WALDO EMERSON
"Ode, Inscribed to W. H. Channing"

THE ASTONISHED MUSE

By Reuel Denney

THE UNIVERSITY OF CHICAGO PRESS

THE UNIVERSITY OF CHICAGO PRESS, CHICAGO 60637
THE UNIVERSITY OF CHICAGO PRESS, LTD., LONDON

Published 1957. Midway Reprint with new Foreword 1974
Printed in the United States of America

ISBN: 0-226-14303-1   LC Card No.: 57-6985

In memory of Sunday evenings
with
SIDNEY AND ALICE COX

Table of Contents

Foreword 1974

BY JOHN G. CAWELTI

Reuel Denney's *The Astonished Muse* was one of those books that made a great difference for me, because, for better or worse, it helped turn me into a student of popular culture. I well remember my feeling of delight and recognition when I first read this book over fifteen years ago. Recently, I decided to go back and reread Denney's work, being somewhat curious to see whether *The Astonished Muse* had become a tired old lady, or whether after a decade and a half some of her vitality and provocativeness remained. I was gratified to discover that there were a few things which, after fifteen years of study, I think I understand more fully than Mr. Denney did in 1957, but only a few. On the whole, I found the book as lively and fascinating as ever with many fresh insights to offer that I had not been able to grasp and appreciate when I first encountered it. It is still one of the two or three best analyses of contemporary popular culture we have, as useful today as when it originally appeared. Therefore, I am delighted that the University of Chicago Press has decided to bring out this new edition.

At the time of its original publication in 1957, the most important theme of *The Astonished Muse* was Denney's insistence that the popular arts "cannot be discussed simply by reference to their producers, messages and audiences; they deserve also to be discussed in terms of the artistic or conventional forms that make it possible or even probable that they will have this or that effect upon their audiences" (From Denney's 1963 Afterword to a new edition of *The Astonished Muse*). The extent to which this principle has become a basic assumption in recent studies of popular culture may well obscure the degree to which it was a controversial notion when Denney constructed his book around it. With certain notable exceptions such as the work of Gilbert Seldes, James Agee, and

Robert Warshow in America and Q.D. and F. R. Leavis and their followers in England, the popular arts were until the 1960s largely the province of reviewers, mass communications researchers, social psychologists and fans. As far as most humanistic critics, scholars, and aestheticians were concerned, the popular arts were examples of mass culture or of low-brow and middlebrow tastes which, however interesting as instances of the mental and spiritual limitations of the majority of the public, were not an appropriate object of serious and sympathetic critical scrutiny. Denney was one of the first important academicians to challenge this set of attitudes, not only by his explicit statements, but by the sympathetic and complex insights embedded in his own discussions of such major popular forms as football, science fiction, the comic strip, television comedy and hot-rod car cults. Nobody who read Denney's discussion of the evolution of American football in "The Decline of Lyric Sport" or his analysis of "Li'l Abner" and "Pogo" in "Children of Thoth" could come away without the realization that these were indeed cultural forms of striking complexity and significance and that their full understanding and appreciation required experience, knowledge, and imagination.

Denney's book can be seen in retrospect as a prototype of two new streams in American criticism and scholarship which have become increasingly important since the middle 1960s. The first is the development of a new kind of journalistic criticism of the popular arts informed by a richer consideration of the social and artistic context of these arts than the traditional newspaper or magazine review. The analysis of cultural forms, fads, and fashions by Tom Wolfe and other exponents of the so-called new journalism; the film criticism of Pauline Kael; the criticism of popular music exemplified in *Rolling Stone*—all show a real debt to the kind of analysis developed in *The Astonished Muse*. The other stream—the recent development of an academic field of popular culture studies which has begun to provide a historical and theoretical base for our understanding of the popular arts—obviously owes a great deal to Denney's pioneering work. It is appropriate that one of the major products of this new scholarship—Russel B. Nye's *The Unembarrassed Muse*—echoes Denney's title.

Significant as it is as a basic document that reflects an early stage in the development of new methods and attitudes in the study of art and culture, *The Astonished Muse* also retains its usefulness for the contemporary reader because it deals effectively with issues and problems which have yet to be resolved. While a number of scholars and critics have, I think, gone beyond Denney in developing more precise and sophisticated methods of structural analysis and have explored more fully the aesthetics of popular culture, there remain two major areas where our thinking has not significantly advanced beyond *The Astonished Muse*. In these areas, Denney's work is still one of the best intellectual springboards for future inquiry.

First of all, there is the problem of finding the right balance between the aesthetic and the sociological in the interpretation of popular culture. Popular culture is art, but it is art which is peculiarly involved with the tastes and attitudes of the public. It is, of course, quite possible to treat individual examples of the popular arts purely as works of art, largely ignoring any careful empirical inquiry into the cultural or artistic implications of their popularity. In fact, many of the most valuable recent studies have developed the aesthetic dimension of popular culture without much concern for the sociological. This tendency, partly inspired by Denney's own insistence on this aspect of the subject, has now reached the point where a new integration between formal analysis and empirical studies of audiences and systems of production would be highly desirable. Aesthetic analysis has produced a great many speculative hypotheses about the cultural meaning and function of different types of popular culture, but there is as yet little substantiation of these hypotheses in the form of quantitative data about the behavior of creators and audiences. In part, this is because the humanist and the sociologist commonly experience great difficulty in reconciling their different purposes. The sociologist is ultimately most interested in firm generalizations about the behavior of groups, while the humanist works toward the definition and understanding of the unique particularity of individual works. Obviously no final integration between these different intellectual goals is possible, but as they pass each other in their different directions, the humanist and the sociologist have a vital middle area of interdisciplinary concern, particularly in popular culture studies. Here, the trained humanist critic can provide the sociologist with richer and more complex conceptions of the forms and varieties of artistic expression, so that the latter's generalizations will ultimately be less characterized by reductionism and oversimplification. On the other hand, the sociologist can offer the humanistically oriented student of popular culture a more precise account of the behavior of audiences and of the social organization of popular culture so that in the end his analysis of the special qualities of individual creations is informed by a better understanding of the dialectic between work, audience, and the network of production and distribution. Few analysts of popular culture have worked as effectively as Reuel Denney in this middle area. His skill at integrating aesthetic and sociological considerations gives us many suggestive patterns of analysis for further exploration.

Finally, *The Astonished Muse* makes an important contribution to another area of cultural analysis: the role of different media. Like Marshall McLuhan, Denney is much concerned with the cultural impact of the new media of film and television, but where McLuhan's brilliant observations on the character of different media so often seem hyperbolic and enigmatic because he tends to interpret every cultural phenomenon as a medium, Denny tries to analyze the relationship between media, artistic forms, and sociological factors. In doing so, he develops a set of distinctions that may turn out to be as important to the understanding of media as the McLuhanesque categories of oral, print, and electronic modes of communication. I refer to Denney's conception of spectatorial, participatory, and literalist modes of cultural activity. These basic distinctions are more than any others the organizing concepts of *The Astonished Muse*, and, while they have important aesthetic and sociological implications, they also represent a means of categorizing the many diverse forms of mediation between people and the objects of their culture. Denney suggests, for example, that we can trace important changes in popular culture by examining the different balance between spectatorial, participatory, and literalist modes of involvement in different areas and in the culture as a whole at different periods. This seems to me an extremely promising approach for further inquiries into popular culture, particularly since it suggests a coherent way of moving beyond our present study of those types of popular culture which most resemble traditional art forms to the examination of such complex forms as games, parties, the news, advertising, shopping, camping, and eating, which cannot be very effectively understood by systems of analysis which derive from the essentially spectatorial tradition of aesthetic analysis. Readers will find many puzzles about this method of analysis which Denney does not fully resolve, but it remains one of the most suggestive attempts at a general theory of popular culture which we have. Therefore, *The Astonished Muse* deserves to be attended to, further developed, and criticized by anyone interested in the fuller understanding of popular culture.

Introduction 1964

BY DAVID RIESMAN

I first met Reuel Denney when I went to live in Buffalo where he was teaching high school twenty-five years ago. We were brought together by Walter Curt Behrendt, an architect and city planner; and I was reminded of this by reading in *The Astonished Muse* the chapter entitled "The Suppliant Skyscrapers," with its sometimes far-fetched and always fascinating discussion of what he calls "the rhetoric of architecture," especially corporate architecture, and his discussion of the way in which the skyscraper began by concentrating its richness at the top (with urns and battlements to be seen there by the top people), whereas today in the Lever House or Seagram Building, the invitation is more democratically extended at the bottom, merging outsiders and insiders—a lovely example of the arabesques of Reuel Denney's thinking. In Buffalo not only did we meet architects and city planners, but in turn, through the Denneys and in company with them, we met a

---

° *In Praise of Adam*, poems by Reuel Denney, University of Chicago Press, 1961.

number of the younger painters, sculptors, and literary folk of
Buffalo—an avant-garde group who, because of the structure
of this industrial city, for the most part absentee-owned, all
knew each other and also knew society people. In larger metropolitan centers, artists, writers, intellectuals, and professional
people would each have found their own specialist coteries;
but in Buffalo there was the great advantage of knowing people in many fields. In those Depression days, Denney and I
used to play tennis (a sport whose pleasures are beautifully
captured in his poem, "Tennis in San Juan," in *In Praise of
Adam*) in the covered courts in the vacant part of a Dunlop
plant; en route to it we enjoyed the spectacle of Buffalo's Lake
Erie industrial waterfront, whose dramatic beauty escaped
most of the city's residents.

Denney was teaching at that time at a technical high school
and writing poetry—some of it recently collected and published. He was the first person I have met who, in teaching
English literature to non-college-bound boys, tried at once to
move within their *lingua franca* of popular culture and to
bring them within his own high culture. From his example I
have for many years tried to interest secondary school teachers
in experimenting with similar devices which would begin with
the materials of everyday life the students bring with them—
the TV dramas, the comic books, the movies, and so on—and
try to make them more critical of this material in terms applic-
able also to what they might read in Shakespeare or Dickens.
Denney himself was aware at the time of many of the dangers
latent in such a procedure: that the teacher might move down
to his students' level without having any influence on their
tastes; that excessive generosity toward banality and triviality
might support the complacency of students rather than challenge their aspirations; and that in fact a vocabulary could not
be found to refine sensibilities through working with unre-
deemable popular material. Yet it is conceivable that such a
program might begin to make a bridge between the genteel
culture of many high school English teachers and the vulgar

anti-culture of the mass media and the street. This gap in turn reflects the most basic chasm—that between men and women —for in American society boys are supposed to escape the socializing efforts of mothers and school marms, aunts and sissies, settlement house workers and preachers, while girls often do well in English, admit to liking poetry, and move out of the working class by becoming schoolteachers. Some male teachers try to bridge the gap through sports or through talk of baseball and the other low-brow pursuits of many intellectuals, just as many writers bridge the gap by describing it, as Mark Twain did so superbly in *Huckleberry Finn*. Denney could manage all that. But he could be infinitely more inventive, as this book may help to show, by his willingness to assume that new forms of mass media can be treated on exactly the same level of critical seriousness as more traditional ones. And this generosity, this catholicity, was evident in his relation to students both as a high school teacher and later, when we were colleagues together in the College at the University of Chicago where many students at all levels of academic performance responded to his engaging curiosity.

Denney is one of the few people in American academic life who has taught both in the humanities and in the social sciences. At Chicago and later he has been principally identified with the latter, perhaps in part because of his departmental association and perhaps because his orientation, as this book makes clear, leaves him basically dissatisfied with the New Criticism and with other such canons of exclusion—especially insofar as they represent, in our hopefully democratic society, the academicians' need to mark themselves off from each other and from the untutored laity. Moreover, Denney's modesty hides his subtlety from some of his literary colleagues.

But this same modesty does occasionally interpose paradoxical barriers between him and audiences who are less sophisticated. For he assumes that everyone can follow his allusions and understandings. Consider, for example, the sheer richness of materials entering into *The Astonished Muse:* the poetry and poverty of advertising; the frontier traditions of American sociability; the socialization of taste in young and old, rich, poor, and bohemian; populism and pastoral in the comics; the qualitative differences between watching a movie and a TV variety show, along with the impact of specific trade union practices on the tiresome documentary realism of these media; the economy of means in Marcel Marceau; the "training" of audiences for football, popular singers, and wrestling; the hot-rod cult seen as a Veblenian satire on Detroit; the quandaries of science fiction and such precursors as Plato, Thomas More, and Milton's *Paradise Lost;* the monumentality of the pyramids compared with that of the modern city, seen vicariously in film or fiction; and a panoply of questions, periodically returned to, concerning how Americans can absorb abundance with grace, joy, and differentiation. This extraordinary gamut of materials is not compartmentalized. Not that Denney does not make critical judgments: he regards fictional distance as being preferable to intransigent realism, irony as preferable to portentousness, invitations to learning as superior to snobbish barriers and obscurities. His own occasional obscurities, as I have suggested, are unintended and spring from his modest assumption that others can see what he sees. And this same assumption leads him, in my own less sanguine judgment, to overestimate the perceptiveness of American audiences, even if he does not overestimate the multiplicity of symbolic meanings that are in some sense "there" and available to them.

It is not uncommon among intellectuals to patronize lowbrow amusements and to be knowledgeable especially about earlier versions such as Dixieland jazz, the Marx Brothers movies, and Ty Cobb's baseball prowess. Much more rare is Denney's willingness to appreciate middle-brow enjoyments. He lacks entirely the spirit of so many self-made American intellectuals who feel that they must demonstrate their superiority to the lower-middle class world of lace curtain taste out of which they have come, and identify themselves on the taste ladder with the aristocracy (which in turn in gentry fashion can patronize the peasant or the working-class folk arts), failing to see the humor of rejections which, had they been iron-clad, would have found no place for the nouveau snob himself.

Denney's appreciation for middle-class and even lower-middle-class values separates him sharply from other, more polemical critics of popular culture such as Leslie Fiedler or Paul Goodman who (whatever their non-violent political beliefs) are sometimes drawn especially to the violent strands in lower-class life and mythology which can be seen as protests against middle-class hypocrisy and repression. In his geniality and tolerance, his critical preference for Walt Kelly over, let us say, Charles Addams, he is out of step with contemporary intellectual modes; the poetry he continues to write often exhibits a whimsical and gently ironic character, a complex combination of the vernacular and the literary. At the same time, Denney is not one of those intellectuals, so common in America, who turns in resentment against other intellectuals and rejects the highbrows. The mucker pose is not for him. He rejects neither the Irish-American side of his heritage (here he is as accessible as is his genial, story-telling uncle described at the outset), nor the classical heritage which he constantly makes his own by reinterpretation, as in many of his side comments on Plato and on Greek attitudes toward work and play.

But the note of disdain is not absent from this book. Denney detests moralizing, finding for example attacks on the comics more unpleasant even than the voices of reaction or vicarious violence in the comics themselves. The world in which the essays that compose this book were written was a more benign one; one might not gather from these pages that Denney has been a peace-walker on streets not far from Pearl Harbor, or that he is committed to any cause more urgent than that Americans gain a greater sense of playfulness and fantasy and become more at ease in Zion.

Yet even when a particular topic is no longer salient, the mode of treatment remains significant. In fact, this very dichotomy between content and mode or form is central to Denney's thought; he insists again and again that an emphasis on content alone demeans the esthetic sensibility and reduces the creator to a sermonizer, the inventor to a technocrat. At times Denney writes with grace and sunny wit; this ease may conceal profundity of theme. And recurrently his task in this book is complicated by the many levels of implication in what he writes. As an encyclopedic literary man and a humanistic social scientist, he is not one to exploit a single academic discipline by means of well-tested procedures. A former writer for *Time* and *Fortune*, he used these employments to widen the orbits of his understanding of our national life; he shared enthusiasm for the movies with his friend, James Agee; an interest in the social consequences of science and technology with his Dartmouth classmate, Robert Colborn (then an editor of *Business Week*); and in his own work on corporation stories for *Fortune*, he enjoyed his contacts with businessmen and bankers.

For ten years we were colleagues together at the University of Chicago. We worked together in the now defunct Committee on Communications as well as in the Social Science Staff of the College. We worked together on a study of sociability, some of whose concerns are refracted in this book in the chapters "The Frontier Host" and "The Sirens' Song," insofar as the latter discusses manners and the role of the media in instructing Americans in etiquette and less formal personal relations. Denney was during these years a generous and responsive colleague who helped evoke and stimulate the latent and half-understood ideas of others. His ability to connect apparently unrelated phenomena may at times lead him astray; and sometimes a point is overstated. But he invites the curious to many new frontiers in American life, whether they had my good luck to know him as a friend and colleague, or encounter him vicariously through the printed page.

DAVID RIESMAN

A chiel's amang you, taking notes,
And, faith, he'll prent it.—Robert Burns

An Accessible Uncle

Some years ago, on a vaudeville stage, a man piled table upon table until there were at least six in a stack. He then climbed all the way up, somehow without bringing the pile down, and stood balanced on the top. Here, he began to sway from side to side, making the table-tower sway with him. After a long series of near tumbles, the tables came down with a crash to one side while he, moving down with pile as if in slow motion, lighted on his feet, free of the tumbling furniture, and stood uninjured. It was wonderful—something devised by the imagination of an acrobat to take its place in memory with the swaying of a tree in a storm, the balance of a wave on its break and plunge.

For this, and for the jugglers, and for a man who rode downstage on a bicycle that gradually fell apart, in imitation of Joe Jackson, a famous earlier vaudeville hero; and for elephants at the New York Hippodrome, and for dancing girls who marched into a tank in the same theater, never to reappear on stage; and for subway recognitions of a fighter named Gunboat Smith, and for a side-street recognition of a blind Negro boxer

1

named Sam Langford, and for views of the night's work by a fighter such as Jack Britton—I am indebted to my uncle. At various times, my uncle also pointed out to me, on the streets of New York, Jimmy Walker, James Farley, James Hines, and an Irishman nicknamed "Bullets," who was a World War I veteran and who was also, like my uncle and my grandfather before him, a New York fireman.

They sometimes say nowadays that few boys have accessible uncles. Boys have to depend on—if they can find them—what I call "social uncles," men from outside of the family. Maybe more uncles are married today, so that they do not have time, as my uncle did in the days before he married, to think up city excursions for a nephew. The statistics suggest, in fact, that they are more likely to be married today, since more people are marrying and marrying younger. This tendency is hard on nephews. On the other hand, my uncle was better than most, and would be hard to duplicate anywhere today, in great numbers, no matter what. He was just a natural genius at being an uncle: a tall, handsome Irishman in a fireman's blue coat trimmed inside with red flannel lining and embellished with brass buttons with crossed firehorns on them. He entered the house every day, home from work, with a headline from the papers, a quote from a celebrity, a comment on a horse, and a story from the firehouse on his lips. As he brushed a sugaring of snow off his shoulders with a meticulous flick of the handbroom, he brought the outside world to us, after a long day that still smells to me of dull linoleum, tea canisters, and hot-air heat.

First storming the kitchen and kissing his mother (my grandmother), he would throw the *New York American* on the cluttered kitchen table and come out with some phrase like "The Vanderbilts are out of yachts!" It was a one-sentence version of some story in the papers. From here he would move with the speed of a tap dancer to the dining room where my grandfather sat in his rope-bottom rocker reading a novel by

Mary Johnston or Winston Churchill or F. Hopkinson Smith. Throwing the *New York Telegram* into my grandfather's lap, he would cry out, "Hizzoner the Mayor says we can't enlarge our pension," and back away from the rocking chair.

"Don't tell me what the grafter says," my grandfather would scream. "I know already!" Having offered these filial comforts to my grandfather's political state of mind, my uncle then returned to the kitchen to continue his daily commentary on "Abie the Agent" or "Joys and Glooms" comic strips, or some other matter where it had been left off the day before. Often enough it was a character in a comic strip named "Barney Google" that required attention; and even more often it was the cat or the dog with the wisecrack in the corner of the box cartoons done by Tad Dorgan. My uncle saw the city through the comic strip, and he saw the comic strip through his sense of the city.

My uncle did not read comic strips and just let them lie. They were, rather, the continuing basic script of a story and a scene not completed until he had read some of the scenes aloud, commented on them, connected them with previous adventures in the same boxes, enacted them with the help of props picked up around the kitchen, and built them by his own imagination and narrative style into a kind of epic. Themes in the comic strip triggered his exploration of similar themes in daily life.

There was a time when Tad Dorgan did a series of box cartoons on the barbershop, focusing part of the cartoon on the fall guys of the situation—the barbers who had to listen to the lies of their customers, the shoeshine boys who had to accept thin tips, the Negro cleanup man who had to keep the floor clean after artist-barbers who tossed the cut hair backward over their shoulders, as they chopped male locks with the dancing abandon of ballet dancers or muralists. Such a fall-guy theme, appearing in a Tad Dorgan box on a winter evening, would launch my uncle into a dramatization of a few months in the public life of a White Wing, or street-cleaner man. The worker's name was usually Tony, and his problem was that he had moved into a new neighborhood with his family and wanted to get a transfer to a district sanitation office in the new neighborhood so that he would be closer to his work. Another point in Tony's mind was that there were fewer horses in his new neighborhood. Tony, like the hero in Franz Kafka's *The Castle*, approached his problem in stages, but unlike Kafka's hero, he knew roughly what his problem was. In successive scenes he met, and was sent on up the hierarchy by, the precinct captain, the ward boss, a borough committeeman, and others. At each stage of the game Tony was accompanied by fixers who had accepted good cigars from Tony for the service of paving the way for him with the politicians. They actually did no more on the day of the interview than push Tony through the office door with the helpful advice: "Speak up, Tony. Don't be afraid. You're just as good as he is anytime." In many weeks of struggles through episodes involving Tony's vote and other signs of loyalty, Tony struggled to go from District Five to District Six. When he finally reached District Six, it had been consolidated with District Five by the newly elected commissioners, the supervisors who were in on the Tony "fix" had been changed, and Tony was sent from District Six headquarters back to the identical horse-paradise of cobblestones and manure-golden gutters where he had been before he ever started his struggle with the machine and the bureaucracy.

This is a book about the popular culture of mass media and sports and advertisements. I have long wanted to say how much of what I learned to see, in the relation between the popular arts and the life around me, I first learned, in a devotee's sense at least, from my uncle. And in more senses than that, I often think of my luck as a child in having an uncle, John Powers, one could call accessible.

All the way from Shawnee Town,
A long time ago.... —Ballad

CHAPTER ONE

The Frontier Host

Pleasure Is Policy

A British traveler of the seventeen-hundreds tells the story of the capture of a predecessor of his, by a strange sort of road agent, on the roads of Virginia. John Bernard, the British stage-comedian, in *Retrospections of America, 1797–1811,* informs us that this traveler, confronted by a man with a pistol at the roadside, was taken prisoner and conveyed to a large, raw clearing in which stood a house whose grandeur was out of all keeping with the wilderness around it. He was imprisoned in a room of the house, a room that happened to be furnished largely with liquor, and told not to come out until he was drunk. That evening, over a dinner of wild game, he learned that his captor-host was a large landowner of the neighborhood who employed a road agent's methods to secure guests for himself in a countryside that offered only few such luxuries a year. The sudden hospitality forced on the traveler by his American host developed into a week-long hunting and fishing party, spiced with conversation about mutual friends in London.

These social rites were assisted not only by Negro slaves trained in the preparation of wild duck and multifarious drinks but also by one of the earliest American leisure machines. The host, in the hottest hours of a very hot day—this first recorded prisoner of southern hospitality had been traveling wild Virginia in the midsummer—called for his bath-wagon. With a skilled Negro at the reins, a covered wagon was drawn up, and the two sportsmen climbed into its shade. While being driven to the pond, the new guest was introduced to the variety of liquors, guns, fishing equipment, and other leisure necessaries that lined the covered wagon. Once at the pond, the slave drove the wagon into a shallow ford; the unexplainable coffer in the rear section of the wagon bed became a bathtub; and the two shaded riders shed their clothes and poured themselves into the water. While the horses were turned loose to swim, the Negro driver now changed roles from driver to barman and gillie; he provided each bather with a drink, set their fishing lines handy, and stood ready to hand them a shotgun if ducks flew overhead. He was also skilled in the placing of bookmarks if a volume of Gibbon should happen to close in the hands of one of his dozing charges. "This Western Sardanapalus," as Bernard calls the planter, who combined "the four staple enjoyments of bathing, drinking, shooting and fishing . . . marked the furnace in the skies burn away, but not with a contented heart" until he had caught his traveler. "If the traveller refused, up went his rifle to his shoulder. . . . The stranger now saw that pleasure was policy; . . . he speedily found himself in the clutches of his human alligator."

No originator of the "captive audience," a social phenomenon already reported in imperial Rome, such a man as the Virginia host might understand the subject of this book if we were to say that one of the more interesting ways of looking at society is to scrutinize its ways of work and play. Since the time of the Romantics, there has been a gradual gathering of interest in that polar pair, undoubtedly because their traditional connections have been shaken by industrialism. In the classic world, as in the world of Virginia, 1750, whole theories of play could be erected on the general acceptance of the presence of slave labor. In the medieval world it was possible to elaborate as a rationale of play, for most adults at least, only the traditional uses of the slack months of the agricultural calendar and the feudal and churchly rituals that allowed for entertainment within their general purpose as collective representations of the social order. In the industrial world it was fashionable until recently to define play as after-hours recreation—a process necessary to undo the evils of industrial work. It has been far harder to build some more positive notion.

The "popular culture" of the mass media—all the products, like movies and comics, that help to pass the time—provide the bath-wagon of the present. Like the bath-wagon, they are technologically elaborate, and like its owner they are aggressively sociable. But one difference is that they "capture" guests, such as stars, only to sell them or give them away to a large audience. Basically, however, the motivations are the same. Industry today provides to many the hours free of labor that the plantation system reserved especially to Uncle Tom's master, along with income to spend on leisure. The chief balm of uncommitted time in the United States, outside of sleep and strong drink, is provided by the mass media—the generators, reporters, and minstrels of a whole variety of other activities in the popular culture ranging from advertising through the fan clubs.

It is to be noted that the nameless planter who stalked his entertainment in the dangerous game of aggressive sociability, deep in the backwaters of Virginia, struck certain native woodnotes wild. In the first place, he was lonely; and this form of human existence still exists, so they say, in the big American cities. For another thing, he anticipated Benjamin Franklin's mechanical-mindedness and the remote-control TV tuner

("Choose what you want from your armchair!") when he dreamed up a machine as a sop to his solitude. And what is most obvious of all is that he was a newcomer to the land. Around the corner there were Indians having their own good time, but it was not his kind; and around the corner there were Africans having their own good time, but it was not his kind. One of the compelling things about popular culture in the United States is that it too is closely related to the old American career of immigration. The immigrants have sought and brought the products of the popular culture, and enlarged their markets, because theaters and vaudeville and movies and all the other forms have always helped to acculturate them to American life. Recent immigrants, coming in numbers from other lands than that of the ingenious British planter, have been great producers of the methods, gadgets, and symbols of popular culture.

Today, only the Christmas-decanter trade in the whiskey industry and resorts that specialize in skin-diving mock the slender leisure resources of the Virginian. Nowadays, his purchasing power could command a tremendous market of goods and services for leisure, a market different from that of his day in that it is full of things that are mass-produced, mass-marketed, and mass-forgotten in the context of a vastly duplicative technology. On a new social frontier of abundance in American life stand the powerful images and managers of mass entertainment, ready to capture as audience any and all wayfarers who come their way. They are the tyrant hosts of our time, and they differ from the Virginia landowner chiefly in this, that they themselves sometimes seem to be the captives of their own audiences. Perhaps that is the modern, mass-media twist on the maxim "pleasure is policy."

The popular artistic uses of technology are keyed to time that people have to spare, and mass leisure has captured us so suddenly that we tend to think about it by drawing on the stereotypes of an earlier era. Thus we take much the same view of modern leisure that people in Jefferson's day took of industry. But, whereas in Jefferson's day there were some hopeful ones like the Englishman, Samuel Ure, who looked to the coming of the machine with enthusiasm, many contemporary commentators view the coming of mass leisure as a calamity. Certainly, it can be argued that we have gotten too rich too fast in our quantities of leisure time and behave with the lack of ease and grace common to parvenus. Most of us, consciously seldom but unconsciously often, flee back to artificially strenuous work—or even to war—in order to escape the perplexities of choice presented by abundant leisure. It follows that these studies, concerned as they are with certain issues in the use of leisure in modern industrial life, employ the term "leisure" to refer not only to time away from workplace or domestic obligations but also to certain demands not to squander unimaginatively the resources that industrialization has opened up for us. Leisure, in that sense, implies a quality of life that we seek to capture or recapture as an element in all our activities.

Certain historical developments provide a background for the better understanding of contemporary leisure. The industrial workweek declined from an average of sixty-four hours in 1860 to an average thirty-nine hours in 1957. This does not take account of such recent institutions as the mid-morning coffee hour or of such old but steadily elaborated ones as the slowdown and the loafing time in most offices and shops. Paradoxically, the relative scarcity of labor in at least the northern part of the United States from the beginning helped promote the mechanization that made reduction of hours look reasonable. Mechanization, given this impetus, more than caught up with labor scarcity, even though the scarcity was artificially perpetuated by barring immigration after World War I. Thus, scarcity of labor led eventually not to long and exhausting hours but to short if not sweet ones. Doctors and other professionals who have made themselves scarce in the 1950's (and

then have forced themselves to keep up with demand by working seventy-two hours per week) can point to the difficulties
of mechanizing the professions, but they may also be liable to
the emotional difficulties the active middle class would encounter if not allowed to work more than, say, railroad hours.

Man-hour productivity—despite the "conscientious withdrawal of efficiency" practiced by labor and management alike
—has been going up in the United States every decade for
eight decades of growing industrialization. If we were willing
to accept the standard of living and of war-making of 1870,
most of us could presumably get by with a five-hour week.
At the same time, the accent on industrial productivity ought
also to be understood in the light of the shift of the last quar-
ter-century in the types of employment. As a percentage of the
total labor force, industrial workers and of course farmers
have declined. The "new middle class" of the clerical and service trades has gained and so has the professional and managerial class, including all the people engaged in the growing education and leisure industries. This markedly affects the kind of
work done; and, as we see every day, the patterns of leisure
differ very much, depending on the kind of work done or on
whether any work is done at all.

Competence in Leisure Today

One important consequence, at the point where leisure and
type of work interact, deserves notice. Rising industrial productivity and shifts in type of employment have moved so fast
that some of the extra time has gotten lost in the industrial
process itself. The multiplication of so-called overhead functions within industrial management may be a response not
only to cost-plus contracts but also to surplus time created
within modern industry. More generally, current concern for
industrial teamwork and beyond that for emotionally meaningful work may represent a similar make-work reaction. Just
as matter in the wrong place becomes dirt, so time at the

wrong time becomes waste, enforced idleness, underemployment, or the occasion for mood-engineering activities.

The same forces reducing the workweek have lengthened the life span, compelling the young to wait in school until the labor force will make room for them. For many of the young, school turns out to be simply a prison with rather inefficient and wholly unhappy jailers. The denizens of these jails have little more pleasure in their free time than prisoners who exercise their ingenuity in outwitting and tormenting their guards. One kind of leisure is labeled "juvenile delinquency," activity in which gregarious theft and gang warfare by the boys and gregarious sexual adventures by the girls appear to be channels for the playful, sociable, and conformist impulses of low-income youth. If, in many areas, we find a lower-income boy or girl who is not delinquent in this sense, we can be fairly sure that he or she is either headed up the class ladder or is psychologically deviant or both, being unwilling or unable to join in the group activities sanctioned by peers. Crises similar to those of time-swamped adolescence appear in the middle-class and upper-class leisure patterns that almost all Americans are aware of as models. Just so, the part-time and summer-job opportunities of the young in the United States during the last decade appear to at least some adults to be jobs in name only. Although actual work is done by baby-sitters and soda-clerks and parking-lot watchmen of tender ages, this work, to older citizens, seems to be the happy by-product of a situation in which the young are paid to socialize with each other away from home, limited by work hours and work practices that make minimal demands.

If leisure constitutes a problem for the idling young just prior to their employment, there is perhaps an even greater problem for the elderly just following their disemployment. Studies show that forcible retirement operates more destructively on men than on women. Even the housewife whose children have all grown and flown suffers less than her husband, most of whose self-esteem, fantasy, and sociability have clustered about his job. These haunt his post-employment life like ghosts, and they are the more ferocious the more intangible the job from which the man has been retired. A midwesterner engaged in adult education recently regularized his meetings of older men and women at the same room in a club building on the same night of each week. Assuming that they knew the place and time, he stopped sending cards to the oldsters to notify them. The next week he was overwhelmed with angry protests. "But you know the time and place by now," he said. "Yes," they replied, "but it's so nice to get the mail."

All this sounds as if time were no problem for people in the society that preceded ours. Then, the leisure perplexities were indeed rare in a nation of early-rising, hard-working farmers and factory hands who were apt to regard leisure as they would an oil strike—as a windfall uncomplicated by emotional excess-profits taxes. It appears that until the Age of Taft, the leisure class held something of a monopoly on the problem; it could occupy itself with perfecting the game of leisure, in ways so admirably satirized by Thorstein Veblen, because of its leadership and the high visibility of its leisure pursuits. In other words, the leisure class took on itself the task of playing on behalf of the whole overworked society; and the very inequality of this distribution of leisure paradoxically gave the leisure class a certain amount of justification for its activities. Yet, in the case of many sensitive and intelligent men and women, this justification sometimes broke down; there was often a pathetic feeling of aimlessness and social imprisonment.

Because the visible uses of leisure are signs and symbols of attachment to social groups, we should remember that it is sometimes more important for social groups of different identity to have vivid notions about each other and each other's movements than to have accurate but dull ones. Such notions are generally based on the visibility of each group to the other, visibility in this instance standing not only for direct interpersonal observation but also for indirect observation and ascription of motives. From this mutual observation arise usable stereotypes of the various social and economic groups. The styles of leisure consumption evidently contribute richly to the imagery on which such systems of recognition are based.

In the nineteenth century, leisure had rather highly defined connotations in terms of the division of labor: the poorer man's leisure demonstrated his freedom from long hours of hard work; the richer man's leisure demonstrated the correctness of his consumption style. Showy consumption of entertainment frequently was meant to demonstrate that the player was free while others worked. The wealthy man at leisure—if he could tolerate leisure at all—was at once the beneficiary of, and the actor for, all the people who made idleness possible for him. He was virtually forced to accept this stress on the social status of leisure whether he wanted it or not. Thus, in his cultivated leisure, the millionaire of the Gilded Age was the "leisure client" less of the architect he employed, the musician he paid, the artist whose work he bought, than he was of the workers who turned out the cash for him.

How different it is today. Leisure and its processes are no longer dramatized so intensively in terms of the social difference between the working-force producers of the income necessary to leisure and the spenders of the income-leisure. The public focus has shifted from inequality of economic opportunity for leisure to the socio-psychological inequalities of access to the goods and services in leisure. The leisure hours of all classes today dramatize, to some degree, the dependence of the leisured person not on the force still at work but on the specific worker who produced the leisure good or service. The collector of paintings or records today dramatizes his "trade" with the musician, composer, or artist in the division of labor, and he plays down more than his ancestors did the social traits distinguishing him from the man who is not yet a customer for the music or the painting. If Veblen's invidious factor continues in leisure consumption, it is an emotion related more than before to the problems of the cultural distance between the consumer and the object, less than before to the problems of cultural distance between the consumer and the non-consumer. To illustrate: the host of today who wants you to praise his new abstract sculpture is more likely to place emphasis on claiming its artist as a friend, thus showing his closeness to the creative source, than he is to place emphasis on the market rarity of the object, as the nineteenth-century collector did, who was concerned with proving, not his closeness to the artist, but his distance from the mob.

In this newer context, it is perhaps understandable that escape motives in the pursuit of leisure arts are more acknowledged. It has become clearer than before that some such motive always existed in the pursuit of art and entertainment. It has become even more evident that many of the contradictions that troubled the taste of the nineteenth century followed from a resistance to accepting this. The Victorian enjoyer of the arts and entertainment experienced a certain pleasure that helped to sweeten the fact that he was enjoying what others lacked, but his guilty glance toward the "have-not" encouraged him to moralize about the arts. Today, new alignments of leisure producers and audiences ready the ground for further liberation from the moralizing we find almost everywhere in the social pragmatism of American critical thought about entertainment and the arts in the nineteenth century. Since no society changes all at once, a good many of these older leisure patterns remain, both in the upper and in the lower classes. If we search far enough, we can find the Huck Finns whose adventures are truant but not delinquent, and we can find gilded youth and wealthy aged folk for whom idleness is not discomfort. Time does not move evenly for everyone, even in our allegedly standardized industrial culture. But this very fact often leads to tragedy. Tragedies of leisure occur for the individual when his life cycle fatefully gets mixed up with some larger social cycle of unemployment, or of suddenly lowered retirement ages, or some other social and cultural development that is at odds with his own development.

The life cycle, in its relation to the individual's pattern of work and play, is always limited of course by the universal law that youth, maturity, and age seek distinct types of leisure and, what is more, that the capacity for leisure, or play, in any of these ages of man is deeply indebted to childhood experience. Notice that we speak of children's play rather than of their leisure. By this we imply the relatively unproblematic but by no means uncomplicated nature of the activity. Leisure has much more ambiguous connotations. In the very young child, work and play are not yet independently organized. Play is viewed by the observant society as preparation for work and, in the investigations of Jean Piaget (*The Moral Judgment of the Child*), for political roles quite as much as for future leisure. Yet children's play, in fact, is both more and less than this. Although it has aspects of localism which the ever renewed child's culture elaborates, it is something we find in all cultures. One great horror of the early stages of industrialization was the harnessing of very young children to factory work and the consequent destuction for these generations of this great, natural resource of childhood play and curiosity. Today, the child's right to play is so fully established that few adult exploiters can stand out against it. Here, at least, industrialism has more than restored to us what it once took away.

We can say, in fact, that the child's play serves as the model for all later efforts to free leisure from its burdens and to cope with the puzzling availability of adult time. Yet here our adult imagery can easily succumb to nostalgia. Studies of children's play by the psychoanalyst, Erik H. Erikson (*Childhood and Society*), show that it is not always free of terror and anxiety and morbidity. Our recollections, when unclouded, often tell us as much. It may well be true, as it appears to be so often, that difficulties in adult leisure arise in conflicts between a given individual's one and only life cycle and the social developments of his time which, in connection with his age, serve to foreclose his growth in leisure—or open the vista of growth too late in life. At the same time, even the most happy coincidence of an individual's life with social changes and fashions favorable to the development of his own leisure satisfaction would not produce, in our society, an approach to leisure entirely free of haunting self-consciousness. We know this because children themselves rarely attain this freedom. We can, however, take from studies of childhood play one other equally important lesson for the adult; namely, that children appear to derive their greatest satisfactions from experiences of mastery and control. Dissatisfactions with contemporary leisure might conceivably be reduced if we did more with the problem of sheer competence—if we enabled people to become more workmanlike and at the same time more imaginative players.

But how can competence be increased? For one thing, through the further development of a critical vocabulary among all users of leisure, the "play-force" of the society. The following chapters are not so much a survey of leisure and the mass media as they are one man's investigation of some of the critical vocabularies that have already been built up, suggesting cogency or lack of it in some of the canons of taste. Talking of a general audience for leisure means little unless the audience is related to the producers of leisure commodities and services, the cultural definitions of artistic form that they employ, the channels through which the commodities and services move, and the persuasions they appear to embody. The very claims made for certain vocabularies of popular criticism confront, of course, a very widespread feeling that little such criticism exists and that the uses of leisure in the United States, especially consumption of the mass media, are intellectual and social drug addictions manipulated by the men of power.

That feeling, as it appears, for example, in the searching work of C. Wright Mills, often seems to be supported by studies of the audience. The way to study the audience, as everyone ought to know by now, is to recognize from the outset that the social and cultural context of the individual audience-member determines much of what he gets out of what he sees and hears in the media or what he does with his leisure. To be in a given social group or to relate to a given social group often makes the difference whether one does or does not come in contact with this or that media event or leisure activity. Mathilda White Riley and Samuel H. Flowerman expressed this very well when they wrote: "Mass media studies have, on the whole, tended to conceive of the audience as a series of discrete individuals characterized by a variety of personal attributes. Actually, however, this conception is oversimplified: in receiving the message, any given person in the audience reacts not merely as an isolated personality but also as a member of the various groups to which he belongs and with which he communicates."

The effect of leisure contact, as we know from many studies, is mediated and restructured by the group affiliation of the audience-member. It follows that studies of audiences often show the captivity of the individual by the spectator-group or participant-group of which he is a member. It is possible, having assembled a variety of such findings, to argue for the ease with which the advertising man and the mass-media managers can manipulate these bondages by cunning selection of their product's form and content. This manipulation, while directed toward the manifest needs of the audience, is often destructive to the satisfaction of more basic needs, especially that of fruitful self-development in a free society.

Since the manipulators can exert some of this power over the audience, it is often interpreted as being total power; yet such total control could exist only on the assumption that the producers always know what they are doing; that media contents always reflect this; that form and content of the media product appear to be indivisible (which is necessary to all artistic and most persuasive effects); that the intended audience consumes the media product; that the media symbols are familiar but not outdated; and that the social reference group of the audience-member fully confirms the media message. Each of these assumptions is challenged in this book, but here we need only examine the implied concept of the audience.

If we think of any audience, we think of a group of people who are conditioned to perceive in a certain way. First, any audience defines itself as a cultural group with conventions of its own: when some groups speak of going to the movies, they mean seeing a British comedy at an art theater; when others speak the same way, they mean finding the darkest spot at the drive-in. Second, the audience as a social group can change its loyalties: it can stop going to movies at a certain age and begin to go to bowling alleys or church suppers. Third, the audience possesses a series of definitions, more or less sensible, of the products it buys, the forms they take, the channels they come through, the symbols they embody, and the producers who make them. Finally, an audience always gropes, more or less successfully, for a definition of the situation it finds itself in when it is being an audience. A businessman may not know why he can read Proust comfortably if fellow executives are doing the same thing in a seminar with the approval of the company, while he cannot do it under any other conditions; but he is aware that a change in his situation as audience-member has led to a difference in his quality as an audience-member.

Studies of audiences and of participating members of leisure-interest groups do not as yet place equal emphasis on all these variables. Since the audience is very often studied as the object of a concerted effort to change minds and tastes (as the object of a campaign, one might say), it tends to be reflected in research as a passive entity. There is a good deal of study of the way in which audiences respond favorably to seeing or hearing their favorite self-definitions confirmed. There is rather less study of the way in which an audience or audience segment chooses among the media leisure alternatives. There is even less study that shows us very much about the autonomy expressed by the audience through its use of the artistic forms that are being employed by entertainers and persuaders. Thus, in contrast with many studies of such quantitative indices as the "number of blows struck" in TV shows beamed at children, there are only a few studies, like those reported by A. J. Brodbeck, of the variations in movie fiction as incitement to aggression in children as related to variations in the ability of the children to distinguish between fictional and non-fictional appeals. These latter studies show, among other things, that children who mistook adventure fiction for "something that really happened" were the ones who more often sympathized with and gave signs of wishing to emulate the antisocial acts represented in the fiction.

The total effect of audience studies so far, then, is to understate the grasp by the audience, or by significant parts of the audience, of the formal and artistic conventions which mediate meanings for them. Many studies encourage us to believe that the media are rich in different artistic genres for the presentation of reality but that there is no corresponding audience skill in differentiating them. Such underplaying of the audience occurs constantly in public statements on children's literature and its effects. We know by investigation that some children, rejecting the seventh shot out of a villain's six-shooter because it is simply improbable, will also reject some of their commitment to the violence portrayed and the immoral agency involved. Yet critics of comic books constantly ignore the differences in genre and the differences in audience that these findings imply, as if all children, by definition, were the aesthetic dullards that the adult viewers-with-alarm are.

Self-consciously humanistic critics of the mass media, unsullied by quantitative sociological studies, have not been any more perceptive about the nature of an audience. They conventionally allege debasement of individuality and art in mass entertainment; at the same time they forgo constructive suggestions. Following the fashion, many literary and scholarly citizens of the United States mechanically snub the mass media. The obvious retort to dogmatically disdainful critics is that they ought not to complain about a popular culture for which they will take no responsibility. Responsibility, to be sure, is a wearisome word; what might it mean in this case? Certainly not direct attempts to change the basic institutions of the media, except, perhaps, when they do things, or fail to do things, with results that might lead to an abridgment of our political and intellectual freedoms. Direct action is the work of those censors whose role it is to watch the managers of the mass media and be the bellwethers of the audience. The humanistic critic can be of most service by acquainting himself empirically, through research of one kind or another, with the channels and the cultural forms (documentary, artistic, and rhetorical genres) through which the media messages move to the public and by acquainting himself empirically with the social organization of the public and its subpublics.

This means a consideration, not only of all those audience-members reached by a specific message, but of all kinds of specific messages that are bundled into a "receiver's package" by specific types of audience-members. Sociological thought tends to study how the audience changes when the stimulus from the mass-media producers changes; political thought tends to study how the public policy or governmental control of the media change when the stimulus from the mass-audience changes. Both more or less take for granted the identity of mass-media form and content—collapsing both into some unit of persuasive effect. The humanist might define his work as critic of the mass media and of the popular culture as a task requiring him to study the media forms themselves as a crucial intervening variable, subject to change by the policy of both producers and audiences but also capable, as all the human communication forms are capable, of asserting their own power over producers and audiences. That is why this study attempts above all to identify some of the documentary, artistic, rhetorical, and spectacle-producing forms that are prevalent in the American popular culture today. Not what the popular entertainment producers directly say, but how they say it; not who hears, but how the form selects that hearer, are the main themes. From this intention develop all the other surmises offered here as touching on the imaginative maturity or immaturity of the American play-force at the mid-century.

Now what are all these arts for?
Always and only to supply a real or an imagined
need or deficiency on the part of
the human patron. . . .—Coomaraswamy

CHAPTER TWO

The Vicarious We

In their use of leisure in the middle of the twentieth century, Americans present a social scene characterized by cross-currents—even by currents that run in opposite directions. Since 1929 American leisure spending has increased sharply to about $40 billion, or one of every six dollars in personal disposable income; at the same time, according to some definitions of leisure spending, it has not kept pace with personal income. Again, since 1929, total box-office receipts of the spectator amusements have risen to $1.5 billion; in the same period, however, the amounts spent for individual recreation increased from $2.5 to $8.4 billion. Since individualized recreations, such as reading, gardening, and participant sports, are sometimes assumed to be more praiseworthy than spectator attendance, this cheers some observers of the American scene.

Similar judgments are sometimes put in other terms; instead of distinguishing between leisure expenditures on the basis of a line drawn between spectatorial mass entertainment and the individual or small-group participant activity, some observers draw a line between the more premeditated and the less premeditated leisure pursuits. The less premeditated or more passively accepted pursuits, such as drinking, home TV-viewing, and casual eating out, amount to about $12 billion of total leisure expenditures; travel, gardening, hunting, and spectator and participant sports lumped together show a much bigger total of some $18 billion. This latter way of looking at the matter has the virtue of conceding that the choice of buying a baseball ticket or an opera ticket may be far from passive or unindividualized, while at the same time pointing to the probability that many "individualized" recreations are not as individually active as they may appear to be. Listening to records, for example, may represent for any one individual mere acceptance of someone else's preferences or of a listening group's trend toward compromised and mediocre preference. This approach, however, assigns the trait of "activity" more to the way in which the leisure choice is made, and the physical effort required to satisfy it, than to the activity itself; it assumes perhaps too readily that the listener who props himself in an easy chair at home to make a choice among specific items on TV and on AM and FM radio is somehow less active in his leisure than the man at the office who has been persuaded by the crowd to see the Big Ten game and goes along for the sake of the company rather than the football.

It may very well be that the "individualized" leisure choices of the mid-twentieth century display an increasing tendency to include personal choices that are subject to group manipulation. Listening to records is as much influenced as it ever was, for adolescents, by the standards of preference of the group to which the individual adolescent belongs; John Johnstone has shown that the opinion-leaders of adolescent fan groups seem to name as their favorites the very records that correspond with the central tendency of the group. The same mechanisms can be found at work in the activities of reading, periodical subscription, hobbyism, boating, fishing, and gardening. It is not unusual in the United States today to find that a

most "active and individualized" hobby such as Sunday painting may represent, for a given individual, a surrender to the
painting club's taste.

As a result of the flattening of the income pyramid in the
United States, new increments of disposable income and leisure time tend to be concentrated in the semiskilled-worker
level of family incomes in the United States. A family's upward social movement toward this level of income (say around
$5,000 a year) has at first the tendency to make leisure spend-
ing decline as an item in family expenditures; a middle-class
family has to reach into the $10,000-a-year bracket before it
ever again spends as great a percentage of its income on leisure as it did when it was at the bottom of the income structure. In transit from the $2,000-a-year income level to the
$10,000-a-year level, the profile of the spending inevitably
changes. In lowest income families, the men are the beneficiaries of most leisure spending; in the $10,000-and-up families,
the participation of women and children increases sharply,
partly at the expense of the men.

The way in which new income and new leisure time are distributed supplies at least one of the reasons why, as new forms
of leisure spending arise, old ones maintain themselves and
even expand. The country appears to be able to sustain easily
the roughly $3 billion spent on gambling and the $1.5 billion
that go into juke boxes, for example; these older-style expenditures continue to rise, even while the goods and services associated with newer patterns, such as the power-boat market,
expand also. At the same time, the heavy distribution of new
income in the lower-middle income brackets probably helps
to explain why books and opera tickets show little or no growth
in sales in the middle of a leisure boom. The bonanza of leisure
spending power and choices has been given, by and large, to
people who are using it to make themselves at home in the
already established middle class.

Because some people are on the move and some are not,

and because among the people on the move different conditions of leisure choice prevail, the currents cross each other
and even reverse each other. Home-centered leisure, for example, is influenced by changes in the nature of housing in the
last two generations. The point of highest average per capita
investment in housing in the history of the United States occurred in the mid-1920's; since then, the average has been
steadily declining. At the same time, the standard of housing
and neighborhood milieu has been visibly improved in many
respects for most of the members of the unskilled and semiskilled workingmen's families. Thus, in a period when good
housing tends to be more widely distributed, its standard of
space has fallen. The markets for gardening and landscaping
goods and services have expanded enormously as a result of
the growth of the one-class suburbs in the lower-to-middle
income groups; yet at the same time the decline of average per
capita family space is such that few houses are built big
enough any more to contain easel pictures of more than the
smallest size. Even among the middle-to-upper income groups,
the personally collected library gives place to a few art books
that stand as a surrogate for the books that used to be there
and cannot be seen any more.

In connection with just such changes, the decline of the old
industrial frontier and the general decline of family living-
space that accompanies the densification of the suburbs have
powerful effects. The densification of social life in the suburbs—which emphasize the public life, the life without privacy,
more than either the city or the farm two generations ago—has
tended to socialize this leisure time rapidly by drawing on it
for group activity. In the new densified situation, there appears
to be less room for the individual's fantasy and privacy—even
while the decline of physical and social elbow room warns that
it may sometime need to be compensated for by an increase in
psychic elbow room. The time that is made available for leisure in the new suburbs tends to be used, perhaps temporarily,

not only for specifically social rather than individually leisure-
ful purposes, but also as a time in which the productive impulses not fully satisfied at work can be discharged.

One of the results is a shift in the relations among the spectatorial, participative, and more individualized forms of leisure
choice and among the market decisions and personal activities
of which each is composed. As spectator sports decline in relative economic magnitude, we see also the decline of sports
writing as a salient source of good writing and of insight into
American life in general. Sports writing, like boxing, does not
have the appeal for the young it once had; and successes in
these fields have moved on to higher status occupations. Likewise, as such sports as bowling grow in participation, snow-
balled by the involvement of women as well as men, they
change their character too. Bowling has asserted its institutional connection with 100 per cent Americanism, played down
its connection with the pool hall, and now is even on its way,
via TV, to becoming a spectator sport.

There are other broad changes. The domestication of leisure
has had the effect of making any and all forms of leisure the
beneficiaries or the victims of the family life-style within
which they are contained. The continued passage of leisure
decision to women and children of all economic classes has
had the effect, in some media, of making it sound as if they
alone were the inevitable trustees of culture and leisure.
Where children are more involved in leisure decision-making,
as in TV-viewing, the heat on censorship is increased; and where
women are more involved in leisure usage, as in home elaboration, the more chance there is that the leisure will be participative and socially conformist. At the same time, the efforts
of men to maintain private and individual leisure pursuits tend
to be channeled, by the way income is being distributed and
by the speed of its changing pattern, into the fishing, hunting,
bowling, and the do-it-yourself and home-productive hobbies
of a more or less literal sort.

Perhaps because millions of families in the United States, the families that have gained the biggest percentage of purchasing power and leisure time, look to this time as a way of finding the realities of the middle-class "core" culture, these families exert a major influence upon the entire meaning of leisure in our generation. This is true not only because these families have new high-income levels but also because our democratized society places few social barriers in the way of their free use of income. They tend to use their leisure to obtain less of the distant and vicarious gratifications, through the movies and the sports heroes, than their rural and immigrant parents and grandparents did; on the other hand, as the figures on playgoing and reading show, they have not yet joined the pattern of the old leisure class in anything except, perhaps, their ownership of a station wagon and an outboard motor. The net effect has been to build up the socially participative leisure activities at some expense to the older spectatorial pattern, without any large addition as yet to the markets for the deliberated arts in their non-popular forms.

This escalation goes far in explaining the general tone of our leisure today, especially its tendency toward the literal. It helps to explain why the mass of all hobby buying continues to emphasize "realism" as one of the major appeals. It helps to explain why some—though by no means all—of the newer problems of censorship, especially in connection with comic books, have risen among social groups that want to control their children's reading without being aware that children's reactions to reading are determined more by their sense of fictional forms than they are by contents.

Contemporary leisure is better understood if we single out three personal stances that are prominent and recognizable. Emphasis on the participative and socialized leisure-time pursuits long ago produced, in social groups as widely different as the fan clubs, the hi-fi addicts, and bird-watchers, the figure of the Participative Purist. The first important thing about him is that he reacts against spectatorship; he *does* things. He would rather direct the symphony orchestra by fiddling with his control board than just sit and listen. The second important thing about him is that he is the member of a group that decides how far you have to go in order to cross the line from spectatorship to participation. Thus the participation is of two kinds: manifestly, in the practice of some advanced leisure activity; latently, in social grouping with people who do the same thing. The third important thing about the Participative Purist is that he works with his group at developing the line between spectatorship and participation, by employing this line as a device for including or excluding other people. The explicit appeal of the Participative Purist is to the scientific, artistic, or cultural nature of the activity in which he and his fellows engage; his implicit appeal is to the heightened morale supplied by agreement on these matters in the fellowship of his peers.

The Participative Purist so dominates the stage of avant-garde leisure in our times that he makes it difficult to pick out of the crowd the Spectatorial Purist. The latter, who may turn up at either the sports event or the concert, represents those of us who manage to hold on to spectatorship by rejecting an older style of it in favor of a newer style. While the Participative Purist is most noticeable among folk-dance, hi-fi, and similar groups, the Spectatorial Purist is perhaps most noticeable among jazz fans; rejecting any claim that he can produce jazz, he seems to know everything about how it has been produced and how it should be. The first important thing about him is his doctrine of the interaction of the artist and the audience. It is one of his rules that the artist depends on the audience and gives the audience work to do, and his stories about the importance of artist-audience interaction in improvisational jazz may bear out his point. The second important thing about him is that he is the member of a spectator-group that has social identity outside the spectatorial situation itself. This group, which renews the integrity of its spectatorship by working at the matter in off-hours, and which even shares a style of life, thinks of itself as an organic audience rather than as a mere collection of listeners.

The third major type is the Reality Purist. He may or may not overlap either or both of the other two types. The first thing about the Reality Purist is that he either accepts or demands the literal in the uses of leisure. As a spectator of games, he is the one who invariably protests if the game turns on an ambiguous decision by the referees, arguing that there hasn't been "any real competition." As a spectator of movies and TV, he is uncomfortable with any form of fantasy. He is the one who builds scale-model railroads while at the same time being contemptuous of a neighbor who paints abstract paintings. In the individualized activities, he is the one who always has the tools, whose shop is arranged so that he can make any kind of cut you want in wood, but whose shop products always turn out to look as if they could be bought in a departmen store. The Reality Purists, if they are in the advance guard, psychoanalyze their children's art and hang around the schoolhouse all the time; if not, they ask their children to burn comic books, in autos-da-fé of the *Blue Beetle*, on the ground that the books will lead to mayhem in the neighborhood. These examples of reactions to comic books are not intended to whitewash the many objectionable features of some such publications; they are important here as illustrations of judgments that fail to take into account the conventions of fiction as a vital link with the audience.

We all share aspects of all three of these imaginary characters; and all three of them are noteworthy for aiming at the right goals, but at the same time overaiming and trying to reach the right goals with the wrong means. Their confusion is quite closely connected with a whole cluster of dubious habits in the play-force at large and helps to explain the connection between vaguely similar phenomena that turn up in widely distant parts of the American scene. Thus, the study undertaken in detail in the following chapters might well be thought of as beginning with a look at the flight from mass spectatorship, as at the movie, to group participation in the reception of entertainment, as in the home TV audience. TV exorcises the distant and private vicariousness of the movie, only to substitute for it what can be called the intimate and socialized vicariousness of the big tube. The sheer decline in the aesthetic distance of the image transmitted by TV as contrasted with the movie, a decline insured by the performer's self-definition as a family guest, leads to entirely new problems of competence in spectatorship: the problems of being critical about a guest. This is little noticed by those who think TV is more "real" than movies because it is more sociable. It is noticed (as we shall see in chapters iii and iv) with alarm and discomfort by the Spectatorial Purist, who has not yet learned how to meet a pseudo-guest.

Far away from the scene of reception, similar uncertainties are thrust indirectly upon the audience by the relation between the producers and the conventions of their craft. The literalism of the media, beloved by the Reality Purists of the naïve sort, is a theatrical convention that functions as a make-work or soil-bank project for thousands of technicians. Without realism, they would be out of jobs; it is bad for them to be out of jobs; therefore, realism must be continued because it keeps them in jobs. The subdivision of theatrical reality by theater-trades jurisdictionalism is reinforced wherever the theater craftsmen themselves are social mobiles into the middle-class core culture. They believe their realism and believe in its necessity; and this permits them not to see that it is their aesthetic subsidy. Indeed, having reinforced realism with their fight for union rights, they now feel justified in violating it: in Chicago, no needle can be placed on a studio disc except by the hand of a musician.

The combination of intimate vicariousness in TV reception

plus the downgraded realism inherited from the movies leads in turn to significant shifts in the possibilities of the art forms. Characterization, for example, changes co-ordinately with shifts in artistic genre. The best illustration lies in the shift of the figures of cops and robbers from early movies through later movies into TV. The most popular TV cop, Joe Friday, is utterly different from the cops who preceded him in film and fiction. His novelty, on closer examination, proves to be closely associated with the degraded realism and intimate vicariousness which are among the two major elements in the artistic mood of TV. One could summarize it by saying that TV rescued and gave a new lease on life to forms of naïve realism that the movies had already disposed of years before.

It is characteristic that the Reality Purist does not notice these changes but that some of the Spectatorial Purists do. The Spectatorial Purist responds by attempting to develop a code which relates him to the cultural definitions of the spectacles that confront him; he tries to understand them in context, not as a mere spectator but as the member of an audience with morale of its own. Interestingly enough, he does not escape the problems of a naïve realism when he turns, for example, to the field of passionate fandom in sports. Football is the supreme case. In the last fifty years it has almost entirely lost its original quality of saying something about Victory and Defeat; to understand these terms in contemporary football means coming to grips with a recruiting, coaching, refereeing, and scoring scene of scholastic subtlety. Teddy Roosevelt, the press camera, and the needs of the business-recruitment system (as described in chapter v) have utterly changed the game, so deeply redefining its symbolic content in American folkway that the spectator today has to become semiprofessionally informed to understand what is going on in the recruitment underground of the conferences.

This ambiguity is matched in the minds of the players and the coaches. The withdrawal of the amateur emotion from football playing is the condition of a certain type of honesty in relation to the game; but the withdrawal leaves a vacuum in the heart of the player which can be filled only by protoprofessionalism. At this point his play becomes redefined as total work, and what an educational system originally defined as a means becomes an end. Football is only one instance. The tension between the amateur and the professional, which involves the code of participative purism for the athlete, of spectatorial purism for the spectator, and of reality purism for the sports-page reader who wants games defined as games and business defined as business, turn up in other arenas as well.

The new pressure on sports is such that recent reportage in the field has become obsessed with fine points of eligibility, scoring, timing, refereeing, and so on. The result of elaborate systems of competition (professional football's brief experiment with radio-controlled quarterbacks, for example) and elaborate systems of rule-making aimed at guaranteeing parity in competition is that some of the non-contest or fictional, sport forms are more clearly "drama" than ever—wrestling, for example. Perhaps it is some of the emotion withdrawn from overcertified or undercertified sports in the public eye that encouraged some young men in the 1940's and 1950's to become hot-rodders. In this almost compulsively concrete and productive activity (as we shall see in chapter vi), participant purism is nicely combined with realism and with an ideology of spectatorial integrity; the builder is the driver is the racer is the winner or the loser. A compelling facet of the hot-rod fad in the United States in the last twenty years or so is its consistently sleazy handling by those parts of the press aimed at readers over the age of eighteen. Newspapers redoubled their criticism of the hot rod precisely during the period when, by holding it down, they could give Detroit time to resist it by partial incorporation. The advertising pages have consistently praised since about 1952 precisely those elements of car design that were attacked in hot rods before that time. Per-

haps the only exception is comic-strip-artist Zack Mosley, creator of "Smilin' Jack."

This example of the press handling of a certain type of flight
away from media saturation and in the direction of participative purism is an example, of course, of the press's conquest,
by subdivision, of the audiences. In such subdivisions (as discussed in chapter vii) the press consciously or unconsciously
arranged its documentary coverage so that its reportorial symbolism did not contradict the symbolism of its advertisements
—hot rods were played down so that the new Detroit cars could
be played up. Again, perhaps guilty at what it was doing, the
press permitted the appearance in non-serious and non-realis-
tic form, such as the comic strip, of themes and attitudes that
could not be expressed literally or that newspapers did not
wish to exhibit in any literal manner. Zack Mosley was able
to say good things about hot-rodders (that is, in effect, critical
things about Detroit) because the comics do not ask to be
taken seriously.

A further example of the function of the comic as serious
jester is found in the transformation of the handling of political
realities by cartoons and comic strips in the last fifty years.

As everyone recognizes, the serious, hard-driving political
cartoon is virtually dead, a victim first of the social revolution
of the New Deal and also of the bipartisan moderation of the
post–World War II years. This has led some rather too hardheaded observers to imagine that the political cartoon itself is
dead. Yet it is far from so. The political cartoon has reappeared
in certain of the comic strips themselves, expressing itself in
terms of new genres of fictional art and concentrating on a
new definition of "politics." For the old box cartoon, politics
was defined as an interpartisan and interpersonal game of in-
sult between big heroes and big villains—Lincolns and Tweeds,
Blaines and Hannas; today, politics is defined as the study of
the sociopolitical resonances of small groups.

In such a time, it is brilliant and appropriate for the political cartoonist to express his feelings in the quasi-fictional form of such strips as "Li'l Abner" and "Pogo." Once this is recognized, it must also be recognized that both strips deal with the problem of "southernism" in the American mentality, as a source of cultural richness and cultural danger. Whereas "Li'l Abner" handles the political scene as a class conflict, in quasi-naturalistic terms, "Pogo" handles it as a study in the disintegration of the New Deal phase of the Democratic party, in terms of fable. The decline of the older "realistic" tradition of political cartooning has given way to a new form the understanding of which depends on some ability to tolerate and interpret the artistic forms of fantasy.

Moving across the spectrum of leisure activities from the spectators of fictions to the spectators of contests, and then to the participant spectators of such industrially related sports as hot-rod building and racing, we move first from the physically passive to the physically active, from the more symbolic and abstract to the more concrete and literal, from the more autistic to the more socialized activities of leisure. Yet, with this mention of the press—of the ways in which the leisure activities that compete with media use are reflected in the press and of the ways in which the press structures its response to changing definitions in major areas of American life—we return, full circle, to more sedentary uses of leisure that we looked at earlier, in our consideration of the conventions of TV. Of these uses, reading remains a vital habit, and one of our problems is to find a truly popular literary product to examine in terms of the themes already touched upon. The fantasy of leisure is today richly expended on science fiction—where dreams are wedded, hot as the Moor with Desdemona, with popular beliefs as to the human meaning of our technological civilization.

Nothing could be less physically active than reading; nothing could be more difficult in many ways; and nothing can both stimulate and assuage this difficulty for some modern readers as science fiction does. Science fiction is the theater, par excellence, of those fantasies of hope and fear that lie deep in the heart of the citizen as Participative Purist in the struggle of morality-and-technology. Do we live in Utopia or in anti-Utopia? Are scientists good or bad? Is the part of ourselves that wishes to purge life of the poetic and non-instrumental statement acceptable? To what extent are our lives a self-confirming prediction?

Some science fiction is pathos; some attempts to be tragedy; some is comedy; some science fiction reminds one of eschatology. Highbrow science fiction today defines the modern individual as helpless in the hands of outside but invisible forces; lowbrow science fiction defines the modern individual as helpless in the hands of forces internal to himself, a battle between body and mind. These differences (as pointed out in chapter ix) involve differences in formal appeal. The fascinating thing is that the audience, especially the young audience, seems to be rather well trained in perceiving these differences; some members of the younger generation can move from comic books to science fiction to *Oresteia* in two jumps. One can see here the process by which Spectatorial Purists in the art of reading rescue naturalism and realism from the Reality Purists and make reading do work that liberates rather than boxes in the imagination. To put it in other words: fantasy re-establishes its rightful power in the hearts of the young reading public not simply by putting on the cloak of science fiction but, what is more, by taking up the fictional contemplation of moral problems far beyond the scope of Jules Verne and the understanding of fictional forms far subtler than the machine-made Poe of Hugo Gernsback.

In no country is reading more debated than in the United States. Debate about it tends to concentrate upon a single human skill all of the various notions about human ability to find reality in symbols. American parents suffer two successive fears: first, that their children will not learn to read; second, if the children do learn, that their imagination will be "over-stimulated." Since American parents are generally unaware that children learn all that is structurally necessary to know about their language by the age of two or so, they are fond of making out that learning to read is harder than learning to talk. So, in a social sense, it is; but largely because children are surrounded by people who hate words, and especially printed words, and especially printed words that mean something. Contact with bored or sadistic attitudes toward language in parents and associates is far more dangerous to a child's reading ability than such moot matters as the phonic system, the right eye in the place where the left eye should be, and palsy of the sitting-nerves in a kindergarten. This is not, of course, the theory of reading experts who regard reading as an exercise similar to recognizing aircraft silhouettes on a translux tape.

As a result, discussions of modern competence in putting one's self in the vicarious world of written fiction by the art of reading too often degenerate in the United States into a debate involving psychological specialists and moralizers. As we shall see, research has shown that the capacity of children to recognize and distinguish fictional and non-fictional forms has as much socializing effect on their behavior consequent to reading as their conscience or their norms of conduct; yet thousands of comic books are burned in the United States on the premise that what they say, not how they say it, is the total test.

This form of literalism in parental attitudes toward the reading skill is promoted, of course, chiefly by the Reality Purists, the kind of people who solve problems of contextual definition of words by going to see what the dictionary says about that one word. It is fought off, now and then, by those Spectatorial Purists in the literary arts who say, but do not say loudly enough, that the relation between words and reality is a dialectic. Even some of the Spectatorial Purists, associating Truth with print and Equivocation with the audio-visual word of the "commercial," forget that it was once the other way around;

the appearance of the alphabet once threatened those who associated integrity with the face-to-face word alone and thought of the written word as a messenger either helplessly open to being taken hostage or already suborned by the sender or both. There is a whole population of Americans who, because they have just learned to read in the last century or so, have lost all capacity to listen to the well-spoken word; they were print-trained out of auditory competence just before the Ear Age of the modern mass media began.

Such problems of competence in the perception of the changing cultural conventions in the world of communications today repeat themselves in the sphere of our visual and kinesthetic control of our technological environment. To illustrate, because advertising and modern architecture define themselves as "functional," they are allowed to be as symbolic as they choose to be; that is to say, the more public opinion allows them to define themselves as spontaneously practical, the more rhetorical they become. The new Lever House is a monument to our ability to produce glass and to our desire to re-form the skyscraper in the direction of a display case for anybody rather than a fortress for Somebody. Yet (as discussed in chapter xi), it is constantly talked about as if it were a sign of social hygiene, which it may be, and never talked about as if it were a development in corporate architecture as rhetoric, which it most certainly is. Explanations based on the motive of "conspicuous production" are helpful but not complete. Is this not a problem in literalism? What is the cultural base of a public opinion whose vicarious identification with urban architecture is based in part on a democratization of the sense of glory but which refers to itself as honoring the architecture because it is "technically advanced"? We have here examples of brilliant performances in the public arts that remain in some sense underdefined; and both the public and its organs of opinion seem to be responsible for the baldness of the critical vocabulary.

There is still another form of literalism that raises an issue worthy of discussion among the instances that have been envisaged in this discussion of certain problems associated with the contemporary mass-forms and their audiences. It is the issue of the motivational "reality" of advertising (scrutinized in chapter x). In the past, advertising was utopian, in the sense that it took motives for granted and proposed real or unreal methods, all involving purchase in the market, to satisfy them. The sense of the simplicity of human nature was strong in the den of the copywriter; and research was brought forth, from time to time, to be used where and when it confirmed what the "creative man" had already divined by instinct. Today we see much of this reversed. The aim of advertising expenditure, shifting toward research and reformulation, is not to point to the satisfaction of motives but to find what motives there might be to be satisfied. The product stands in the limelight, taken for granted; what is thought to be mysterious is why anyone should want it, at a certain time, in a certain circumstance, in a certain way.

One might say then that someone who resembles at a higher level the Reality Purist is at work at the advertising business; he is the agent who works for a business-management class which claims to know enough about motivations to deserve positions of leadership but also to know so little about human motivations that it has to have them researched all the time. Making allowance for the fact that the purpose of much advertising-associated research is to present the mood of certainty that research encourages and then to attach this mood to conclusions that the research did not actually arrive at, it is the search for motivation that puzzles. The definition of a leader is that he supplies motives. Why is it that American business spends so much time asking to be supplied with motives? It cannot be explained entirely by the democratized mood of American corporate life at the moment. It must be explained in part because of a failure of motives in the business groups.

Perhaps, to go back to the theme of vicariousness, American business has finally become vicariously rather than centrally related to the American scene. It feels, perhaps, that it is not at the center, that it does not quite belong, that it can acquire motives only by imitating something else that is going on in the society. What is that other thing that is going on? The best guess is physics; the businessman is gradually relaxing his motivation and passing the tension on to the psychologist and the physical scientist. They live the real lives with reality; the businessman lives vicariously through them and is pleased by the occasional identification he can achieve with them. This is amply reflected in the messages of the media, in the declining morale of the advertising profession, and in the transition from Business Romance to Science Realism in so many stylistic adjustments of the media today.

The "vicarious we" are dealing, it appears, with a time in which the technical multiplication of likely or unlikely stories, in our reading, our advertisements considered as amusement, our games, our hobbies, and our audio-visual forms, is immense. It is a time in which the documentary likeliness or the unlikeliness of the story seems more important to us, because of the social atmosphere we are living through, than the artistic probability or the improbability of it. Our vicariousness seeks for the true thing and in TV mistakes social intimacy for artistic form, in sports mistakes old-guard amateurism or business expedience for the true thing, in hot-rodding mistakes the overorganization of the peer group, trying to be at once strong, rebellious, and respectable, for the true thing, and in the visible accretions of our cities mistakes the apparent hygienic functionalism of a building for the true thing. Doesn't this deal harshly with the possibility that, since appearance is more evident than reality, much of the best that we know and are is fiction, self-confessed?

> *. . . Things scarcely would have for us features*
> *and outlines so determined and clear that we*
> *could recall them at will, but for the*
> *stereotyped shapes art has lent them.*—Bernard Berenson

CHAPTER THREE

The Seeming Real

Some Popular Concerns

On Sunday, December 12, 1954, the British Broadcasting Corporation produced Nigel Kneale's adaptation of George Orwell's *Nineteen Eighty-four*. It was viewed by between one-fifth and one-quarter of the entire adult population of the United Kingdom. Within a few minutes after its first scenes, the BBC began to receive messages of protest, according to BBC's own chastely statistical reports, "about one-third of its viewers on Sunday reacting violently against it, its horror tending to blind them to its moral." While there was some protest against its being shown on a Sunday, some of the defense of the presentation came from the most churchgoing people in the islands. Although some viewers seemed to be protesting its brutality, their form of protest seemed to carry with it the implication that they had seen the program as an attack on socialism and resented the totalitarian coloring it associated with a socialistic way of life. Many of those who protested said simply that it was "not entertainment," which may very well have been so. There was every indication that BBC was surprised by the results of the broadcast and of the careful poll on the play that it organized shortly after the presentation itself. All this was the result of the appearance on TV of a pure fiction containing recognizable motifs drawn from the political life of our age.

A radio station in Detroit, as reported by John Crosby in the *New York Herald Tribune*, presented not long ago a documentary show called "Kidnap." It was based directly on the experiences of a seven-year-old girl who had been seized by a sexual pervert; its presentation was followed by a discussion of the problem exemplified in the incident. Commenting on the program, Crosby asked whether the intent of the program was to expose and thus to aerate a public problem of some importance or whether the intent was to shock. He mentioned the possibility that the very reportage of the event might lead, as some police officials think, to duplication of the event. No one doubts the practical judgment of the police that this sometimes happens, even though it is extremely difficult to weight the media-event "cause" of crime with all the other causes that may be operating. Is there any doubt, furthermore, that some mass-media forms evade responsibility for providing within the context of the presentation itself some sort of artistic and intellectual controls which assure that a human rather than a dehumanized reaction follows the viewing?

Recently, Marya Mannes, in the *Reporter* magazine, reviewed several thought-provoking programs aired in 1955. She finds herself sympathetic with the handling of the deviant in social life in an NBC-TV discussion program led by a young scholar, Richard Heffner. Such topics as homosexuality and anti-Semitism have already turned up on his program without, apparently, suggesting to her that they were producing homosexuals and anti-Semites. Nor did they impress her as presenting in a "scientific" plain-paper wrapper materials that were to be used by the audience in some clandestine or antisocial way. Her regret, on the contrary, is that the program on anti-Semitism lacked an anti-Semite: "The real test of a proper attitude is to confront it with an improper one." Although this repeats the high-moralizing turn that Miss Mannes displays in some of her TV criticism (a "test" could be supplied not equally well but significantly by the appearance of an anti-Gentile), her discussion is a fruitful one.

Miss Mannes explored in the same article a somewhat different though closely related problem of the media. She described the film study of the Wassaic School for the Mentally Retarded, which was made for CBS by Bill Leonard and presented along with an interview by Leonard of the New York State Mental Health Commissioner. The network originally showed some opposition to the idea of presenting this material and was persuaded to accept it, apparently, by the letters of people who had had parental experience with retarded children and of people employed in their care.

The form of each of these media events was different from all the others. Orwell's *Nineteen Eighty-four* was fiction; "Kidnap" was a journalistic documentary in the criminal vein; the Heffner programs were discussions of our social milieu; and the Leonard program on the retarded children was based on social research. All of them, however, share two major characteristics: their unabashed references to the unpleasant side of the contemporary world and, as a consequence of this, their willingness to arouse popular concern and controversy. They are cited here because they supply as well as any recent examples some idea of the variety of problems that turn up in connection with such materials. The most general of these problems is that of control: we see here the actual workings of informal control in the doubts of producers about production and the protests of the receivers against reception; we also see the very conditions that sometimes lead to direct censorship. This problem itself, however, is one that immediately raises questions of artistic and documentary and rhetorical form. Did some members of the BBC audience feel that their broadcasters were wrapping too much seriousness in the format they felt to be reserved for less challenging forms of fictional entertainment? Apparently so. Was Crosby protesting that "Kidnap" seemed to him very close to a documentary excuse for satisfying a dubious taste for crazy violence? So it seems. Was Miss Mannes demanding that the covert side of public opinion on the status of Jews be represented fully (despite anti-Semitism's practically professional covertness) as a part of the documentation of a social "case in public opinion"? Undoubtedly. Finally, is it possible that the program dominated by *one* major method of presentation, such as Heffner's, is more responsible than the program that employs two disparate methods of presentation (narrative and discussion) like "Kidnap"? Yes—if one suspects that in "Kidnap," as in so many double formats, the narrative was less sensitive because it was to be followed by discussion, and the discussion was less cogent because it had been preceded by narrative.

There are as many policy problems induced by the willingness of the media, often out of a sense of great responsibility, to educate the public in various matters as result from a desire to retain public attention at any cost in sensationalism. There are also artistic problems; and the main purpose of this chapter is to discuss the artistic problems, especially insofar as they serve as the conventions through which all the other problems get defined. It is only with artistic problems that we shall see how certain basic mechanisms such as the public-private equilibrium of the media are constantly at work; how special themes such as violence command public attention; how stereotypes of character on the audio-visual screen spark protest from veto groups; how the very realism of the modern camera creates problems for censorship that did not exist before. It is only with this sort of background that we can then go on to discuss the way in which certain kinds of realism are built into the occupational structure of the audio-visual industry; how ideas of criticism, control, and censorship based on "quantitative" approaches to media content get off the track; and how some of the more recent sophisticated forms of movie realism serve as "violence comic books" with respectable covers.

Miss Mannes, writing about the appropriate criteria to be applied to such presentations as that of the retarded children, suggests that the test is whether the program can help to make "compassion supplant aversion"; and one could hardly suggest a better test. In her concluding remarks, however, she speaks darkly of how these programs "mercifully stopped short of that line beyond which contemporary fiction has gone to its great detriment—the point where the presentation of 'reality' is an end in itself, and a sordid end at that."

This could hardly be called the test that is appropriate *both* to contemporary documentary footage and to fictional footage, however realistic; and thus her proposition stands as an example of that confusion of genres which is so important in our general judgment of what the media do. Miss Mannes should have stuck to the test of an effective public "compassion" and explored this theme with the fulness it deserves. For it breaks open immediately the question of the public-private equilibrium in media publicity, a question that is so general in all media presentation that it must be discussed here.

Taking Miss Mannes' materials as the major example, let us notice that the point of the network argument preceding the public presentation of the film of the retarded children is that the program was made possible by the appeal of those who had a non-fictional stake in the problem it portrayed. This, in some sense, constituted a useful pre-test of the audience or at least a part of it: it tested the reactions of people, not merely unfortunate parents but also, above all, simply parents. This quite reasonable probe into the real-life identifications of the audience provided just the sort of test appropriate to the case.

It may not have gone far enough. The patients might have been asked, and, if they gave no reply, this might have been interpreted as meaning that they could not care or that, being unable to care, they should be left unexposed as human beings unable to protect themselves from publicity. True, this would run the risk that the dramatization of the need for trained personnel to aid the retarded would be lost as a media message; but it might be better for retarded children to be miserable and private than to be publicly exhibited and better cared for. The problem of "dissipating the stigma and concealment attending this common human problem," noted by Marya Mannes as one of the aims of the program, was clearly aimed at the consolation of the parents far more than it was at the welfare of the children. In this sense, the presentation of the materials has an entirely different meaning in addition to all those mentioned by Miss Mannes, even though we recognize that such a program may result in an improvement of the children's lot because it alleviates the state of mind of their parents.

The point is that whereas Miss Mannes writes as if the seeing of these children by the general audience is the major effect, the major effect could well be on the parents of these children, an effect brought about by seeing that these children have been seen by the general audience. The price paid by the rest of the audience is to have to identify, through a documentary lens, with ill-fortune that is not at the moment theirs; it is on the basis of this price paid by the general audience that the "victim audience" can redefine and purge its own emotions relating to the problem. Thus, one of the criteria that Miss Mannes does not mention, which is more important to non-fiction than to fiction, is whether accessories to the pathetic, tragic, criminal, or shameful in the public documentary have both obligations and rights. Their rights might be exemplified in the right of the criminal's family to protection from the TV lens in the courtroom. Their obligations might be exemplified in the responsibility, often violated with the help of the networks, of the unfortunate on a "misery" program not to show his bitter misfortunes beyond the limit of the consensus of public opinion. Although there is no intent here to argue that the

parents of retarded children are exhibitionists of their problem—we know, indeed, that they are the reverse—we may
argue that *all* successful efforts to make the public look at what
it first does not want to look at constitute a coercion—like com-
pulsory education! And the coercion involved in the airing of
the retarded children contains the perplexing possibility that a
private-public equilibrium is being arranged so that the private
onus of the parents will be less, not merely because the children
are better cared for, but because the public onus has become
greater.

One test of the documentary is where, when, and in what
circumstances this change in the public-private equilibrium
should take place. This question of the balance between the
right not to be informed and the right to be informed is so deeply rooted in the mass-media relationship that it had better be
illustrated by less portentous examples. It is a question that
turns up in connection with the frequency with which the media present some social types at the expense of others and with
varying tones of implicit approval or disapproval. The media
can either confirm or resist a strong stereotype—tending to confirm the stereotype in order to build recognizable dramatic
character, tending to deny it in the hope of doing something
original and perceptive. The American media generally follow
the popular vote, for example, in presenting doctors in a highly
favorable light, thus maintaining a certain equilibrium of public relations information in favor of the doctor. The British media, on the contrary, are not afraid to show doctors as bad men
or bunglers for the reason that doctors are not so high in the
popularity scale in Britain. Now, the stereotyped portraiture of
specific social and occupational types is such that its conventions can rarely be flouted by the media, and wherever the media
have to choose between not informing the public and following
such a convention, they choose not to inform the public. A case
in point might be high-school teachers who are surprised,
amused, and occasionally needled by the presence of "Our Miss

Brooks" on the TV screen. It is clear that they are being involved willy-nilly in the creation of a new stereotype of themselves, just as detectives feel the same sometimes uncomfortable process going on when they watch Joe Friday.

Are there any rules of the game that control this sort of thing in the American audience structure? Of course there are. Hollywood has long prohibited the attribution to men-of-the-cloth of certain actions that are considered a slur upon their profession; and the degree to which professional and trade associations put pressure on the mass media not to handle their members in a cavalier way is well known. There are well-organized beliefs to the effect that some occupational and social roles are above the laws of art while others are not; and these beliefs are sometimes closely related and sometimes not at all closely related to such indices as the public rankings of professions, by prestige, in the United States. In TV-life, the villains are likely to be, of all things, diplomats and businessmen; many of the heroes are doctors; and lawyers are sometimes good and sometimes bad.

In all these instances, however, there is hardly a taboo of the formal or informal kind that cannot be circumvented either by what some people might call code evasion or by what others might call artistic transcendence of the problem of representation involved. The soda-jerk in American life was fully defined for Americans largely by minor players who did things that the audience accepted with total gullibility largely because they were dramatic characterizations offered as transitional bits in plot or on the periphery of audience attention. Yet note that praise or blame for a character-type from the audio-visual media, even within the framework of artistic intention, is taken at a quasi-realistic, even advisory, level by some members of the audience. Western films and western novels are most popular in western states for an understandable reason observed by Leslie Fiedler: westerners need character-typed westerners in their media to keep on believing in themselves.

These comments on the public-private equilibrium and on the formal elements in media presentation that encourage or discourage change in that equilibrium suggest the complications of media control when it operates, as it must, not only on a differentiated social actuality and a differentiated audience, but also on forms that are different in their principles of organization. All these issues tend to come together when we consider public concerns with violence in audio-visual presentations, a concern that includes an anxiety not merely about the violence itself but also about the moral character of the fictional or nonfictional agents who commit it. We might well begin by considering the cross-cultural ambiguity of acts of violence in the audio-visual world. When we see how differently two different cultures look at violence, we can see more readily how different artistic conventions and different knowledge of these conventions, in different audiences, bedevil our judgment. Some of the best comments on the prevalence of violence in American films come, to be sure, from the British observers. They react sensitively partly because they have not seen so much violence in British films, partly because this code itself reflects the morals and manners of a society in which even a casual brushing physical contact is considered an invasion of privacy and in which the monopoly of violence is in the hands of the state, parents, and semi-sacred custom. British distaste for our movie violence is sometimes muddied by a sociopsychological confusion: the British are more systematically dominated as children than we are, and violence (or absence of fondling) is part of this system. One result is that the British associate violence either with the Bad Boy or with the Perfect Father, and hardly with anything in between except sports and hitting lower-class women on the fanny in vaudeville shows. This makes it hard for them to digest American movies, where violence is frequently enough associated with very Bad Boys but most tensely associated with Good-Bad Boys and hardly ever with the Perfect Father. The figures of authority in American movies are monopolies of good will alone, rarely ever possessing that godlike right to strike, as in the British Chief Justice, which is so often associated with British film fathers, detectives, bosses, and other authorities on the "right" side of any dispute between man and man or man and state.

It might be interesting, however, for the American to have a chance to see and to think about those sections of American films that are cut by European censors because of their violence. Some small movie theater in the "art circuit" could do this easily by superimposing on the screen during European-cut sections the image of a transparency with, say, a big $\times$ written across it. Doubtless such a policy, even on one night a week, would be interpreted as a variation on the old exhibitor game of using ostensibly reportorial means to call attention to "dubious" film-footage in its current show. If the experiment were tried, however, a few more American movie-goers would become familiar with the objections that are voiced, for example, by an interested and genuinely concerned English-born critic of "popular iconography" in the United States, Geoffrey Wagner.

He notes that research into film content shows that recent American films average 6.6 scenes of violence per film and that only 7 out of a sample of 80 movies contained none at all. He is especially to be listened to when he points out that the "good" characters in Westerns "try to kill two men for every one that the bad characters do." Thus, while some of his comments on the non-moralized violence and mayhem of films seem overdone, his comments on the moralized violence—the violence willed or performed by the "good" agent—seem profound. We must recognize that a real threat is contained in American movies' license-of-violence for the righteous. Part of the point of identifying scenes deleted by European censors would be lost in the American showing, to be sure, because the American showing could not include for the sake of comparison the sections censored by American authorities. It could not be demonstrated by example that Europeans tolerate scenes of sexuality that our code forbids while snipping scenes of violence that our code allows. Thus it would be impossible to see exemplified the thesis of G. Legman (*Love and Death*) that excess sex censorship in United States films creates a vacuum that sadism fills up.

This selection of certain problems of the mass media in the presentation of materials held to be deleterious by some parts of the audience has emphasized an admittedly narrow selection of current popular concerns. The adverse criticisms cited here are based, it must be remembered, on a variety of presuppositions. One is that the effect of certain themes on all or parts of the audience can be reasonably determined; another is that, given the determination of the effect, it can be characterized as good or bad for the audience. Another is that both these functions can be carried out by formal and informal policies of control. Still another is that, in the process of applying control, something like a consensus of popular opinion, balanced between the judgments of the majority and the minorities in the audience, can and should be arrived at. Here we bypass all except the first question in order to concentrate on the determination of effect.

Our available ways of talking about desirable effects tend to be contradictory. One way consists of asking the mass media to present people as they ought to be; and this, of course, is always translated consciously or unconsciously into "people as our cultural definitions of the moment say they ought to be." This rule is applied most often to products beamed at children by the mass media. Another way consists of asking the mass media to present no more and no less of certain types of acts and consequences than are believed to occur in real life. This of course is always translated consciously or unconsciously into the critic's image of the social order. If he believes, against the facts, that crime is increasing more in urban areas than in non-urban areas, he will react more unfavorably against crime-associated violence in a rural than in an urban scene. Still another way consists of detouring these approaches and saying: "Present what people will accept, not what they refuse to accept." The problem here always turns out to be a question of who "they" are and who "their" representatives are.

Yet no one takes these approaches seriously, either singly or in combination, without regard to other considerations. Everyone knows, though few say so often enough, that mass-media effects are a function also of form; and forms are the product of their histories and their ideologies. If the "real" is equated with the "sordid" by some members of the audience, then the forms feel the influence of this. If forms are dominated by shifts of medium, as from stage to film and film to TV, with the result that the camera eye moves to a new sampling of documentary and fictional reality, then the forms feel the influence of this.

Surely film and TV have disturbed the uneasy peace previously existing among the various criteria of audience effects: they have permitted a mechanical agent to select the detail that composes the totality of what an audience sees. Modern audiences are still struggling to come to terms with the difference between what a camera sees and what the human observer sees. Clearly, censors are as much troubled by such problems, originating in shifts of media and genres, as they are by the content of the genres. Audio-visual realism has sparked a series of shifts in the cultural audibility and visibility of aspects of life; the morale of "realism" interpreted as a denigration of human dignity has been bolstered by these shifts, especially under conditions of mass-audience accessibility; and critics and censors realize that the ethos of "realism" is itself just another form of fantasy but cannot bring themselves to deal with it as such. The only self-organizing fantasy that exists in the human world is the human dream; all others presuppose struggles between form of a certain kind and content of a certain kind—struggles that are not resolved, as they are in dreams, by partial

suspensions of waking attention. Perhaps the only self-consist-
ent criterion of modern film realism would derive from asking
whether a given product constitutes the simulacrum of a culturally acceptable dream. Yet this is the criterion that the censor cannot learn to apply. He cannot apply it, to be sure, because, while all audio-visual presentations, whether documentary, fictional, or rhetorical, are objectified in some sense, they
are subject to various rules of interpretation. One of the major
rules is that one must ask in connection with any audio-visual
presentation how many of the audience are seeing it as documentary, how many are seeing it as fiction, and how many are
seeing it as persuasion. This is one of the questions about form
that censorship often begs.

It is necessary to turn to specific illustrations of these problems in the popular vocabularies of criticism. First we must take
a sample of the production process and see how the literalism
that creates problems for the censors is sustained in the labor
organization of production. Then we must turn to an audience
segment and see, by illustration, how a misplaced criterion of
content analysis can lead to ambiguous criteria of censorship.
Finally we must return to a case of the "realistic" genre itself
and observe how changes in artistic fashion induced by neo-
realism result in a distortion of urban-rural, urban-suburban,
and labor-management aspects of our current social scene.

Naturalism and the Theatrical Crafts

The appearance of color TV has already committed the industry to another step in the historic process of technological
advance by which movie, kinescopic, and studio presentations
cyclically add new sensuous dimensions to realism, increase
capital costs of equipment, and increase technical and craft
personnel costs. The artistic effect of the shift, if it follows the
pattern set up by such previous developments as the movie
conversion to sound and the early days of TV itself, will be to
make sensuous realism the major issue and dramatic realism

the minor issue of TV fiction. The secondary effect, after the novelty has worn off, will be to direct TV toward a renewed pursuit of dramatic realism. Dramatic realism will be defined, of course, within the general terms of an aesthetic of naturalism. The two stages of adaptation to the new are, first, high sensuous probability and low dramatic probability; second, high sensuous probability and somewhat higher dramatic probability than in the first stage. Since a major task of "dramatic probability" in the second stage is to exploit to the fullest the quasi-documentary effects introduced by technical innovation in the first stage, it is taken for granted in the second stage that a naturalistic aesthetic is the one and only criterion of dramatic probability.

This sequence repeats at a more advanced technical level the successive stages of the use of natural color in the movies. Some of the earliest and most effective uses of movie color were in documentary film; still later, some of its most publicized effects were connected with "epics" such as *Gone with the Wind*. It required all the years between *Gone with the Wind* and *An American in Paris* for the movie industry to develop a conviction that natural color might be manipulated for fantasy effects; and it appeared to have learned this not from uses of the color-sensitized film directed toward natural objects but from the "synthetic" color effects of the cinematic cartoon-makers. In the years between these two films, the general assumptions about color could be described as follows: (1) it adds a new sensuous dimension; (2) this new sensuous dimension is interesting in itself; (3) after it ceases to be so interesting in itself, it becomes an added tool in the artistic armory of dramatic realism; (4) the aesthetic of naturalism, of course, provides the framework in which color achieves its most appropriate uses as a variable contributing to dramatic realism.

This technical pressure toward literal effects in the movie and TV arts has been criticized often enough for the disruptive effects it has on pre-established traditions of production and form. Audience veterans recollect that Movietone and related systems made obsolescent some matinee idols with poor voices. It seems correspondingly certain that color TV will have influences unforeseen even by reference to experience with color in Hollywood. Disappointment with such ambiguous "progress" in the movie and TV arts is often expressed in terms of Aldous Huxley's comic hyperbole of the "feelies" in *Brave New World*. The argument implicit in Huxley's satirical fiction of the "feelies" is that the art of the film or TV is reduced toward an aesthetic of sensationalism and, indeed, hedonism; the latter is regarded by Huxley as a public sin, the former as an artistic error. This prophecy, however, exaggerates the cultural, if not the technical, possibility of keeping everyone at a Cinerama level. Without pausing to debate the sin of hedonism, it is clear that "literal" techniques when new occupy only a brief period of high status in their own terms; their more durable effect is to drive both producers and audiences beyond the latest tricks of a sensationalistic aesthetic toward a more highly elaborated aesthetic of naturalism.

Naturalism means, in the first place, a notion that fiction is good if it is a slice of life—a slice of life recognizable as such because it exhibits certain social phenomena that are associated by both the producers and the audience with real life. The movie or TV fiction, according to naturalism, is good if it meets these external tests of probability; and these tests of probability are, furthermore, the only relevant tests for fiction. Such artistic standards were taken over by the film from other media, and these other media, especially painting and writing, acquired them partly as the result of a culture contact with photography and phonography in early stages of their technical development. The documentary and topical effects in early movies were not so much the result of naturalism as an artistic theory-at-work; they were nature unself-consciously at work in front of a lens which happened to be turned in its direction. Dramatic naturalism came to the film later, as a cultural preference for watered-down versions of the genre.

Given this relationship between new theatrical techniques and the aesthetic of naturalism, we must understand how much this has had a crucial effect on the occupational structure of the movie and TV industries. Enormous efforts at scenic, historical, and social versimilitude, which are ordinarily regarded as being dictated largely by the tastes of the audience and the producers, are perhaps made even more inevitable in movies and TV by their institutional roots in the skills of the technical and craft personnel. Could it be that the proportional thinness of non-naturalistic techniques in film and TV is as much a function of the supply of technical skills aimed toward realism as it is of any other factor? The technician and the craftsman in movie and TV industries have a heavy stake in naturalism and in continued cultural definitions that work in its favor. This stake, in fact, composes an important part of the general social goodwill that becomes, in part, an element of their occupational bargaining power. This power of displaced craftsmanship resembles the power and persistence of all such "high-finish" producers in American life, from the weight-reducing beauticians to the smiling air-line hostesses.

We must remember that in the early development of a new cinematic or TV technique the technicians occupy a crucial role in the production process. A relatively informal production team, working with unstandardized devices, labors with a will to turn out the best technical product that it can. The functional subdivision of tasks is such that scene-building, lighting, wiring, and a whole host of other variables have not yet been defined in terms of their precise interdependencies. Partly because decisions as to their interdependence have to be made on an off-the-cuff basis, the technical team itself has an amorphous sense of its professional identity. In later stages —and this was most recently noticeable in TV—the techniques of lighting, camera work, and scene-building become more rationalized. The technical and craft group enlarges; its operations become routine and bureaucratized; and its sense of professional identity grows. Many of the skills of the early men are built into the machines or the production techniques employed by the later men. The technicians and craft people themselves, reacting in some instances to memories of their early exploitation, in a medium that has proved to be more profitable to its owners than anyone first dreamed, seek collective security vis-à-vis their employers. Their tactical bargaining position emphasizes jurisdictional specialization aimed at standard effects of realism, as understood up to that point, and binds each craftsman to the support of it. When labor standardization and standard production practices become fully institutionalized, a whole style in theatricality becomes fossilized in technical fact. It is hard to dispense with any realistic item of production because all the labor resources necessary to attain it have, in a sense, been budgeted into production plans in advance.

In 1947, for example (as I reported in *Fortune*): "Members of two Hollywood unions, the Make-up Artists and Hair Stylists and the Motion Picture Costumers . . . disagreed with each other over the right to install false bosoms. Probably only a few close students of labor followed the case far enough to notice that the jurisdictional dispute arose from an ambiguity in the falsies themselves. Some are made of cloth and some of rubber. In Hollywood or elsewhere, jurisdiction is frequently determined by the materials used or fabricated. . . ." Although this proves more about the suzerainties of specialists in illusion than it does about realism, it does no great harm to be reminded in detail how in all the arts the worst sort of AF of L practices prevail. It is not merely that the musicians' union prevents living composers from taking tapes of the rare public performances of their new works but also that academes and journalists develop a monopolistic mentality.

The pride of the Hollywood craftsman in doing things right also showed during an interview with a former bucket-and-wall-style painter who rose to power for a while as the head of Hollywood Painters Local 644, a group of artists with heavy responsibilities to realism. He liked to talk about the subtler abilities of his painter-members. "One time the studio wanted some pictures of birds flying backward like they were in Shanghai. They hired a Chinese painter to do them like in the tradition. He gave up in a couple hours. Our man finished it up, all right. Why, we can paint birds flying upside down if necessary."

All this is of no little importance to the largest Hollywood labor group, the various members of the solidly established International Alliance of Theatrical Stage Employees, with more than fifty thousand members all over the United States, many in Hollywood. Its agreements in the 1940's and some recent ones called for Sunday rates five times the week-end standard in some specific labor assignments. "These rates," said Richard Walsh, onetime head of the Alliance, with the rapt air of a bird-lover listening to a rare warbler, "are called golden hours."

The technicians and craftsmen of the expanding team take over from the small group of their predecessors a compulsive nicety about lighting, wiring, and scene construction. It can be called compulsive because in some senses it becomes less relevant in later and more standardized phases of the technical game than it was in the earlier stages. Thus in early TV programs audiences took the trouble to notice and laugh at scenic and lighting anomalies. There are far fewer of them now. But even if there were more than there are, who would care very much? Many types of scenic and illumination perfectionism would go unnoticed now that people are interested in what TV exhibits dramatically more than they are in what it is technologically. Yet it is easy to understand why the technician prefers to be a perfectionist. It is the craftsmanly tradition; it links him as a technically indispensable heir of his technical predecessors; it makes him important and employable.

The technicians and craft people, during any cost crisis of the industry, are economic inflexibilities. They resist most alternatives that would bypass older technical requirements or render them artistically irrelevant. The cost-ratios induced by this feeling were striking in early TV. Even today, the technical cost of a single one-hour program of a standard sort on a national network from New York runs from five to fifty times as high as the payment to the scriptwriter. This ratio, seen in context, is not necessarily scandalous. It is impossible to project the Pacific Ocean in which four flyers are adrift in an open boat from a studio location without considerable expenditure of time and equipment. It is probably even more expensive to reproduce a home or hospital scene of the improbable scenic luxuriousness deemed appropriate to soap opera. Nevertheless, in a period when most people in the industry are worried about costs and advertisers threaten to withdraw some of their "free" entertainment to American TV-viewers, the budgetary issue is of some importance.

The issue is important because it points toward the very real problems of the artistic basis of cost-and-income distribution in the movie and TV industries. Yet we must recall the complications of labor history: the technicians of Hollywood, in the old days after some careless treatment by the producers and stockholders, organized for their own protection. They were followed by the semiskilled technicians, some of them migrants from the stage industries. In the late 1920's and the 1930's the International Alliance of Theatrical Stage Employees was suddenly assisted in its union tasks by the Chicago bad boys, Willie Bioff and Jack Brown, who used gangster methods to enforce collective bargaining. In a still later stage the Hollywood painters and others, partly as a reform move against the IATSE and partly as a result of the Communist caucuses, staged another series of battles for control of the workers and the producers. Few hands were completely clean, and no hands, including those of the unions influenced by Communist caucuses, were completely dirty.

One of the old lessons relearned in the movie-union battles

of the 1930's and 1940's was that the industry itself was a poor judge of its relation to its own technicians. It was often in too much of a hurry to know how much it depended on the gaffer up among the lights; it was often in too much of a hurry to know that he was unionized or a goldbricker. All entertainment industries are full of indispensable and dispensable *standby* labor, and of all types of labor this type is the most difficult for both co-workers and employers to tolerate psychologically. The standby worker in entertainment industries often retaliates psychologically on an occupational prestige basis by a profound cynicism about everything that transpires in production "above" his level of operations.

For all that, not the technician's job is at issue here but his "stickiness" in the job. When theatrical skills are highly subdivided and when interskill jurisdiction becomes important, many technical workers are forced into stickiness. Becoming socially and economically identified with one aspect of the production craft, they are looked at with understandable suspicion if they try to take control of other aspects of the craft in the work situation; and they may be looked at with suspicion if they attempt occupational mobility even of a horizontal type from one craft to another. They live, compared to directors, actors, and entertainers, in quite a different world. Associating themselves less with the changing fashions of the industry and more with its permanent technical base, they consider themselves more permanent than the others. Vice-presidents and stars and writers disappear; they remain.

Employment in the film industry is not what it once was; in late 1956, the number of studio workers declined to about 12,054, according to the reports of a West Coast bank—a figure that suggests that more applicants would be looking for the roughly 4,000 craft jobs in the West Coast TV factories. Part of the 1956 decline was correctly attributed by the Hollywood AF of L Film Council to the increase in production abroad. Such production began, we recall, in the late 1940's, when studios began to use real-life settings, blocked credits abroad, and the lower all-round costs of production outside of the American price structure. One of the results of the practice was to increase the number of open-air quasi-documentaries; another was to get Hollywood production away from some of the cost problems and many of the artistic problems of the subdivided reality of the jurisdictional movie lot. In late 1956 the Hollywood AF of L Film Council, in the face of multiplying labor-shortage reports in almost every semiskilled trade in the United States, announced publicly that it intended to ask producers to reduce the 55 films out of a total of 255 in shooting that were being produced overseas. Vague though not necessarily exaggerated charges that overseas production policy took jobs from free-union American labor while handing at least some of these jobs over to Communist-tied unions in Europe were made by the Council. From available reports, the Council took no notice of the possibility that success in their policy would add to the arts-tariff system that already operates to deprive American consumers of leisure products manufactured abroad at qualities equal to or better than the American brand and at lower prices. Its logical extension might be a policy forbidding American travel abroad beyond a certain limit on the principle that it took jobs away from American hotel and resort managers and personnel.

What is so interesting in this case is the apparent economic stickiness of this and perhaps other segments of California skilled labor. One almost gets the idea that, having moved to California as a heaven, these craftsmen have been "tetched" by a state nationalism which makes them take it for granted that the American consumer, in this instance the movie-goer, should be compelled to accept their products whether they want them or not—and accept as a matter of course the artistic limitations on production that flow out of the Hollywood traditions of the craft system.

Viewing the inertia of the crafts and the enormous cost of

producing "realistic" shows, the scriptwriters or their self-appointed spokesmen sometimes complain of underpayment. Nevertheless, writers, producers, directors, and audiences all share in maintaining the high cost of realism. Influences of neo-realism from Europe, to be sure, were successfully incorporated into a general mood of cost-reduction rather than cost-expansion in the years when Hollywood was suffering most from TV's inroads; but this was only a special case of change demonstrating what happens when realism has its fat taken off in one industry while the calories are being shifted to produce artistic obesity in a competing industry. In the audio-visual field as a whole, in spite of the rise in power and prestige of writer-producers and writer-directors, the power to determine artistic form as contrasted with the power to fill up by formula artistic conventions already accepted, has not changed radically in recent years. A superabundance of technical means in both movies and TV, but especially the profitable networks of TV, is hard to resist using. Where audiences for Belasco productions once generated a need for craftsmen because realism was the commodity they wanted, we now generate a need for realism because crafts and techniques stand wanting to be used.

There is, to be sure, a mutually confirming relationship among the class audience, the aesthetic convention, and the institutionalization of realistic techniques. For one thing, as long as organized craft people lead the industry with the services of naturalism, they impose the aesthetic of naturalism on the audiences they are supposed to serve; and it is probable that they rationalize their own tastes in the arts by doing so. If TV were less artistically muscle-bound, could it afford to develop more scripts outside the formula of naturalistic drama or melodrama and dispense with a few million man-hours of carpenters who might better be building real houses for real people than expensively imitative cottages for TV characters?

Naturalism as a Test

In one of his poems, Ralph Waldo Emerson, commenting on the growth of the democratic spirit in the nineteenth century, spoke of the "astonished Muse" who found "thousands at her side." Television in the United States undoubtedly astonishes all the Muses. The Calliope of epic fictions finds herself unexpectedly presiding over reruns of old western movies, and Clio, the Muse of history, is invoked daily by the newsmen who report world events over TV. Today the Muse who mentors the multifarious creativity of mass information distribution and entertainment has millions at her side. At the beginning of 1957, with some 40 million TV sets in operation, the TV audience numbered about 100 million. This is the audience that gives 30 million viewers to *Hamlet* as well as many more millions to Milton Berle.

Television undoubtedly has produced an alteration in the relative importance of the mass media. One of the first things it did was to strike hard at the profits of the movie industry, which resulted in many changes of policy and management, including "theater TV" and the recent sale of hundreds of old movies to TV networks. As for new footage, all the large studios have to compete with a number of small new firms who have been producing film for TV on a "quickie" basis, with costs, until recently, quite as low as the dramatic probabilities sometimes encountered in their scripts. The rate at which TV can eat up old film is suggested by the sales of numberless British films of ancient vintage, a welcome postwar credit in British film profits and the United Kingdom balance of trade.

Observers do not differ widely in their estimate of the ways in which the media fare of the people of the United States has changed since TV began to elbow out movie and radio time among set owners. In the first place, it is clear that a whole group of special-interest audiences are pleased. TV has made it possible for sports spectators to see a major sports event almost every day in the week. The children of the United States are probably more gratified, more unexpectedly, than any other audience: they have found on TV something they long dreamed of—free movies every day. Soon after TV gained its first sizable audiences, it was reported that children between the ages of two and fourteen spent as much as four and one-half hours per day at their sets. This employment of the after-school and evening hours by the children exploded a series of noisy battles among educators, parents, and the media men.

In TV's earlier stage an American ex-educator named Angelo Patri, who has long advised parents about their problems through a syndicated column, signed a paid testimonial in which he declared that the child who was deprived of TV for other reasons than parental lack of funds was close to being deprived of his cultural birthright. Appearing in a large advertisement for TV interests, this challenge was greeted with indignation by many parents who either refused TV to their children or carefully monitored their children's hours with it.

Stirred by the possibilities for some immediate research into attitudes toward the media, a Chicago student in the field of communications, Margarete Midas, began to investigate a city neighborhood, asking householders about their attitudes toward the Patri debate. She obtained a small sample of opinions in a neighborhood where social and economic class affiliations range from millionaire status almost to slum-dwelling status. She was surprised because many TV-owners had never heard of the controversy; because *none* of the respondents of lower socio-economic status were concerned about the Patri proposition; because virtually *all* those of upper socio-economic status took a stand against Patri and to some extent against TV whether they had heard of the controversy or not. This distribution of attitudes, considered along with other probabilities, suggested very strongly that a larger sample would yield a similar, if not sharp, correlation between class and attitudes toward TV.

Such findings were reinforced by studies of the attitudes expressed in magazines and in groups of parents of homogeneous occupational and socio-economic status. The *New Yorker*, for example, consistently employed its cartoons to identify TV with middle- or lower-middle-class social status and with parent-child tensions within this context. Not long after TV became widely distributed in the United States, it began meeting high resistance from academic communities, where children of all ages were being shielded from it by a more or less conspicuous non-ownership of sets. The same tendency was noticeable for a while, though with much less intensity, in middle-class families associated with the intellectual trades and the free professions. In all these social regions TV was said to be bad for children, specifically in its vulgarity, its bad taste, its disturbing emotional effects. A major TV critic in the United States, John Crosby, has dismissed these parental concerns as projections of adult anxieties having little or nothing to do with the impact of TV on children.

In any case, the attacks on TV, especially in the earlier days, are less interesting than certain failures to praise it for its virtues. Thus, many who are unsympathetic to TV and its fare tend to dismiss the brilliance of its sports coverage partly because the reportage of sports seems to them a trivial matter. What is more important, the one or two fields in which TV has been and is superb are neglected. Take the matter of theatrical dancing. American theatrical dancing, the product of a confluence of folk tradition and the entertainment business, is acknowledged as one of the liveliest popular art forms in the world. It is partly inspired and keyed up, of course, by the rich treasury of American folk music, especially in jazz idioms. For all that, although TV gives weekly presentations of superb theatrical dancing, many in the audience seem to be unable to find the words in which to appreciate and criticize the achievement. Yet who can deny that the proper performance of a dance is one of the great achievements of a culture finding its form and that American TV is learning to become a great channel for it?

Arguments for and against the quality of TV fare in general have been drawn from studies either of its content or of its emotional, intellectual, and physiological effects, especially on children. To take first the problem of the effects, little has been proved against TV except that children grow bored with over-exposure after a time and become more selective; there exists no basic research that proves seriously harmful effects on children. TV seems to have reduced only temporarily the hours spent in reading and on homework by public school students. On the other hand, high TV attention has never been success-fully correlated with a decline in school achievement. In only one clear-cut instance does TV have some measurable effects: it appears to extend somewhat the period of wakefulness and uneasiness in children just before they fall asleep at bedtime. For all that, it would be far more to the point to ask, not how good or bad TV is, but how good or bad its competition is in the everyday cultural life of the family.

Recent discussion based on TV content analysis owes much to the work of Dallas Smythe and his collaborators, highly trained students of communications who monitored and quan-tified TV program content on a full-week basis in three major cities of the United States. They found that crime drama for children took up a larger segment of time (about 20 per cent) than any other classification except the one that included drama, variety shows, and popular entertainment music (about 70 per cent). They found also that, according to their method of classification, only about 4 per cent of program time could be claimed as educational. Although these statistical results were employed by editorializers to reinforce their charges of TV terrors to children, the investigators themselves made no such claim. In the first place, they claimed only to have mon-itored the content and format of TV fare; they did not infer from the high percentage of crime stories for children that TV invited children to emulate criminals. Correspondingly, they did not admit the argument of the media men, that because most crime programs wind up by saying that "crime does not pay" they are therefore either a positive force for public morality or good drama. In assessing the educational achievements of TV they demanded that any program with educational claims should demonstrate a clear-cut intellectual purpose. They excluded quite correctly from the educational classification all the dramatizations of information-giving, problem-solving, and attitude-building which are incidental and atomized parts of entertainment programs.

These studies were among the most useful materials employed by the Americans concerned about TV who carried out a drive in 1951, in Federal Communications Commission hearings, to make TV a tool for education in the United States. With great expenditure of time and effort—and against opposition by some of the commercial broadcasters—educators, parents, and their allies fought the issue on two grounds. They charged and proved that commercial broadcasters did not live up to the FCC code which enjoined an educational function and that therefore the educators had a potential right to use new channels of TV for educational purposes. As a result, early in 1952 the FCC awarded to educational combines in various regions of the country the right to acquire and exploit a group of wave channels which in terms of commercial broadcasting were worth millions of dollars. The record of educational TV so far is not what some self-confident Ichabods thought it would be, a glorious revolution. It does have a lot to be proud of.

What is most compelling about program-contents evaluation, perhaps, is the more than faint suggestion given that the literal number of blows given in TV might have some directly dubious effect on the upbringing of children exposed to the medium, although none of the investigators asserts this relation, most of the people who took such tests seriously as a black eye for TV actually did. This interpretation stands as a classic example of a certain simple-mindedness about how a work of fictional art gains its effects on its audiences. It suggests that Americans find most to fear in a "realism" representing forbidden acts and that they believe control over such representations will reduce the inspiration to such acts. Whatever the political morality of this stand may be, insofar as it affects censorship developments, its aesthetic is clear: realism is dangerous, not when it is bad art, but when it is the representation of disapproved actions, characters, and thoughts. This attitude, of course, reinforces documentary realism of the cruder sort, since the way to get the rough stuff on the screen is to claim that it is based on research into actuality.

All this and more was demonstrated by research into the audience for the famous Orson Welles invasion from Mars broadcast of October 30, 1938. There were some, no one knows how many, who made no attempt at all to check on the authenticity of the story. There were others who checked the authenticity of the fictional "news broadcast" by external evidence, as, for example, by tuning in to other stations to hear whether such terrible news was coming over them. Finally, there were those whose familiarity with the voice of Welles or the genre or whose dissatisfaction with internal evidence of probability (such as the unheard-of speed with which the "gas" was spreading, according to the fictionalized reports) led them to doubt the veracity of the broadcast virtually from the beginning. This tendency toward the misinterpretation of the media message, since it was associated with those who were plainly ignorant of distinctions between the fictional and the nonfictional conventions, appears at first to justify those who express fears about the impact of comic books and TV violence on children. "If many adults cannot tell the difference between fact and fantasy," they say, "then how many children cannot tell?" But this misses the point. It shifts the attention of the would-be censor to questions of mere media content, as if everyone in the world were insensitive to fictional form. Without dismissing attention to content, the invasion-from-Mars story suggests that children have a right to develop their sense of fiction as an art form and that, indeed, the public interest has the obligation to help them develop it. It is a mistake, on finding that illiteracy in artistic form is the cause of a public problem, to recommend that the question of forms itself should be disregarded; it is more reasonable to recommend that skill in the perception of fiction become every child's privilege, to the degree of his ability.

Westerns and Urbans

This chapter began by considering a sample of audio-visual presentations with the idea of spelling out some of the problems that are generated for their publics by media form itself. Starting from the concept of a public-private equilibrium of information on this or that issue, we saw how the various fictional, documentary, or persuasive formats play their part in the web of conventions that connect the audience-member with his idea of "reality." Frequently enough, illiteracy in forms is encouraged by an industrial and occupational structure that knows only one form—expensive realism. Frequently enough, criticism and incipient censorship of the media are confused by hoping to remedy young illiteracy in fictional forms by monitoring mere content. Always and everywhere, the very range and exactitude of the camera eye and the sound track originate novel problems for criticism and censorship: first, by substituting for the word the uncontrollable curiosity of the audio-visual track; second, by involving the whole public imagination in simplistic notions of how "reality" gets onto a screen.

This might make it sound as if only hayseeds and other provincials faced such problems, but it is a fact that new twists in sophisticated realism in the film today bring the same problems home to everyone. Two major influences bring about a new tendency to use naturalism in dubious ways in film production.

One is the greater freedom of film in contrast with TV, so that film tends to respond to TV competition by emphasizing the sexuality and violence that have never been allowed to flourish on the more puritanically controlled home screen. The other is Italian neo-realism. This productive and impressive form, learned in part from earlier American films, is not easy to describe. Beginning with such films as *Open City,* it has achieved for its audiences a remarkable blend of tragic and comic handling of everyday subject matter, with fine outdoor photography, informal casting, superb individual performances, and a sensitive cutting of film that has been turned on real-life scenes and on actors and actresses conspicuously not "smooth" in their preparation for the camera. It is not too much to say that the virtues of neo-realism taught Hollywood a new way of art, that its low costs taught Sunset Boulevard a new budget concept, and that its stereotypy, while helping to revive some aspects of the American urban crime film, has also encouraged some very self-conscious responses on the part of American film people. Neo-realism has especially turned attention back to the American urban scene, doing so in a way that sometimes seems extraordinarily "dated" in its implications.

Now that the United States is becoming metropolitanized, the suburbanites outnumber the city families and the farm families in the United States. The interesting thing, however, is that the film industry produces only two generalized types of "regional dreams" in all its movies—dreams that we can call the Western and the Urban. Westerns are all films of any kind that are organized around outdoor chases, as, for example, *Moby Dick* and *The Red Badge of Courage.* Urbans are all films of any kind in which the social organization of industrial life is portrayed with some pretense to documentary excellence, with or without chases. These two classifications, for our purpose, cover all films produced anywhere, with the possible exception of some cartoons and short films dealing with the life of woodpeckers.

The Western is generally, at the moment, the export vehicle of American culture. Its form has been taken over and readapted for a variety of purposes by other cultures in all parts of the world. It deals in general with a scene of transition from the pastoral to the agricultural and commercial and, often enough, with the transition from the social disorganization of war to the settled ways of peace. One of its major themes is the marginality of the lone wolf after the society builds up around him, as the old frontier declines. We have seen its adaptability to chases as various as those involving the Sicilian beyond the law, the Japanese medieval soldier in the land wars, and "bicycle Westerns" of the Italian rice fields.

The Urban used to be the export vehicle of American culture when, in the 1920's and 1930's, it employed the gangster formula or variants thereof to tell the tale of American city life. It has lost its shape in the last twenty years for reasons that no one is quite sure of but which may stem from the increased metropolitanization of all United States regions and the pell-mell movement of second- and third-generation immigrant groups from the central city to the suburbs.

This emigration has already had several marked effects on the Urban. It has helped to produce, for example, a film such as *Marty*, which, in movie form at least, appears to see the lower-middle-class residential "ring" of the metropolis through the eyes of people who have already moved to the suburbs, or to exurbia, or to the Gold Coast. For all its many virtues, the movie *Marty* had a TV air of condescension to its characters. Thus, the emigration has reinforced the tendency to use the urban setting and urban character as the scene upon which to project scenes of social disorganization that may or may not be urban in their origins or transit. This tendency always existed in a sort of agrarian form; now it has added a suburban dimension. At a time when social disorganization has been shifted heavily into the suburbs, with their improbable tax structures, overcrowded schools, problems of law enforcement, TV culture, and so on, the suburban drive-in still shows movies in which all these aspects of social reality are projected, as a matter of course, upon the big city. The major exceptions to such a trend have occurred where there has also been a shift in genre: several science-fiction films, *The Invasion of the Body-snatchers* in particular, take up the suburban scene as a symbolic milieu in a way parallel to the manner in which the Urban used the city scene. This hints strongly that it almost takes a new genre to discover a new scene; and there may be reasons (see chap. ix) why this particular genre has begun the exploration of the suburb. In any event the withdrawal of the older feelings of identification with the Urban on the American scene is under way.

On the Waterfront might stand as the best example of this, since despite the excellence of the film, especially the acting, it manages to convey a most distorted picture of what it portrays. The cowardly "crowd" portrayed in this movie is shown as the captive of the shipping industry and its managerial and labor organization. What the film does not say is that since World War II this bondage has been almost entirely a matter of inertia. The labor market outside of shipping has done more than anything else to change the morality of the waterfront from murder to mere threats of it; and this has led to greater increases in the self-determination of waterfront labor than anything else in the last fifteen years. What the film should explain, within the documentary terms of reference it appeals to, is why anyone is left on the waterfront. What it appears to be explaining is (1) that the situation is terrible and (2) that dockside labor wants to stay.

This may indeed be the unconscious content of the film, and, if it were recognized as such, it might have produced a semidocumentary in which the stickiness of immigrant and second-generation semiskilled labor in the heavily Irish and Catholic groups of the waterfront labor force could be explained. In the meantime, it is clear that the reaction against totalitarian violence among the dockside workers in their new economic situation is something that they value as a new "luxury" of labor-organization sentiment. They gained it with the long-time assistance of the legal forces, and they have been graduated above the homicidal level of industrial organization. *On the Waterfront*, however, manages to take the feelings associated with freedom from violent conditions in this labor force and transfer these to the moral armamentarium of the filmmakers and the audience. Whereas the fact is that the dock workers themselves have recently gained the luxury of considering murder a non-necessity in labor organization and are thus in a position to reject it and affirm new values, the film invites us to imagine that it is *we* who have risen above violence by our rejection of its totalitarian use by agents in the film. While we who have not worked on the docks are asked to revel in our moral superiority to a labor mob portrayed as masochistically passive, we are encouraged to forget that it is *they* who have recently made the upward move.

It would be fairer to the entire audio-visual industry if we were to remind ourselves that its confusions in the theatrical subdivision of reality, and the confusions of its audiences, are part and parcel of a culture generally struggling with an overstated literalism in all its attitudes. Moreover, the same compartmentalizations that prevent integrally developed artistic or documentary or persuasive forms from becoming true channels between producer and public also operate to prevent reasonable statement of the problems involved. The student of media behavior in the context of public opinion and governmental action does not know enough about the restrictions on the industry to understand how desperate can be its struggle to be at its best for its best audience. The anthropologist who berates Hollywood or Radio City for low tastes often fails to consider that the American child has to train himself to literacy in the mass-media cultural forms and conventions against the resistance of parents and schoolmasters who themselves maintain childish views of media forms. The professor of literature often enough is forced by his craft union to spend a lifetime learning so much about the written text that he must neglect contextual study of the actual conditions of performance of fine fiction, documentary writing, or rhetoric. The economist, especially in regard to studies of demand for cultural products, has generally shown only a perfunctory and mainly statistical interest in the making and the marketing of mass entertainment. Yet the time is right for a more unified view of the way in which the forms of media presentation provide centers from which economic, institutional, and cultural definitions gradually grow to such strength that they are accepted as unshakable facts of life by almost everyone.

Kenneth Boulding (in his book, *The Image*) asks whether we can learn how the organization of the image of a social unit such as an industry or a firm gets started. "A guess may be hazarded that one of the most important conditions for the initiation of technological change is the development of rather isolated and perhaps somewhat persecuted subcultures within the larger society." The matter of persecution is uncertain; but the idea that an "isolated subculture" may form a master image which develops to the point where it is an organizing principle seems highly probable. In the audio-visual arts of today it may be that some sort of literalism based on the aesthetic revolutions of the late nineteenth century has become just such a fertile image. Indeed, it sometimes seems so strong that it can subvert the vocabulary directed against it. Even the attempt in this chapter to speak in terms of distinctions between "form" and "content" constitutes an intellectual tax paid to a set of terms that are themselves at once too analytical and not analytical enough to describe the transactions of mass communication.

For when a sign is given me, if it finds me not knowing
of what thing it is a sign, it can teach me nothing,
but if it finds me knowing the thing of which it is
the sign, what do I learn from the sign?—St. Augustine

CHAPTER FOUR

Real and More Real

A Mediator of Fantasy

These comments about the pressure toward realism say little concerning the ways in which style is chosen and employed to achieve the persuasion of reality on the screen. To examine style, we must go to stylists, in this case comparing and contrasting three well-known television performers of the medium's first ten years. Important elements in the work of comedian Herb Shriner and of producer-director-actor Jack Webb, the Joe Friday of "Dragnet," can be scrutinized in contrast with that of pantomimist Marcel Marceau, who travels a different path toward artistic reality.

Before discussing them individually, however, we may observe that television producers have experimented with a number of ways of telling stories, fictional and non-fictional. Story-telling format, as Gilbert Seldes has suggested, is dominated by three types of dramatic writing: series, serials, and "single shots." Successive units of a series program are linked by the presence of continuing characters, although the weekly episodes may be and usually are self-contained. The serial, of

course, is based on the cliff-hanger principle, and its major requirements include: subdivision, hence prolongation of all important dramatic events; flashbacks; reminiscence; and reca-
pitulation, especially at the beginning and end of each episode.
Although these large-scale elements of format are more or less
recognized by viewers as well as producers, some other ingre-
dients of narrative form, the subjuncts of TV presentation as
spectacle, have not been so widely discussed.

One such element is the personal mediation of narrative. In
some programs, fictional enactment or documentary reportage
come to the audience only after the audience has acquired a
set of expectations about what it is to see through the direct
intervention of a narrator, a master of ceremonies, a live an-
thologist and commentator. Thus in comedian Herb Shriner's
earlier TV shows, before his give-away days, he himself provided an introduction to a weekly story. In Dave Garroway's
original Chicago show, Garroway provided a highly informal
introduction to personality interviews, "improvised" skits, and
dramatizations and pantomines. In both instances, the form
and content of the dramatized episodes were regarded as ex-
tensions of the personality of the master of ceremonies, and
audience expectations were molded in part by the identification of their viewpoint with that of the master of ceremonies
himself. It might be helpful to discuss more fully some of the
techniques employed in this mode of presentation and the
general setting in which it has been employed.

The Shriner program, presented weekly from New York,
ordinarily introduced itself by a view of Shriner at something
like theater distance from a first-row audience in front of the
curtain. On that stage he was defined as an Indiana boy who
took it for granted that his recollections of small-town life in
Indiana during the Depression would amuse his audience. He
played on the strong contrast between city and country, the
past and the present; he made the country a symbol for a lag
that connects us with the past, while the city by contrast was

defined as the present and the future. His own rural origins gave him the dignity of the rural observer—the hick who can make such good fun of country ways that he acquires the cognate right to apply country wit against urban pretensions.

It was noticeable that the nostalgic aspect of Shriner's stage personality was echoed in a sophisticated manner in the commercials for the sponsor, a shirt manufacturer. Shriner's style at one point was to pretend that he had made home movies of the shirt factories; shown adjusting his rickety home projector, he then took his TV audience on a tour of the plants. The home movie screen loomed on the TV screen, and the film footage, shown with a verbal commentary by Shriner himself, proved in fact to be snippets from old movies, showing the typical workmen and factory-girl stereotypes of the days of the one-reeler—snippets dominated by fragmentary situations heavily laden with nickelodeon notions of life within the factory. The sheer photographic blurriness, upside-downness, and discontinuity of these bits of film dramatized Shriner as the bungling home movie-maker. The dramaturgically heavy style of the view of factory life presented in these film strips also provided Shriner with an object to make fun of (images of old industrial life in America made maudlin by rapid movement, melodramatic conflict between boss and worker, or romance between boss and collar-ironing girl)—The Bad Old Days of Capitalism.

Within this framework, Shriner made clean fun out of a whole series of obsolete ideas about factory life. What struck Shriner as funny was the sharp melodrama of old-time themes in the movies; what struck his live audience as funny was his unwillingness to satirize this artistic convention directly, his deft way of passing from scoffing to mock-serious and then nostalgic attitudes toward it and back again. In part, he was achieving a parody of the industrial documentary film, with its long-winded statements about the quality control exerted over the cotton bolls that finally go into the shirt; yet at the same time he seemed to want to accomplish at least two other ends for the sponsors. First, he achieved contrast that was strongly felt when the screen suddenly shifted from Shriner's zany movies of old factories to a few brief views of the new factories: the message here communicated the idea that the workers in the two situations were in different worlds. The older workers were overmanipulated; the newer workers are freer, better dressed, and work in less dangerous places. This meaning, established by contrast, led to the second accomplishment: the sponsoring manufacturer's shirt was to be accepted partly because it was made by happier workers. The time spent in arguing that the shirts ought to be bought because they are better was negligible compared with the time spent dramatizing the argument that the shirts ought to be bought because they are a product of the "new" industrial scene as opposed to the "old."

The tension set up by Shriner with his audience around the old-new and city-country polarities took on importance both in his commercial and in his story material. Since Shriner was dramatized as the country boy making good and at the same time telling how amusing his origins were (here the continuity exploited Shriner as a biographical fact), it became appropriate that he should wear the costume of a recently urbanized man. What was his costume? It was the dress style based on the proper selection of the best in ready-made and department-store apparel; Shriner himself became an approved wearer and advertiser of a great standard ready-made brand. Shriner's suit as well as his shirt fitted this role—he never wore Broadway, Loop, West Coast, or Madison Avenue clothes.

One of the more winning repetitious elements in the Shriner format was the presentation of a short sentimental play. The actual presentation involved what might be called successive lyric, narrative, and, finally, dramatic sections. In his character as commentator, Shriner almost unnoticeably broke off to begin to talk about "someone he knew back home"; this was the lyric section, in which Shriner's mood dominated the moment. Then came fabulation by Shriner as he began to tell about the character of the scene and the incident; this was the narrative or epic section, in which the audience's interest was transferred to the story. At this point, Shriner walked back toward the curtain as it was being drawn aside and personally introduced the audience to the scene of the story about to be presented—introduced the audience, that is, by permitting the TV screen or camera to take over his vision of the scene. In the fadeaway, the audience became Shriner, and Shriner became the audience; and this initiated the dramatic section.

In the beginning of the lyric section, Shriner fictionally lived in a perpetual youth, or memory of youth, in a small Indiana town: the period was the Depression, and the people were sad and tough and funny. In the middle or narrative part, the past life of Shriner indefinitely extended backward into rural times, which became a figure of speech for all the time between the Civil War and now. Shriner seemed to be able to remember people who were born and died before 1918, the year he was born. In the concluding or dramatic part, the audience was drawn back to a world in which the old are more important than the young; the heroes are sixty-five-year-old postmen and white-haired ladies in white houses; and as soon as the drama began, the rural scene and its people were treated in pathetic rather than comic terms.

Such a detailed examination of a master-of-ceremonies technique of a certain type should remind us of its major causes and effects in TV. The technique, however it happens to be used, reminds us that while the vicariousness of the movie is offered to the small audience-group or audience-chamber in a darkened, public place, away from all other aspects of sociability except candy-exchanging and hand-holding, the intimate vicariousness of TV is offered to a small audience already organized, in many instances, as a social group. The "performer in the home" reacts to this image of his reception by reducing the manifest aspects of make-believe and art in his performance and increasing the elements of sociability. This is what encourages the news commentator on TV to strive to be the greatest master of some sort of dramatic persuasion, while it leads the actor enacting a part on TV to strive to be as inarticulate as the boy or the girl next door. For well-rounded men like Shriner and Dave Garroway and Steve Allen, who are at their best when they are acting themselves, nothing abstract is left in their art because they allow no distance between the audience and themselves. All their artfulness is involved in sociable presentation of themselves as people who would not rub out a cigarette on the furniture.

Perhaps we identify many of TV's activities as attempts not at informing or fictionalizing but at what Richard Wohl and Donald Horton call substitute sociability. Given the pressure toward this mode induced by the intimate vicariousness of TV, the effects on the conventions of art and history and rhetoric can be listed fairly clearly. Everything that assists make-believe by establishing psychological distance and elaborated abstraction in the work of the actor suffers on TV. He can be perceived enacting suffering; it is difficult to perceive enactment of his own perception of himself suffering; the result is a certain absence of seriousness, which is then reinforced by the miniature scale of the image. This histrionic context established by TV undoubtedly influences its choice of scripts and the way they are deployed for the audience by the attention of the camera; it may have even more to do, as an influence, with the rise of the newer acting styles.

Although movie and TV actors often have enough talent to act with their whole bodies even while the camera selects only part of them for observation, they seem to be driven by the intimate vicariousness of TV to very group-conscious styles of interaction with each other. TV acting tends always to represent human individuality as something that has to be torn like living flesh from the circle of group membership, and most of the time

cannot be. An image of gestural explosiveness and verbal in-
articulateness seems to be the TV standard. The deepest feelings of life are expressed in heavy breathing and frenzied shifts
from cataleptic rigidity to an idiotically plastic motility.

The impacts of the intimate vicariousness of TV on documentary and reportorial formats are rather different. Like fiction, these formats are far less popular than the ones that emphasize the informality of the personality enacting himself. As
studies of the return of General MacArthur show, TV lies to its
audience about the actuality it is supposed to be reporting. It
portrayed the General surrounded in Chicago by welcoming
crowds—crowds that existed for a few minutes at only a few
points in his city-wide tour. Yet, as studies of political conventions and speeches show, it often tells much of the truth about
the people and the events it portrays. The trouble is that few
people care one way or another except on election night; they
would rather have their news come to them through a medi-
ator of feelings about the news, like those superbly pompous
headwaiters in the café of history, the news reporters and commentators who enact each night the total subtraction of meaning from human events. Perhaps the only successful TV reportorial format is the interview with the unexpected character, who is dragged onto an improbable scene to be talked to
in an irrelevant way, then to be dispatched beyond the tube-
margin forever.

Of all the forms that it might try to use, TV fails most
directly at persuasion. The fundamental rhetoric of TV, based
on the idea that each audience-member is quite all right as he
is, utterly thwarts persuasion. All attempts to persuade on TV
are attempts to argue that the audience already approves what
is being argued, and, while this is often successful enough as
an advertising method, it has little to do with persuasion. TV
attempts at persuasion begin by trying to get audience approval for something, and they end by conceding that, since this
is impossible and undignified, the audience must be irritated

into not forgetting something. The best advertisements on TV in terms of effectiveness are self-consciously bad and cannot be anything else. Since TV entered the American scene, its one successful strategy in selling a product or an idea has been to encourage some culturally laggard members of the audience to believe that they are good enough to have a good car or a good idea; and it has succeeded as a marketer largely as an upgrader of the self-esteem of consumers. This is no mean achievement; but it is a very special form of persuasion that has no sense of value for what it is selling, which the plugger usually despises. It feels pride only in bringing people up to the level of taste that TV producers and performers already have and now even more, since they sell them, must run away from. TV persuasion believes so much in "people" that it has no energy left to believe in anything that is aspiringly human.

This may help to account for some of the disappointing experiences met with by TV and many of its stars in the 1956/57 season. That year TV attained a new plateau of audience saturation and at the same time sensed a weakening of some of its appeals. It may be starting to experience the difficulties of a medium aimed at total mass appeal. Yet, if it is to be more selective in programming, it will have to give up its "rating-systems" habit of acting as if every audience-member is as important as any other, regardless of taste, income, or condition of cultural servitude. TV is a buckshot medium, sprayed in all directions.

Paradoxically, this is why TV is so brilliant, as a remolder of American culture, in the field of the "soft sell." Every day, TV simply puts before people an art form, a feeling, an idea, that they would never have found in a book, because they would not have looked into the book, or because it isn't in a book. TV's exploration of the game of consumption and sociability is, by the nature of the medium, on a far more subtle level than anything ever done by the movies. It can dramatize and expose and suggest ways of transcending social banality that are impossible to the screen, largely because of the very "actuality" and "interview" format of TV that at the same time produces so much of its rubbish. It is terribly true that TV has probably elevated ten times as many family conversations in Sourwater, Georgia, as it has degraded there. The central consideration is the intimate vicariousness that makes the medium a peep show into personalities.

The Plainest Plainclothesman

A technique quite different from that of personal mediation is employed in Jack Webb's "Dragnet" to achieve the appearance of reality in action and characterization. Let us look at how he works by examining first the synopsis of one of his weekly dramas, one that appeared on TV the same day Webb was portrayed on the cover of *Time* magazine.

Joe Friday was after shoplifters at 8:00 P.M. on Thursday, March 15, 1954, out of the Chesterfield shift on CBS. Friday traced the thefts to a `Irs. Bruce Sterling, "upper-middle class," wife of a surgeon. She promptly analyzed herself as having done it out of loneliness; she said she wished she could find the answer to her troubles, and Friday told her that she wouldn't find it in jail. The pattern of Mrs. Sterling's kleptomania was to rob mostly the same stores and then jettison the stuff on the way home; she wound up on the blotter.

The realism was familiar to followers of "Dragnet." It employed semi-swallowed voices, many close-ups and uninterrupted eye-contacts, and Webb's talent for not having to blink until he has just come to the last three words of any speech, however long. (When he does finally blink, a trap is heard to shut.) The realism depends also on a documentary style of facial expression and, to a much lesser degree, on the choice of material for the tales. The realism is rooted in Webb's Belasco touch; as reported by *Time*, "Dragnet's sets exactly simulate the offices at the Los Angeles Police Department."

"Dragnet" has quite its own pattern of attitudes about the cop and society; fictional and real cops, the detective-story formula and genres of dramatic art, and reality and fantasy. Possibly the sharpest contrast to what "Dragnet" is up to, in the popular detective vein, is to be found in the supercilious fantasy that used to appear in the episodes of "The Penguin" in the old funny section of the comic book named *Batman and Robin*. Detectives Batman and Robin lived up to a playful relation with the criminal, The Penguin. Crime was a sporting game in which The Penguin repaid his law-man foes by never attacking persons, only the unfastened property of society. Batman and Robin could view him somewhat as real detectives sometimes viewed bank-robber Willie Sutton: detectives had to be amused when Sutton, asked why he robbed banks, replied, "Because that's where the money is." The adventures through which Batman and Robin chased The Penguin were written in a comic frame; he was a relatively innocent "Raffles," compared with their usual vicious adversaries. Above all, the author permitted them to fly through the air to catch The Penguin on their batwings, because the story was defined from the outset in just such fantasy terms.

In the realistic "Dragnet" series, the most interesting terms of the make-believe involve the relation of the cop to the society. Friday is not the patrolman whose uniformed visibility gives rise to helplessness and therefore to appropriateness for comedy. He has no connection with the manhole-disappearing, Model-T-reversing Keystone Cop (when the Law couldn't tell a lamppost from a man, and a kid couldn't tell a tootsie-roll stain on the screen from a beauty-mark on the cheek of a starlet). He is the plainclothesman whose concealed identity gives rise to some of his power and information, thus fitting him for the genre of pathos or tragedy. He is the Listener, who asks first, unlike the old-time cop, before he makes the arrest. Again, Friday is not the private and perhaps even amateur sleuth; he is the public and certainly professional one. As such, he plays a more impersonal, bureaucratized role, backed by vaguer and higher sanctions of juristic, as contrasted with moral, force than the private or the amateur. His definition as the public's servant rather than as a client's agent is a major part of his authority, and this in turn is closely related to his choice of orientation. He is more oriented toward the police profession than toward its clients; and he appears to be liked by his audience, for some reason, because he is a cop's cop.

So much for his general dramatic outline. It would have little of the dramatic magnetism it actually possesses if the role were not filled by a highly defined personal character. A cop can be shady, or moralistic, or something in between which is neither; the last is Friday. A cop can identify only casually and segmentally with his occupational role, as in the famous instance of Sherlock Holmes, or he can lead no imaginable life outside it; the latter is Friday. In his investigative method, the cop can work chiefly as a muscle man or as a system man; the latter is Friday. Most important of all, the fictional detective appears to have the possibility of maintaining one of four relations between his craft and his emotional involvement in it. Both craft and involvement can be high; both can be low; or one can be high while the other is low. Mickey Spillane's Mike Hammer is high in emotional involvement and not so high in competence (even if he owned a steel blackjack, it would be made away with by a blonde menace). Sherlock Holmes was high in competence and involvement. The "stupid constable" of English detective fiction is often low in affect and low in competence. Friday is the fourth case, high competence and low affect. If he could only become *more* apathetic, we assume, he would become that much more competent. But he always listens, no matter how impassive his ultimate arrest of the malefactor is; he has been the Great Listener of dramatic TV.

Surely the most interesting thing about any fictional cop, however, is the kind of crimes he happens to get to solve. You might think because Friday is a dramatization of just a good plainclothesman that he realistically solves all kinds of crimes in all kinds of ways. This is not what a closer examination

of the story line suggests. The vulnerable point in "series" realism is that sheer volume of episodes finally makes the stereotypical repetition show through, and the stereotype points to
where the fantasy is, in the minds of the producers and the
audience. To go back to Mrs. Sterling, you will have noticed
her crime was not a professional but an amateur crime; that it
was committed by the wife of a white-collar professional; that
it was not an example of "organized" crime; that it involved
aggressions against persons—herself and her husband—more
deeply than it involved aggressions against property, the stolen
articles being interpreted as the symbols of her deprivations.
Some such pattern fits most "Dragnet" storylines.

"Dragnet" *has* chased down professionals, organized criminals, and those who have committed crimes against property.
Such cases are not frequent, however; in general, that sort of
crime does not invite the solution that Friday prefers to commit. The ideal type of a "Dragnet" operation involves the arrest
of malefactors who are hard to find because they look something like our neighbors and something like the people on
soap opera. Few characters on "Dragnet" have ever had the
healthy greed to commit a crime just for the sake of money.
In the terms of a real detective, Friday's favorite prey are the
"high" people, moralistic respectables who break the law,
rather than the "wide" people, whose breaking of the law is
both an ethos and a business.

While "Dragnet's" selection of crimes is far from being realistic in representing the police blotter, it is close to being
fantastic in its grip on the audience; that is, it capitalizes most
effectively on our fears about our own hostilities among those
of us who claim to be not professional criminals but, at the
most, semiprofessional or simply amateur. We must compose
the larger proportion of the 80 million listeners. We are not invited to watch a pursuer whose activity might bring fright to a
"big-shot," as in the comfortable old gangster films where only
the higher-ups of society were bad men. We are invited to

watch a pursuer who brings fright to respectables such as our-selves. The realism consists in documentarily tracking the crimes that the audience might commit, not in getting off into a sample of crimes they would probably avoid. This is a special form of intimate vicariousness.

In the Kefauver hearings, viewers saw the society at the mercy of the aggressions of corrupt higher-ups; in "Dragnet" we see the society at the mercy of aggressions that are simply our own. Naïve moralists will applaud this for bringing responsi-bility home to each viewer in his own terms. The media critic might answer that the media message, by confirming the audi-ence in the belief that its own aggressions are a danger, makes its members doubt their own morale and confirms them in their drabness. The fully confirmed member of such an audience, if arrested for stealing white rats from a bubonic plague labora-tory, would naturally expect to be picked up, not by an indi-vidualistically colorful genius like the nineteenth-century Sher-lock Holmes, but by someone who looked like the non-union-ized skip-tracer at the end of a bad day—in short, by a Friday.

Crime and Punishers

The discussion so far may suggest that social definitions of such characters as policemen exist only in the fictions of popular culture and that it is necessary to look only at these images to gain hints of social reality. Nothing could be further from the case. The films (as Wolfenstein and Leites suggest in their pioneering volume, *Movies: A Psychological Study*) represent certain scenes and agents with great emphasis and repetition not because they are so frequently found in fact but because they are so frequently absent from the factual world. One must compare the fictional composite of a type, such as the detective, with evidence outside the fantasies of the media to see whether the media figure is rooted in some social reality upon which, in turn, his interest as a dramatically probable figure in fiction actually rests. Joe Friday does mirror a particular conception of a particular kind of detective in the historic sequence of real detectives; the particular type he is modeled on and the particular way in which the modeling is achieved serve to tell us something about the way in which we control our contemporary imagination.

The position of the policeman within society, no matter what public stereotypes are associated with it, is closely connected with, and mediated by, changes in the concept of social control and law and follows its own stages of development and change. Some of these changes may not be especially noticeable to the policemen who implement them, the public that is influenced by them, or the fiction-writers who respond to them. Along these lines, it need only be suggested that the policeman always operates in a complex of sanctions, some of which originate in shifting preoccupations in the philosophy of law. Joe Friday should remind us that the twentieth century has seen the American policeman affected by at least one major intellectual movement in this field.

The plainest plainclothesman represented by Jack Webb in his mask of Joe Friday, the cop without emotions, represents one historic type in the development of the cop figure in fiction in the twentieth century. Through this type, as through any other widely popular product, we get vague inklings of changes in general attitudes toward law enforcement or, more generally, techniques of social control. The scene that police fiction presents today was affected by World War I, the Prohibition law, the industrial violence of the Depression, and the restricted immigration pattern. The scene has also been changed by the rapid social mobility of millions of people in the United States since the beginning of World War II. The media themselves have changed. The movies, rarely originating any police figures except comic ones, have picked up and elaborated the available stereotypes of fiction, from Sherlock Holmes to Mike Hammer. They have familiarized the audience with interna-

tional differences in crime, police theory, and detection. Radio
and television, for commercial purposes, have continued to develop a series of marginally differentiated brands of detectives
and policemen. The audience structure of the "police romance"
has changed. Comic books have taken over at the lower literary
levels; "psychological drama" has taken over some aspects of
the detective story at the highest literary levels. Middlebrow
readers have shown a tendency to lose interest in fictional police work, while taking more of an interest in "documentary"
reports.

The decline of the comic cop in the movies may be connected with an attempt on the part of the movies to depart
from lower-class appeals and connected also with an attempt
on the part of the audience to rise above lower-class responses.
It can be supposed that the Hammett private detective, who
was sensitive to industrial injustice, was a kind of Robin Hood
of the Depression and that his appearance in fiction was connected with a need to create a Popular Front counterstatement
to the industrial Pinkerton. Such at any rate was the role of
some of the "investigators" in Hammett's brilliant melodrama
of capital-labor violence and intrigue, *Red Harvest*. It is a good
guess that the "low-pressure" cop represented in "Dragnet" is
symbolic of the new alliance between the lower class and the
white-collar class suggested by analysis of the Eisenhower victory in the 1952 elections. Hostility to the police, as recent
research shows, is one of the social habits given up by the
poorer people as they increase their stake in the middle class.
"Dragnet" appears to dramatize, for the medium with the biggest and lowest-status audience, precisely this respectable definition of the cop. How much the media image of the profession
has to do with the more general public image of it, or with the
realities of the profession itself, raises other questions.

To put it briefly, the urban police of the United States in the
early twentieth century operated within a legal tradition of
positivism and liberalism. This does not mean that they swung

their nightsticks more correctly and more softly than they did before or after this fashion in law; it does mean that their "higher-ups" and the judges who decided the cases they brought to them operated in a more impersonally professionalized and meliorist way than earlier. One feels that this ethos was more than vaguely echoed in the "craftsmanlike" writing-up of the craftsmanlike case in the British and American detective story up until about 1930. Focus on scientific method in police work went with a "preventive and corrective" attitude toward crime, and these attitudes in turn went with a brand of detective fiction in which the class structure was firm and predictable. The policemen and the detectives of the detective novel up until about the end of the first quarter of the twentieth century were Comteans and Benthamites, one might say; at their moral and fictional best, they were men who dealt with criminals and with themselves in the terms of nineteenth-century social thought of the more optimistic brand.

In the years since the Depression and World War II, the reappearance of Natural Law (partly as response to Nazi successes in making murder a stateway) has dulled some of the edge of positivistic and utilitarian legal thinking. Where the older detective had to face the "instinct toward crime" and the criminal ruined by a bad society, the newer detective faces crime that arises from the ambiguity of a whole culture and from Dostoevskian criminals who have been engaged in "suspensions of the ethical." Nevertheless, the older image of the bureaucratic cop persists. The audience heartbeats induced on the home-cardiogram by the TV efforts of Jack Webb, as Joe Friday, may be responses to a professional stereotype that emphasizes the routinization of that older image of the cop. For it appears on the evidence that Joe Friday is a sort of "tired" version of the scientific cop—tired, that is, in the sense that he psychologizes all human motives while at the same time remaining supremely uninterested in motives as such, especially his own.

This discussion of two modes of naturalism is not intended to suggest that either Shriner or Webb was wrong to exploit the mode or to modulate it in his own particular way. Both have been highly and deservedly successful entertainers with many an innovation to their credit and a real feeling for their craft. The search for the dramatically literal is not merely a matter of Belasco-like techniques; it is also the organization of an appeal to a whole set of attitudes on the part of the audience. Moreover, some of these appeals of certain types of current naturalism bring a further issue forward: what has all this to say about the definitions of the public and the private that are taken for granted by the audience for such shows?

In these shows we see two major principles at work. In Shriner's show, the principle is that if you can believe in the real man, Shriner, then you can believe to some degree in anything that he presents himself as being connected with, even if it is a fiction of rural life. It is connected, of course, with a certain unwillingness on the part of many in the American public to honor a dramatic artist for what he artistically appears to be, rather than for what he actually is. The general encouragement given to this attitude by the mass media in the last fifty years has had the effect of confusing millions of Americans about that relation between the private life and the public life which is represented in the special relation between the natural and the fictional. This attitude runs through censorship groups, congressional committees, all kinds of public attitudes. It amounts to a public dictum that "fiction is not to be trusted" and thus reverses the major claim of fictional art considered as such, which is that good fictional art can remind us that appearances of natural reality are precisely what cannot be trusted. The idea that a fictional construct might be and has a right to be a partly self-sufficient test of what life could be is a privilege that millions refuse to accept. The result is a pervasive literalism that is one of the major characteristics of the core culture and that, in earlier sections of this book, was singled out as a major deterrent to the progress of mass-media style. It should be added that the same literalism, the same appetite for atomized fact, the same hatred for theory and speculation, seem to be evident in much of our so-called high culture—the "Notes and Queries" approach.

In the Joe Friday shows, the effect of this literalism seems to be much multiplied by the cleverness of the format employed: the emotionlessness of the hero and the crimes that he detects suggest a sullen relationship between the viewers of the law at work and the law they hope to see upheld. Fundamentally authoritarian in its attitudes, this audience seems to be invited to take the position that the law is something that somebody else made. To find one's self against it is simply to find one's self in a fated position prescribed by the social psychology of one's upbringing and the uncontrollable disorders of one's own self-distrust. There is no tragedy; all is pathos, and all is deterministic pathos. The anxiety is for an "actuarial self"—the self that one is or might be when one thinks of one's self as the member of a social aggregation and not as an individual. In Webb, the law and the enforcers are unambiguously right, and there is never the possibility that the cop or the miscreant may share a perception of the imperfections of the law. At base, the law is equated with a brute force operating with no basis in democratic consensus but simply because it is there, like the limestone blocks of the courthouse. One could hardly find a more disconcerting symptom than this of secularized determinism at work in the culture at large.

The implications for the relation between the public and private in this audience stance run along the following lines: lower-middle-class attitudes toward the law, which were once enlivened by seeing law as an objective protector of class privileges for the few, no longer take the law as a quasi-tragic, quasi-comic antagonist. It is no longer "public" in this sense; it has become a half-realized projection of the authoritarian psychology of a sociopsychological class and hints that this group's oversubjectivization of the law is essentially cynical and self-defeating. Cynical, that is, in the way that "Little Orphan Annie's" most devoted readers must delight in the social circumstances that rationalize Daddy Warbucks in settling all his problems by a kind of private feud-right resembling lynch-law.

Audio's Silent Foe

The in-your-lap realism, intimate vicariousness, and substitute sociability of TV make it, as everyone knows, the most voluble medium in history, a medium in which sound effects are almost as important for their prevention of silence as they are in their function as dramatic signs. When silence found its voice, the brief answer it made to the babble of TV turned out to be the work of French pantomimist Marcel Marceau. Like many a Frenchman in the modern arts, he practices the craft of achieving expression by reducing rather than multiplying the cues available in a given medium. Could he have been liked half as well if TV had not prepared for him the most favorable advance contrast effect for a performer since non-Aryan Jesse Owens triumphed in Hitler's Olympics?

Most of Marceau's audiences, both on and off TV, seemed delighted by what they could see when they didn't have to listen, by what their eyes could tell them about things that otherwise would have to have been said. He even renders linear perspective: at the close of one of his scenes he walks away into the distance. The actual stage footage covered by Marceau in this departure does not exceed five yards, but he makes it look, in that five yards, by successive transformations of his pace and posture as if the character he is portraying has traversed half a city block.

It is wrong of Marceau to argue that pantomime is a better medium than gesture-plus-voice because gesture alone is more honest—that actions are more honest than words. Anyone who has watched a baby-girl drum major walk in a Legion parade knows that this is not true. No matter how much his silent communication is offered as a naturalistically superior corrective to an age that despairs of the integrity of its words, that is not the point. Pantomime is not "better" or "worse"; it is good in itself. And it is good because it practices a fictional economy of means; and it is especially good in this age because it contrasts with redundant TV.

It is wrong of his appreciators, on the other hand, to talk about the universality of his language of silence, as if they meant that the gestural keyboard he employs were a cultural universal. True, all people make expressive gestures, even to the point where some people in some cultures spend some of their time in making counterexpressive gestures. This, however, is different from claiming, as some of his admirers appear to claim, that the gesture sentences and phrases that he uses mean exactly the same thing to the French and to the Americans. They do not. His repertoire of gesture is built from European stage experience of the last two hundred years, modified and codified through the physiological and psychological studies of French investigators in the nineteenth century. It forms a constellation in which each part can be related to another, like noun to verb in a French sentence when read by the American on the page; it does not form a language immediately evident on every level to an American audience any more than a French taxi-man's prose is lucid to a Smith graduate.

What is culturally universal in his keyboard of gesture is, in the first place, the European body image and manipulation and, secondly, its gradual transformation into a canon by psychological science and dramatic art. It is universal in having a physiological base and a cultural inflection; it is locally European in selecting as the vocabulary of mime a very few of the millions of "kines" and "kinemes," or basic gestural units, available in that cultural system. The essential universality, however, is artistic; it is not so much the precise things he says by gesture that count, but the transfer to the audience of a total narrative and a total emotional effect derived from the succession of these details.

The contrast power of his silence is so great that few of the audience would have quarreled with the momentary loss of empathy induced by, let us say, his French manner of throwing dice. Frenchmen don't *throw* dice, apparently; they *drop* them, like petals of roses to the attar bins. After you learn this from Marceau, you can forget it; the anxious moment comes just before the context makes it clear to you that what must be going on is a crap game, not perfume-making. All that he says is not self-evident in meaning as a unit; it must be given meaning by applying to the sequence of gestures all that we know from other actors, from ballet, and so on. How is it that Marceau, whose gestures constitute an ethnological museum of gestural meanings that Americans do not use at all in the same way, is an artist rather than an animated waxworks? Because, since everyone has to move expressively, and move in a culturally defined way, his exploration of one rather pervasive, culturally defined way, even if not American, is at least comparable. Its enhanced contrast with the American system prevents us from projecting so many ambiguous meanings into it that it would lose its exotic clarity.

How does Marceau tell us anything about the practice of realism, intimate vicariousness, and substitute sociability in TV? Or, to put it another way, what happens to our sense of these TV-originated tones of entertainment performance when a Marceau dramatizes for us without the use of words? In the first place, naïve realism is driven off the stage by his work; it is neither possible nor appropriate for a medium that, by definition, reduces the sense cues and the perception cues that are available in the real world. The audience is relieved perhaps because it realizes that no one is going to fire a gun or burst into charm.

The intimate vicariousness is gone. It seems to be in the nature of Marceau's tradition of pantomime to sustain the most pleasing sociable distance from the audience. He enacts a chalk-colored silhouette that sometimes seems to be a moving aperture through which the light of a reality is sensed. He allows the reality to be transmitted through him; he does not try to throw his biographical self onto the stage as a substitute for it. At certain points in the performance he creates an illusion that makes it appear that Marceau himself is somewhere offstage manipulating a puppet with strings. He does not dramatize himself as anything like a guest in the TV-owning household, appealing to a small social group whose intimacy he is at once invading and fearing to trespass on.

No substitute sociability can appear as an element in this format; the absence of speech makes it impossible for the actor to make those reflexive remarks about the viewing situation itself which are the para-language of TV—"If you're thinking of getting a drink of water, get it now, because the guest star will be here in a few seconds." Nor is one inclined to talk back to Marceau, even when he appears on TV. One cannot say to him, as one so often says to TV speakers, "Oh, yeah?"; and the distance permits illusion to flourish.

This scrutiny of certain aspects of form in three TV performers claims to be only an illustration of certain general conventions that could be studied equally well, and perhaps to better effect, in other regions of the TV world. It would have been inappropriate here to single out such ambitious programming as "Omnibus," or to spend much of this chapter on the quiz shows, or to attempt an evaluation of the more pretentious dramas available on TV. Yet, while making a nod to the commercial product in its purer forms, it is important to acknowledge the interest associated with the younger writers who, for example, have been doing some good things with the "single-shot" play on TV. They have developed a form that might be called the "tragedy of manners"—actually a kind of tragicomedy in which popular psychological and sociological themes of the time are explored. Horton Foote, the author of an interesting TV play called *A Young Lady of Property*, Gore Vidal, and others, have done striking work in the form. In some senses, their work amounts to moving the short story from the magazine page to TV. As interest in written fiction declines and as the general audience magazines that supported the good American short story go under, their effort is important.

Today, the written short story becomes arty in most instances, a claustral form like the sonnet of yesteryear. In TV it takes on some new life by reverting to the nineteenth-century form of the "tale"—a form at once more vulgar and somehow more in search of a life of its own than the "art" short story, which seems to be the burnt-out end of the tradition established by Chekhov, Mansfield, and others at the height of magazine and newspaper reading.

The getting up of the Spectacle is more a matter
for the costumier than the poet.—Aristotle

CHAPTER FIVE

The Decline of Lyric Sport

The Big Game

The realism and the fantasy of the audio-visual media never can and never will exhaust the play impulse, and we know that many people in many ways seek less vicarious uses of leisure time. The impulse toward sports is one of these ways, even though an individual who is a spectator rather than a participant may find his vicarious thrills in the game the other fellow plays. To turn away from the big media, one might look first at the Big Game in the United States. Even when received as a media experience, over TV, it involves a different relation to the world of leisure than looking at anything else on TV.

Here we must ask again how a specific entertainment form— in this sense the form of a game—gets to be what it is and how the audience has developed its current vocabulary of response and criticism. The question leads us to look at the mechanisms of sports production and distribution and at the forces that lead to the dominance of certain cultural definitions shared by audience, participants, and manager. The most significant aspect of the spectacular mass-appeal sports in this decade is their absolute growth in gate receipts and appeal, along with their decline relative to other ways of spending the leisure hour and the leisure dollar. Audio-visual entertainment, new uses of transportation, and other new leisure habits have cut the ground from under all but the top-drawer leagues and teams.

Historically, Herbert Schoeffler shows in papers translated by Donald Levine, our American sports pattern is the direct descendant of the Glorious Revolution. It was in the late seventeenth century, especially in the 1690's, that England revolutionized the European sporting ideal. It made the aristocratic sports, especially racing, a social property of all classes; and it permitted the plebeian sports to rise and suffuse the sporting pattern of the whole male culture. The last master fencers in England became its first boxing champions.

The magnetism of the sporting world in Britain and the United States is associated, moreover, with its meaning as a reaction to industrialism. Industrialism makes men feel a shift or disturbance in the traditional relation to their bodies; they wish to re-create it through sport. Again, as Helmuth Plessner has argued, the relative insignificance of the individual in subdivided industrial roles makes him search for acts of aesthetic completion and expressed, even if channeled, physical aggression. Out of these historical backgrounds rise some, if not all, the harmonies and contradictions of the American sports world today, especially that part of it which strains to make a commodity of sport in the mass-entertainment market.

The imagery of competition, as represented in the Big Game and in media interpretation of the Big Game, contributes to the system of expectations holding among various parts of society. Sport can be studied as social imagery—spectacle from which the media draw symbols that are then employed in the supreme court of folkway.

The integrity of the symbol system derived from sports is largely a function of two things. First, sports recruitment draws on habits built up in the imaginative generosity of childhood and youth, draws, that is, on a pre-class, pre-caste system of social interaction. Second, sports recruitment is a big business with a market to satisfy, a business that trains its own critics and virtually pays to have them trained. These two characteristics of the sports world must surely go far to explain why sports, like entertainment, are usually ahead of churches and schools, for example, in responding sensitively to the moral pressure for freedom and equality in our society. Thus in the segregation issue, for instance, sports and some kinds of popular entertainment have established community between the races before other social institutions could or would.

The association of dominant advertising images with sports is significant. The first Coca-Cola advertisement (1905) showed a young man with golf clubs and a young lady with a tennis racket. It is another reminder that the Coca-Cola advertising campaign may have been the greatest in advertising history. It not only had a dominant color, red, and an amusingly shaped bottle, and a faintly medicinal taste to sell; it also always repeated its message and associated the beverage with illustrated health, beauty, and sports. All that remains to be suggested is the probability that the ads themselves acted as advance agents, among some customers, for sports. They must have made tennis players out of some young men and women who would not otherwise, even at the urging of the women's magazines in the first decade of the century, have learned to cry "Love," to the delight of kids at the fence.

United States sports history is a social process, paralleling change in the rest of the society, the rise of industrialism, the softening of puritanism, the needs of war, and the process of ethnic assimilation. These themes give meaning to dramatic figures like Jim Thorpe and "Alabama" Pitts, incidents like the White Sox scandal, and brittle scenes like that of Theodore Roosevelt advising Taft to avoid the "dude" game of golf.

Most commentators, however, are more familiar with the literature of physical recreation than with any other. They have never been particularly lucid on the theme of amateurism versus professionalism. In the United States, that issue was joined more sharply in the 1920's—the years in which Thorpe and Paddock were penalized for accepting small amounts of money in connection with athletic appearances. Those were also the years in which the Supreme Court held that baseball was not to be interpreted as interstate commerce under the Sherman Antitrust Act. (This has been recently reaffirmed, two justices dissenting.) During the 1920's, in the field in which sport was already *most professionalized,* our legal advisers refused to regard it as such; and in the field in which sport was *most amateurized,* Olympic experts refused to regard it as sufficiently so. From the point of view of the athlete, one might define this as a situation in which the possible gains of professionalism were not fully acknowledged and in which the penalties of amateurism were fully applied. Marginal status, indeed.

The confusion of this period was brought about by a variety of factors in the sports world. Purist amateurism was in some senses an upper-middle-class stand about sports; it had the effect of penalizing men who combined amateur sports with industrial work. On the other hand, the refusal to grant full professional status to the baseball player was part and parcel of a general reluctance to define leisure marketing services as industries in the full sense of the word. Out of that situation in the 1920's certainly developed part of our image of the athlete as a sacrificial victim, a man between two worlds. It seems possible that the movies and the comic strips and the novels have employed him as just such a hero to a greater extent than any other kind of professional character in our social history. Movies about boxing heroes are only the latest development in a thematic development that is beginning to acquire the classical stereotypy of the Western. In the Western it is the ambiguity of violence and law, in the pistol of the morally indeterminate man facing the Trampas walk (the formalized cowboy duel named after the bad man in *The Virginian*). In the fiction about the sports world it is the ambiguity of violence and love, in the right hook of the morally indeterminate boxer who is facing the fixed fight.

This theme of the conflict between the amateur and the professional is important not only because it has this generalized meaning but also because it suggests models of social process. If baseball and football players and track stars suffered from this indeterminacy in the past, we can be sure that some auto racers and some modern dancers are suffering from it now. In its more preindustrialized stages, a leisure fad tends to draw on organizers and exemplars who feel that it is not right to ask money for what they can teach in the skills of performance and the skills of spectatorship. The result is a twilight area halfway between amateur and professional status.

The uncertainty of this situation is suggested in the following excerpt from a *New York Herald Tribune* column by John Crosby, critic of television and radio programs:

"The other night Kraft Theater unfolded a play, 'The Fair Haired Boy,' which dealt with college football and rang out all the stops. As a scholar of the old-fashioned or classic type of football film, I found this a very interesting deviation. In the old days, there was a big scene in the locker room.

" 'So you *lost* the signals, eh? Kirk, you're through! Turn in your uniform and keep away from the stadium tomorrow. Rivkin has confessed everything—and old Yarvard is going in there to *win!*'

"In 'The Fair Haired Boy,' there was very little football at all. The story, as briefly as possible, dealt with a college football quarterback caught at cheating, an idea they picked up somewhere. His professor, a monument of incorruptibility, insisted that he be flunked and thereby rendered ineligible rather than be allowed to drop the course. The whole resources of the university were then concentrated on winning this professor into some understanding of the importance of the gate receipts and the relative unimportance of good grades.

"The forces of evil, I'm happy to say, were defeated. The player was dropped from football. The nasty old coach and the highly corruptible dean and a little creep of a college press agent were routed. Skulking in the the background throughout was the big star of the class of 1936, now a lush, who symbolized, I guess, the corroding effects of football on the young.

"It was all so different from the old days when football, as I recall, was considered a great character builder, when Pat O'Brien, the ultimate in moral uprightoutness, always played the coach."

Why and how has the grand old game changed that much—if, indeed, the particular media image of the game that Crosby saw is a fair image and if Crosby's own reporting evokes the image in a perceptive way? Why has the relation between the audience and the game changed over the years since the turn of the century? Why does football tend to become involved, as many of our other sports, in a complex tissue of connections with the emotional and moral ambiguities of the society as a whole? Why does almost everyone feel some vested interest in the symbolic structure of a game of football, experiencing a sense of historic occurrence and discontinuity if that symbolic structure seems to be undergoing change?

One way to investigate this is to take a closer look at the way the game of football developed in the United States and at the ways in which the game (including the doctrine of coaching as well as playing), the critical observers, and the large audience have also changed. The investigation can well begin by taking note of the air of moral and financial crisis that seems to have gathered over American football, and its place in campus culture, recently. It is a chapter in the decline of lyric sport in the United States.

Football: Origin of Species

On October 9, 1951, Assistant Attorney-General Graham Morrison instituted an antitrust action against a number of universities because of their efforts to limit TV broadcasts of their football games—efforts dictated by the terrible burdens of what we might speak of as "industrialized football." This action occurred only a few weeks after the scandal of the West Point student firings, which, along with the William and Mary palace revolution, indicated that football was indeed reaching another crisis in its adaptation to the ever changing American environment. Small colleges such as Milligan—a church-supported school in the mountains of eastern Tennessee—were discovering football so mechanized that they could no longer afford the necessary entry fee for machinery and personnel. Milligan spent $17,000, or two-thirds of its whole athletic budget, and did not get it all back in the box-office net. Football had come to resemble other industries or mechanized farms, into which a new firm could move not by relying on an institutional lifetime of patient saving and plowing back of profits but only by large corporate investment.

As a result of successive changes in the game since its post–Civil War diffusion from England, the production of a college football team today involves the heavy overhead and staff personnel characteristic of high-capital, functionally rationalized industries. Thus, the growing scale of college football is indicated by its dollar place in the American leisure economy. In 1929, out of $4.3 billion in recreation expenditures by Americans, the college football gate accounted for $22 million. In 1950, out of about $25 billion in such expenditures, it accounted for $103 million and grossed ten times the income of professional football. The 1950 gate of $103 million suggests that a total capital of more than $1 billion is invested in the college football industry. The revenue figures, of course, do not include the invisible subsidization of football, nor do they hint the place that football pools occupy in the American betting economy.

It would be wrong, however, to assert that football has become an impersonal market phenomenon. Rather, its rationalization as a sport and as a spectacle has served to bring out more openly the part it plays in the ethnic, class, and characterological struggles of our times—meaning, by "characterological struggle," the conflict between different styles of life. The ethnic significance of football is immediately suggested by the shift in the typical origins of players' names on the All-American football teams since 1889. In 1889, all but one of the names (Heffelfinger) suggested Anglo-Saxon origins. The first name after Heffelfinger to suggest non-Anglo-Saxon recruitment was that of Murphy, at Yale in 1895. After 1895, it was a rare All-American team that did not include at least one Irishman (Daly, Hogan, Rafferty, Shevlin); and Jewish names appeared before the turn of the century. On the 1904 team appeared Pierkarski of Pennsylvania. By 1927, names like Casey, Kipke, Oosterbaan, Koppisch, Garbisch, and Friedman were appearing on the All-American list as frequently as names like Channing, Adams, and Ames in the 1890's.

Although such a tally does little more than document a shift that most observers have already recognized in American football, it raises questions that are probably not answerable merely in terms of ethnic origins of players. There is an element of class identification running through American football since its earliest days, and the ethnic origin of players invites theorizing about the class dimensions of football. Most observers would be inclined to agree that the arrival of names like Kelley and Kipke on the annual All-American list was taken by the Flanagans and the Webers as the achievement of a lower-class aspiration to be among the best at an upper-class sport. The question remains: What did the achievement mean? What did it mean at different stages in the development of the game?

Hasn't the meaning worn off in fifty-odd years, the roughly two generations since Heffelfinger and Murphy made the grade?

One way of answering is to study the interrelations between changes in the rules of the game (since the first intercollegiate contest: Rutgers, 6 goals—Princeton, 4 goals, in 1869) and to analyze the parallel changes in football strategy and ethos. All these developments are to be seen as part of a configuration that includes changes in coaching, in the training of the players, and in the no less essential training of the mass audience.

Football as a cultural inheritance from England may be analyzed for its intercultural diffusion and variation. Just as the French have transformed American telephone etiquette while retaining some of its recognizable physical features, so Americans have transformed the games of Europe even when, as in track or tennis, the formalities appear to be unaltered. Within the Western industrial culture, there are great varieties, on a class or national basis, in the games, rules, strategy, etiquette, and audience structures of sport. In the case of college football (leaving aside the derivative and symbolically less important professional game) the documentation of sports writers—themselves a potent factor in change—allows us to trace the stages of development.

Football in its earliest English form was called the "Dane's Head," and it was played in the tenth and eleventh centuries as a contest in kicking a ball between towns. The legend is that the ball was at first a skull and only later a cow's bladder. In some cases, the goals were the towns themselves, so that a team entering a village might have pushed the ball several miles en route. King Henry II (1154–89) proscribed the game on the ground that it interfered with archery practice. Played in Dublin even after the ban, football did not become respectable or legal until an edict of James I reinstated it. The reason was perhaps less ideological than practical: firearms had superseded the art of bowmanship.

During the eighteenth century, football as played by British schoolboys became formalized but was not changed from its fundamental pattern of forceful kicking. In 1823, Ellis of Rugby made the mistake of picking up the ball and running with it toward the goal. All concerned thought it was a mistake. Ellis was sheepish, his captain apologetic. The mistake turned into innovation when it was decided that a running rule might make for an interesting game. The localism, pluralism, and studied casualness of English sports made it possible to try it out without securing universal assent—three or four purely local variants of football, football-hazing, and "wall-games" are still played in various English schools. Rugby adopted "Rugby" in 1841, several years after Cambridge had helped to popularize it. A commemorative stone at Rugby reads as follows:

THIS STONE

COMMEMORATES THE EXPLOIT OF

WILLIAM WEBB ELLIS

WHO WITH A FINE DISREGARD FOR THE RULES OF

FOOTBALL, AS PLAYED IN HIS TIME,

FIRST TOOK THE BALL IN HIS ARMS AND RAN WITH IT,

THUS ORIGINATING THE DISTINCTIVE FEATURE OF

THE RUGBY GAME

A.D. 1823

This establishment of the running, or Rugby, game, as contrasted with the earlier, kicking game, had several important results. One was that the old-style players banded themselves together for the defense of their game and formed the London Football Association (1862). This game, abbreviated to "Assoc" appears to have been the starting point for the neologism "soccer," the name that the kicking game now goes by in many parts of the English-speaking world. A second result was that the English, having found a new game, continued to play it without tight rules until the Rugby Union of 1871. As we shall see, this had its effects on the American game. The third and most important result of Ellis' "mistake," of course, was that he laid the foundations for everything fundamental about the American game between 1869 and the introduction of the *forward pass*. (The forward pass is still illegal in Rugby and closely related football games.)

Football: The Media Intervene

In the Colonial period and right down to the Civil War, Americans played variants of the kicking football game on their town greens and schoolyards. After the war, Yale and Harvard served as the culturally receptive importers of the English game. Harvard, meeting McGill in a game of Rugby football in 1874, brought the sport to the attention of collegiate circles and the press—two identifications important for the whole future development of the game. But if Harvard was an opinion leader, Yale was a technological one. A Yale student, D. S. Schaft, class of '73, who had studied at Rugby was instrumental in persuading Yale men to play the Rugby game and was therefore responsible for some of Yale's early leadership in the sport.

Soon after, it became clear that American players, having tasted the "running" game, were willing to give up the soccer form. It became equally clear that they either did not want to or could not play Rugby according to the British rules. "The American players found in this code (English Rugby Rules) many uncertain and knotty points which caused much trouble in their game, especially as they had no traditions, or older and more experienced players to whom they could turn for the necessary explanations," wrote famous Yale coach Walter Camp, whose book on football, co-authored by Lorin F. Deland, was published in 1896. An example of such a problem was that the development of Rugby rules in England was accomplished by admitting into the rules something that we would call a legal fiction. While an offensive runner was permitted to carry the ball, the condition of his doing so was that he should only happen by chance to be standing behind the tangled players at the moment the ball popped back out to him. Deliberately sending back the ball was not permitted. The British rules of the mid-nineteenth century appear to take it for granted that the difference between a deliberate and a fortuitous sending-back of the ball would be clear to everyone. This aspect of Rugby rule-making, called "heel-out," had important implications for the American game.

British players, according to tradition as well as the rules, could be expected to tolerate such ambiguity as that of the heel-out rule just as they tolerated the ambiguity of the "dead" ball. They could be expected to tolerate it not only because of their personal part in developing new rules but also because they had an audience with specific knowledge of the traditions to assist them. In America it was quite another matter to solve such problems. Rather, however, than drop the Rugby game at that point, because of intolerance for the ambiguities involved, an effort was undertaken, at once systematic and gradual, to fill in by formal procedures the vacuum of etiquette and, in general, to adapt the game to its new cultural home.

The upshot of American procedure was to assign players to the legalized task of picking up and tossing the ball back out of scrimmage. This in turn led to a variety of problems in defining the situation as one of "scrimmage" or "non-scrimmage" and to the whole question of the legality of passing the ball back to intended runners. American football never really solved these problems until it turned its attention, in 1880, to a definition of the scrimmage itself. The unpredictable English "scrum," or scramble, for a free ball was abandoned, and a crude line of scrimmage was constructed across the field. Play was set in motion by snapping the ball. Meanwhile, Americans became impatient with long retention of the ball by one side. It was possible for a team that was ahead in score to adopt tactics that would insure its retention of the ball until the end of the period. By the introduction of a minimum yardage-gain rule in 1882, the rule-makers assured the frequent interchange of the ball between sides.

The effect of this change was to dramatize the offensive-defensive symmetry of the scrimmage line, to locate it sharply in time ("downs"), and to focus attention not only on the snapping of the ball but also on the problem of "offside" players. In the English game, with no spatially and temporally delimited line of scrimmage, the offside player was penalized only by making him neutral in action until he could move to a position back of the position of the ball. In the American game, the new focus on centering, on a scrimmage line, and on yardage and downs created the need for a better offside rule. From that need developed offside rules that even in the early years resembled rules of today. American rule-makers were logically extending a native development when they decided to draw an imaginery line through the ball before it had been centered, to call this the "line of scrimmage," and to make this line, rather than the moving ball itself, the offside limit in the goalward motion of offensive players. At first, lined-up players of the two sides were allowed to stand and wrestle with each other while waiting for the ball to be centered; only later was a neutral zone introduced between the opposing lines.

A problem posed for the student of cultural diffusion at this point can be stated as follows: What factor or factors appear to have been most influential in creating an American game possessing not only nationally distinct rules but also rules having a specific flavor or intense legality about many a point of procedure left more or less up in the air by the British game?

We can now go beyond the rule-making aspect of the game and assert that standardized rules chiefly met the needs of ever more widely separated college competitors and their spectators. The English rule-makers, it appears, dealt with a situation in which amateur play was restricted to a fairly limited number of collegians and institutions. The power of localism was such that many an informality was tolerated, and intended to be tolerated, in the rules and their interpretation. American football appeared on the American campus at the beginning of a long period in which intercollegiate and interclass sportsmanship was a problem of ever widening social participation and concern. Football etiquette itself was in the making. Thus, it appears that when early American teams met, differences in opinion could not be resolved between captains in rapid-fire agreement or penny-tossing as was the case in Britain. American teams did not delegate to their captains the role of powerful comrade-in-antagonism with opposing captains, or, if they did, they felt that such responsibilities were too grave. "Fifty years ago arguments followed almost every decision the referee made. The whole team took part, so that half the time the officials scarcely knew who was captain. The player who was a good linguist was always a priceless asset," writes John W. Heisman, who played college football in the 1890's.

Into just such situations football players thrust all the force of their democratic social ideologies, all their prejudice in favor of equalitarian and codified attitudes. Undoubtedly, similar considerations also influenced the audience. Mark Benney, a British sociologist who is familiar with the games played on both sides of the Atlantic, points out that, whereas the American game was developed in and for a student group, the English game was played before quite large crowds, who, from a class standpoint, were less homogeneous than the players themselves, though they were as well informed as the latter in the "law" of the game. Rugby football was seldom played by the proletariat; it was simply enjoyed as a spectacle.

Held by the critical fascination the British upper strata had for the lower strata, the audience was often hardly more interested in the result of the game than in judging the players as "gentlemen in action." "The players," Benney writes, "had to demonstrate that they were sportsmen, that they could 'take it'; and above all they had to inculcate the (politically important) ideology that legality was more important than power." The audience was, then, analogous to the skilled English jury at law, ready to be impressed by obedience to traditional legal ritual and form and intolerant of "bad form" in their "betters."

The early Yale games, played before a tiny, non-paying audience, could not promote a class-based ritual of "good form." When the audience came, later on, their attitude toward upper-class sportsmanship was much more ambivalent—they had played the game too, and they were unwilling to subordinate themselves to a collegiate aristocracy who would thereby have been held to norms of correctness. The apparent legalism of many American arguments over the rules would strike British observers as simply a verbal power-play.

Such differences undoubtedly speeded the development of the specifically American variant. Native, too, are the visual and temporal properties of the game, as it developed even before 1900: its choreography could be enjoyed, if not always understood by non-experts, and its atomistic pattern in time and space could seem natural to audiences accustomed to such patterns in other foci of the national life. The mid-field dramatization of line against line, the recurrent starting and stopping of field action around the timed snapping of a ball, the trend to a formalized division of labor between the backfield and line, above all, perhaps, the increasingly precise synchronization of men in motion—these developments make it plausible to suggest that the whole procedural rationalization of the game which we have described was not unwelcome to Americans. It fitted other aspects of their industrial folkways.

Spurred by interest in the analysis of the athletic motions of men and animals, photographer Eadweard Muybridge was setting out his movie-like action shots of the body motion (more preoccupied even than Vesalius or Da Vinci with the detailed anatomy of movement) at about the same time that Coach Woodruff of Pennsylvania (1894) was exploring the possibilities for momentum play: lineman swinging into motion before the ball is snapped, with the offensive team forming a wedge, charging toward an opposition held waiting by the offside rule. In Philadelphia the painter Eakins, self-consciously following the tenets of naturalism and his own literal American tradition, was painting the oarsmen of the Schuylkill. Nearby, at the Midvale plant of the American Steel Company, efficiency expert Frederick Winslow Taylor was experimenting with motion study and incentive pay geared to small measurable changes in output—pay that would spur but never soften the workman.

Because there is no such thing as historical inevitability or necessary cultural homogeneity, the previous remarks do not mean that football developed as it did out of cultural compulsion. The culture supplied some of the conditions, but the game has a dynamism of its own. Indeed, the very effectiveness of momentum play, for example, led eventually to a rule that the line must refrain from motion before the ball is snapped. For the bulldozing of momentum play led, or was thought to lead, to a great increase in injuries. At first these injuries were coped with at Walter Camp's training table (his men had their choice of beefsteak or mutton for dinner, to be washed down with milk, ale, or sherry), but the public outcry soon forced further rule changes, designed to soften the game. After a particularly bloody battle between Pennsylvania and Swarthmore in 1905, President Roosevelt himself took a hand and insisted on reform.

Writes Frank G. Menke: "In a 1905 game between Pennsylvania and Swarthmore, the Pennsy slogan was 'Stop Bob Maxwell,' one of the greatest linesmen of all time. He was a mighty man, with amazing ability to roll back enemy plunges. The Penn players, realizing that Maxwell was a menace to their chances for victory, took 'dead aim' at him throughout the furious play.

"Maxwell stuck it out, but when he tottered off the field, his face was a bloody wreck. Some photographer snapped him, and the photo of the mangled Maxwell, appearing in a newspaper, caught the attention of the then President Roosevelt. It so angered him, that he issued an ultimatum that if rough play in football was not immediately ruled out, he would abolish it by executive edict."

Notice here the influence of two historical factors on football development: first, a president of the United States who was a self-conscious patron of youth, sport, and the arts; second, the relative newness in 1905 of photographic sports coverage. Increased photographic reporting of popular culture was the direct result of the newspaper policies of William Randolph Hearst, beginning about 1895.

Coach Walter Camp's colleague at Yale, William Graham Sumner, may well have smiled wryly at this. Hard-boiled sociologist Sumner was exhorting his students to "get capital" and cautioning them against the vices of sympathy and reformism—a theme which has given innumerable American academes a good living since—while Camp was exhorting his to harden themselves, to be stern and unafraid. In spite of them both, the reformers won out; but the end of momentum play was not the end of momentum. Rather, with an ingenuity that still dazzles, the game was gentled and at the same time speeded by a new rule favoring the forward pass. But before going on to see what changes this introduced, let us note the differences between the subjects of Sumner's and Camp's exhortations, on the one hand, and Taylor's on the other.

Frederick Taylor, as his writings show, was already seeking to engender a YMCA morality in a work force increasingly drawn from non-Protestant lands, whereas Camp was inculcating the same morality in young men of undiluted Anglo-Saxon stock and middle-class or upper-class origin. Not for another fifty years would the sons of Midvale prove as hard, though fed on kale or spaghetti, and only intermittently, as the sons of Yale. Meanwhile, the sons of Yale had learned to spend summers as track layers or wheat harvesters in an effort to increase their stamina, moral toughness, and cross-class adventures.

Nevertheless, certain basic resemblances between the purposes of Taylor and those of Sumner and Camp are surely present. By contrast with the British, the Americans demonstrated a high degree of interest in winning games and winning one's way to high production goals. The Americans, as in so many other matters, were clearly concerned with the competitive spirit that new rules might provoke and control (British sports, like British industry, seemed to take it more for granted that competition will exist even if one does not set up an ideology for it). Much of this seems to rest in the paradoxical belief of Americans that competition is natural—but only if it is constantly re-created by artificial systems of social rules that direct energies into it.

Back of the attitudes expressed in Taylor, Sumner, and Camp we can feel the pressure of not only a theory of competition but also a theory of the emotional tones that ought to go along with competition. It is apparent from the brutality scandals of 1905 that President Roosevelt reacted against roughhouse not so much because it was physical violence but for two related reasons. The first and openly implied reason was that it was connected with an unsportsmanlike attitude. The second, unacknowledged, reason was that Americans fear and enjoy their aggression at the same time and thus have difficulty in pinning down the inner meanings of external violence. The game of Rugby as now played in England is probably as physically injurious as American football was at the turn of the century. By contrast, American attitudes toward football demonstrate a forceful need to define, limit, and conventionalize the symbolism of violence in sports.

In England we see a game in which shouted signals and silent counting of timed movements are unknown—a game that seems to Americans to wander in an amorphous and disorderly roughhouse. Rugby, in the very home of the industrial revolution, seems preindustrial, seems like one of the many feudal survivals that urbanization and industrialization have exploited and not destroyed. The English game, moreover, seems not to have developed anyone like Camp, the Judge Gary of football (as Knute Rockne was to be its Henry Ford): Camp was a spark plug in efforts to codify intercollegiate rules; he was often the head of the important committees. His training table, furthermore, was one of the signs of the slow rise in "overhead" expense (an optimistic risk like the watering of United States Steel stock), as against the British need for parsimony. But at the same time the rise in costs undoubtedly made American football more vulnerable than ever to public relations considerations: the "gate" could not be damned.

Football: The Modern Ethos

This public relations issue in the game first appears in the actions of the rules committee of 1906—the introduction of the legalized forward pass in order to open up the game and reduce brutal power play. Between 1906 and 1913 the issue was generally treated as a problem centered about players and their coaches and thus took the form of an appeal to principles rather than to audiences. However, the development of the audience potential that we shall show unfolding after 1913 was not autonomous and unheralded. If public relations became a dominant factor by 1915, when the University of Pittsburgh introduced numbers for players in order to spur the sale of programs, it had its roots in the 1905–13 period. The rules committee of 1906, by its defensive action on roughhouse rules, had already implicitly acknowledged a broad public vested interest in the ethos of the game. Let us turn to look at the speed with which football was soon permeated by broad social meanings unanticipated by the founders of the sport.

By 1913, innovation in American industry had ceased to be the prerogative of Baptist, Calvinist, and North-of-Ireland tycoons. Giannini was starting his Bank of America; the Jews were entering the movies and the garment hegemonies. Yet these were exceptions, and the second generation of immigrants, taught in America to be dissatisfied with the manual work their fathers did, were seldom finding the easy paths of ascent promised in success literature. Where, for one thing, were they to go to college? If they sought to enter the older eastern institutions, would they face a social struggle? Such anxieties probably contributed to the fact that the game of boyish and spirited brawn played at the eastern center of intellect and cultivation was to be overthrown by the new game of craft and field maneuver that got its first revolutionary rehearsal at the hands of two second-generation poor boys attending little-known Notre Dame.

The most significant of the two boys, Knute Rockne, was, to be sure, of Danish Protestant descent and only later became a Catholic. During their summer vacation jobs as lifeguards on Lake Michigan, Rockne and Gus Dorais decided to work as a passing team. Playing West Point early in the season of 1913, they put on the first demonstration of the spiral pass that makes scientific use of the difference in shape between the round ball used in the kicking game and the oval that gradually replaced it when ball-carrying began. As the first players to exploit the legal pass, they rolled up a surprise victory over Army. One of the effects of the national change in rules was to bring the second-generation boys of the early twentieth century to the front, with a craft-innovation that added new elements of surprise, "system," and inventiveness to a game that had once revolved about an ethos of brawn plus character-building. Rockne, after becoming the best-known American coach, said, "After the church, football is the best thing we have."

With the ethnic shift came a shift in type of hero. The work-minded ability of an all-round craftsman like Jim Thorpe gave way to the personality glamor of backfield generals organizing deceptive forays into enemy territory. (Of course, the older martial virtues are not so much ruled out as partially incorporated in the new image.) In saying this it must not be forgotten, as sports columnist Red Smith has pointed out, that the fictional Yale hero, Dick Merriwell, is openly and shamelessly represented as a dirty player in the first chapters of his career. But his deviation from standard sportsmanship consisted largely of slugging, not of premeditated wiliness. In fact, the Yale Era, even with Camp's reign, was characterized by a game played youthfully, with little attention to the players' prestige outside college circles. The change that came with second-generation players is marked. A variety of sources, including letters to sports editors, indicated that a Notre Dame victory became representational in a way a Yale or Harvard victory never had been, and no Irish or Polish boy on the team could escape the symbolism. And by the self-confirming process, the Yale or Harvard showing became symbolic in turn, and the game could never be returned, short of intramuralization, to the players themselves and their earlier stage of innocent unruliness. American heterogeneity that had made it impossible to play the Rugby game at Yale finally transformed the meaning of the game to a point where Arnold of Rugby might have difficulty in drawing the right moral or any moral from it. Its "ideal types" had undergone a deep and widespread characterological change.

For the second-generation boy, with his father's muscles but not his father's motives, football soon became a means to career ascent. So was racketeering, but football gave acceptance too—acceptance into the democratic fraternity of the entertainment world where performance counts and ethnic origin is hardly a handicap. Moreover, Americans as onlookers welcomed the antitraditional innovations of a Rockne and admired the trick that worked, whatever the opposing team and alumni may have thought about the effort involved. One wonders whether Rockne and Dorais may not have gotten a particular pleasure from their craftiness by thinking of it as a counterimage to the stereotype of muscle-men applied to their fathers.

It was in 1915, about the same time the newcomers perfected their passing game, that the recruitment of players began in earnest. Without such recruitment, the game could not have served as a career route for many of the second-genera-

tion boys lacking the cash or impetus to make the class jump
that college involved. (This is ably documented in a pioneering study by George Saxon, "Immigrant Culture in a Stratified
Society," *Modern Review*, February, 1948.)

The development of the open and rationalized game has
led step by step not only to the T-formation, but also to the
two-platoon system. These innovations call for a very different
relationship among the players than was the case under the
older star system. For the game is now a co-operative enterprise in which mistakes are too costly—to the head coach, the
budget, even the college itself—to be left to individual initia-
tive. At least one institution has called in an anthropologist to
study the morale problems of the home team and to help in
the scouting of opposing teams. To the learning of Taylor has
been added that of Mayo, and coaches are conscious of the
need to be group-dynamics leaders rather than old-line straw
bosses.

Today, the semiprofessionalized player, fully conscious of
how many peoples' living depends on him, cannot be exhorted
by Frank Merriwell appeals but needs to be "handled." And
the signals are no longer the barks of the first Camp-trained
quarterback—hardly more differentiated than a folk-dance cal-
ler—but are cues of great subtlety and mathematical precision
for situations planned in advance with the aid of camera shots
and character analysis of the opposing team. Industrial, mili-
tary, and football teamwork all have a common cultural
frame.

Yet it would be too simple to say that football has ceased to
be a game for its players and has become merely an industry
or a training for industry. In the American culture as a whole,
no sharp line exists between work and play, and in some respects the more worklike an activity becomes, the more it can
successfully conceal elements of playfulness. Just because the
sophisticated "amateur" of today does *not* have his manhood
at stake in the antique do-or-die fashion (though his manhood

may be involved in very ambivalent ways, in his more generalized role as athlete and teammate), there can be a relaxation of certain older demands and perhaps a more detached enjoyment of perfection of play irrespective of partisanship.

Today the game is no longer the brawny battle of the days of Walter Camp, when football could be compared to the work of the steel-puddler or the farmer and the team captain could be compared to some simple self-made capitalist like Andrew Carnegie. It is a game in which anthropologists are hired as scouts, recruits are acquired in a labor market, and Monday-morning TV quarterbacks employ charts that make a Wall-Street analyst look amateurish. Some people fear that the constituencies of football-minded alumni, press agents, and coaches constitute a Praetorian Guard of state lobbyists and pressure groups; while at the same time former football stars write sob stories of their corruption by monopolistic merchandisers. The Reality Purist who remembers sand-lot football is sometimes driven to shift his interest to the professional game, where he finds pace cultivated as an element of drama. The Spectatorial Purist, ever hopeful of finding ritual "integrity" in football that will permit him to make some of the same semireligious claims for an American fullback that an Andalusian can make for the toreador or the bull, wavers in his hopes.

The role of football tutor to the audience has been pushed heavily onto radio and TV announcers (some of whom will doubtless be mobile into the higher-status role of commentators on politics or symphony broadcasts). The managerial draining of local betting pools into several big oceans has also contributed to the audience stake in the game. Yet all that has so far been said does not wholly explain alumnus and subway-alumnus loyalties.

Oddly enough, the college-football audience of all ages is more simple-mindedly loyal to the game than the promoters themseves. The sport generates so much distrust within collegiate circles themselves that those really unhappy with it are its producers. No one hates the game so much as some former players and some coaches, except perhaps a few prexies. In addition to all its other disadvantages, its team organization tends to be authoritarian; and its distinction in prestige between backfield stars and proletarians-in-the-line is at odds with American myth. Such things as the offensive and defensive platoon systems encourage the public to feel that football is a game—whether this be true or not—that develops routinized specialists who, even when they are brilliant blockers, are performing as robots. Increasingly, football's major rationale as a part of higher education is that it plays a part in the American class-mobility system. As we shall see in the next chapter, it symbolizes, especially with respect to amateur purism and recruiting practices, the American drift toward monopoly through efficiency and the subsequent anxieties over the sense of "real competition."

This history of the game and its audience suggests strongly that the football spectator today, if he is to feel competent, had better be a veteran of the game. There seems to be a parallel between the way in which the late nineteenth-century conventions of naturalism control our audio-visual media and the way in which legalities resembling Sherman Antitrust legislation control the American football game. In the one case a literalism of the imagination sets undue limits to both fictional and documentary forms; in the other the elaboration of rules and loopholes concentrates the spectator's sensibility on conference meetings that resemble sessions of the United Nations.

Is it inevitable that one of our great national sports should become a bureaucracy? Some of the moral, aesthetic, and merely procedural strains of the sports bureaucracy are what we must look at now, as we turn to the cultural rifts that underlie our spectatorial forms.

For all life is a game. . . . —Plotinus

CHAPTER SIX

The Spectatorial Forms

Spectator and Participant

To play golf, tennis, baseball, or what you will in childhood or maturity engages one in a series of deep and persisting identifications. To play is to belong to some kind of group of more or less definable social and age status. Within this playing group, many aspects of the non-playing role are "suspended." Some players display one kind of personality on the field and another off it. The artificial time and space limits of the Game permit fluid interpersonal experience that would never occur so rapidly and with so much permutation in "real life." Error and recovery from error, for example, are possible within a single inning of a baseball game. The mere physical objectification of "in" and "out," "batter" and "fielder," "winner" and "loser," occurs in terms of a social rhythm perceptible to all players and shared by all in a system of expectations.

A general childhood experience with the Game is regarded in America as a skeleton key to the secrets of society. Considering that the nation has often been defined as a nation of spectators, the overlap in spectator and participant roles is high.

The overlap probably provides one of the symbolic centers of that American tendency to emphasize mutuality and interchange of roles at the expense of their complementary separation. The interesting thing in a rich society such as ours is that many sports consumers can be classified readily as spectators and performers. (Sports such as mountain-climbing and skindiving, of course, do not involve much spectatorship.) And though the ethos of the spectator is closely related to the ethos of the player, it is less tangible, less certain.

In the 1920's Ernest Hemingway began to work out a code for spectators as one of his themes. In much of his work he presumes that his readers feel guilty and unsure of themselves in a spectator's role. To them he suggests that there are good and bad spectators and that they have different points of self-reference in relation to sports and to the competitors in the sports. An important quality of this self-reference allows the spectator to perform some quasi-ritualistic act in which he acknowledges the vicariousness of his experience and at the same time resists envy or fear of the competitor's situation. Why this should have turned up as a major motif has been explained often enough in terms of Hemingway as a personality. This does less than justice to the social environment of the 1920's and to his understanding of it.

It could be argued that the crisis of spectator ethos in the 1920's was part of American feeling because of the international dilemma of the time. Isolation and intervention are crucial political magnifications of the theme of spectatorship and participation; and in World War I the United States began to suffer new ambiguity and self-doubt about its relation to the world. The experience was made personally and historically concrete in the lives and deaths of Americans who sealed a new culture contact with Europe during the war. The people of the 1920's began to question the traditional American ideals of individualism and detachment. They asked whether detachment, spectatorship, "keeping one's powder dry," might not be degradations of an obsolete ideal. They were facing, among other things, the specialization of sports, the industrial expansion of sports, and the consumption of sports by a population seeking at once to escape an old morality and to find a new morality, in play.

Of all the social scenes in which the spectatorial crisis could find a symbolic reference, the world of sports presented the most generally known, fertile, universal and organically interrelated universe of terms. Some observers, like Ring Lardner, found it compelling to explore the locker-room dimension of reality. His stories were stories of working stiffs in baseball uniforms that only required a few moral and pathetic mudspots on them to look like a clown's attire. Some found it meaningful to explore the relation between the small-business purveyor of sports, such as the fishing or hunting guide, and his clientele. This is one of the crucial role relationships from which Hemingway develops his dialectic of work and play. The 1920's can be characterized, among other things, as the decade in which Americans thought more and made more discoveries about the spectator-audience relationship than in any period before or since. This tends to be obscured by more recent writing which perhaps overemphasizes the self-destructive exhibitionism and voyeurism that haunted some of the famously creative lives of the period.

Amateur and Professional

The specialization of sports may be documented in two ways: by observing the business methods necessary to a university's department of athletics; by observing the decline of interest in sports activities among younger Americans. The business methods have already been commonly observed. The fan in the stadium on Saturday knows that contemporary football requires comptrollers, personnel directors, public relations counselors, and so on. Depending on the size of the athletic department's business, a few men or many perform these functions. The decline of interest among young Americans has not been so much observed or so well understood, but it is a fact.

Some of those who have observed the fact associate it with the low marks on physical aptitude scored by American youngsters as compared with European ones. Whether or not that is a legitimate association, many young athletes from Europe and "lesser developed" areas of the world undeniably look healthier than American youngsters of the same age. In general, the American standard of living and nutrition, which is two or three times higher than that of other countries, produces the pastiest lot of children in the world. Doubtless, American inferiority results partly from overconsumption of milk, a food overrated by Americans and popular in the United States chiefly because of its importance to immigrants as a symbol of class status. But milk is not the only potion that threatens the health of young Americans. "Toughness" and athletic skill are profoundly and widely confused with one another; individual sports like tennis, suitable to urban dwellers, are slighted; and old-fashioned moralizing, muscle-building ideas of physical education prevail in the schools.

It can be interpreted in various ways, then, that recent research directed by Eugene Gilbert shows that interest in active sports declined among young people between 1951 and 1956. It would be rash to associate the decline with the hashed and rehashed problem of physical softness in America; it might mean simply that young people have found other and more interesting things to do. Socially compulsive participant sports have been in the past producers not only of physical fitness but also of that mental unfitness which we find in the marginal participant who later becomes a moralizing or bloodthirsty or vainglorious spectator. Precisely because it is very hard to prove that sports, as contrasted with a physically active life of work and play, are crucial to health or hardiness, it is important to detect in sports-mindedness a desire to feed the sources of

100 per cent Americanism, spectator benches, and the star system of the Big Game.

Industrial sports cannot generally create basic traits in our culture, but they can serve to confirm what we admire and what we dislike in the culture. To the degree that big sports pander to a taste for violence, they may encourage it as well as rechannel it. To the degree that they build the entertainment system rather than individual participation, they may distort our ideals of human growth in a free society. The debauching of colleges by "hardheaded" alumni pressure groups may lead to conditions not so different from gangster control of unions.

For who denies that American sports are specialized, centered on the "star" system? We see also that the public supporting sports suffers contradictions, inconsistencies, and uncertainties about amateur and professional status. There are three standards of sports participation available in the United States today.

The first and most powerful, the one supported by the most massive forces in the culture at large, is the business standard. By this standard, the ultimate goal of any athletic ability is to provide sports entertainment for cash. There is clearly nothing wrong with this standard except when, as in any other kind of business, it becomes disconcertingly illegal, as, for example, the purchase of college basketball teams for the benefit of gamblers. Players in a variety of sports ranging from bowling to baseball consider themselves as members of the general American "farm system" that provides stars to the commercial circuit. Their major problem, for years, has been to decide how much they wanted to bargain as a group with their employers or their sponsors and how much they wanted to bargain individually, as stars. The tendency in recent years has been to extend the claims of the proletarians in the wage-bargaining process. Professional football and baseball are the highest developments, probably, of this system.

The second most powerful standard of participation involves social class and has two major variants. The form of participation defended by Avery Brundage of the Olympic Committee and the American Lawn Tennis Association is the participation of the amateur gentleman. This standard prescribes that the athlete's family may buy his practice time and coaching for him but that it is quite unthinkable for anyone else to buy it for him. The important thing is that the athlete should be free from school or employment duties which would hamper his development as a great contender. The second variant is the upwardly mobile standard of the "non-gentlemen" and is represented best by the subsidized college football player. According to this standard, athletic ability is the commodity that must be marketed in order to complete an education, rise in the world, and overcome the disadvantages of a poor social start in the world. Rising in the world fits very well with the dominant business values of society in the United States, but completing an education does not. The "mobility" standard and the more traditional standard of Brundage both have roots in a theory of the relation between sports and social class. Where the standards conflict, we must hope that Brundage's standard will not be routed. At the same time we must hope that Brundage's standard will be applied with more social and cultural sophistication than it has been in the past.

The third, and less important, standard of participation is the type indorsed by the educational community. Here, participation is based on bona fide registration as a student, passing marks of studies, and certain controls over compensation which pretend to resemble the iron-clad standard of amateurism espoused by Brundage. The educational standard is caught squarely between the two class variants mentioned and, at the same time, stands in conflict with the values of the business system. College football is so much larger, as an industry, a career, and a way of life, than most organized sports in the United States that it naturally becomes a major scene of conflict among all these approaches to what organized sports should be in America.

It might be well to point out that there are cross-cultural implications in all this. The American sports code is largely an adaptation of the British code, and America is one of the two English-speaking countries in the world that have carried the cultural context of sports to a keener degree of social intensity than Britain herself. Australia leads the world in the degree to which its sports interests and sports organizations reflect the total social and political ideals of the nation. Sport in Australia is virtually the invisible government of an egalitarian semi-socialistic community based on generations of lower-middle-class immigration from the old country. The development of mass sports and spectacle sports is not out of balance with the development of individual sports, and there is no professional-amateur friction to speak of. Any Australian in sport is believed by his countrymen to be a sort of gentleman to begin with, deserving all the support he can get from the rest of the gentlemen, even if it amounts to providing him with a welfare state and fringe benefits. All this results in part from the ethnic and linguistic consistency of the Australian population, which in turn creates the image of a whole social group going up the social scale all together. In the United States, the greatest complication of sports standards has arisen from the rapid inflow of non-English-speaking immigrant groups.

Yet the United States, along with Canada, deserves to be classed near Australia as one of the countries that has continued the British tradition of associating sports closely with the whole class and political texture of the society and especially its nineteenth-century revolution of making sports available to the rising middle class. In the English-speaking industrial democracies "youth movements" tend to be contained within the ethos of a sporting world associated with industrialism and high consumption; the absence of such connections is one of the things that makes "youth movements" in other countries, especially the Latin and Oriental countries, so utterly different. The ethos of sports for the young, of course, is closely related in highly industrial countries with mass educational opportunity and especially the growth in numbers of secondary school students and college students. The older British ideal of sport tends to hold more in English-speaking countries where sex segregation is practiced in schools, and it tends to decline sharply in countries emphasizing coeducational practice, chiefly the United States.

In comparison with Britain and Australia, the cultural meaning of American sports occupies a tense position between those two. Britain is able to maintain its amateur traditions because its class revolution has proceeded at an orderly pace since the 1880's. Australia is able to maintain a commercial concept of the amateur because it has judged that all of its sportsmen and spectators are gentlemen, and what gentlemen decide about sports, no matter what they decide, is correct by definition. The egalitarian traditions of the Labor party in Australia create the context in which aid to a young athlete is nothing more or less than *noblesse oblige*. The United States gyrates nervously between these two alternative class perspectives of sport because it is not sure what relation it wants to hold as between the athletic organizations and the class system as a whole. We lack the desire to take the Australian way; it would seem socialistic and patronizing to us. We reject the British way because it seems to us unfit for society such as ours in which social mobility proceeds at a faster pace, for more people in a greater variety of social circumstances. We cannot, of course, accept the Latin and Oriental standards of sport, which are still based, except in the "revolutionary" countries where sport is likely to be an industrial display, on a clear-cut difference between master and slave.

Sports opportunities in the United States today, especially in higher-cost individual sports such as tennis, are unequally distributed. The country can afford to support both the spectator system and the participant system, but today the spectator system still serves to mask the deficiency of the participant system. It might cease to do so as soon as it had to pay part of the bill. That is to say, despite our resources and the millions we spend on an athletic star system, many children, especially among minority groups, are growing up with few sports opportunities.

Given this desideratum, it would be wise to define every athlete as professional from the outset and then—only then—to establish certain forms qualifying him for amateur status for a particular event in a particular sport. The first rule of such events would be that no athlete could compete as an amateur in his major sport; for that sport, of course, is the one in which he is professional. The second rule would be that a portion of the income tax paid by sports corporations, including colleges, and by athletes, including college athletes, go to a national Amateur Committee charged with promoting sports for participants without "earning" power in sports.

If the United States is to build the participant system from the receipts of the spectator system, however, and especially if it is to avoid welfare-state sports, the American corporation and the American labor union must work out new ways to stimulate the spirit of amateurism. So far they have lagged. Business stumbled into subsidization of sports more or less accidentally and has not taken stock of the cultural implications. Labor unions seem too sleepy to care.

Meanwhile, the sports industry even tries to dominate its consumers into a sort of "yellow-dog" contract of spectatorship. In the previous chapter we noted critic John Crosby saying indirectly that football is "so different from [what it was in] the old days." He appears to belong to a relatively small group of sophisticates who can afford to wish for the old game that presented a clear-cut, sportsmanlike ideal and that introduced no ambiguities of subsidies, scholastic qualifications, and big-university politics. His view is perhaps the view of the de-

manding man who wants his entertainment to remain entertainment. To demonstrate a quite different approach to the
question of sports spectatorship, we may quote from an article
about sports in general: "America is becoming a nation of bad
sports. It's about time we stopped coasting on our reputation
and looked at the facts. The blunt truth is that Gus H. Fan is
proving himself to be a rowdy, unruly, brawling pain in the
neck. . . ."

This is the statement with which a writer known as Adie
Suehsdorf opens an article entitled "Are Americans Bad Sports?"
in *This Week*, a magazine that often prints such articles dealing with the art of consuming mass entertainment. The purpose
of this article is to raise the standards of sportsmanship in
American mass-attended sports.

The article gives four reasons for bad sportsmanship, i.e.,
verbal and physical violence of an exaggerated character, at
mass sports. The first is ignorance of the game on the part of a
new class of consumers who do not know the rules. The second is that the games are too complex. The third is that betting
money is involved. The fourth is that people seem more interested in identifying with a winner than in enjoying the game
as a spectacle.

Let us consider reasons for bad sportsmanship not included
by Suehsdorf, excluded really, because he sides with the industry against the consumer:

First, management has favored a situation in which players
fight against rules and umpires, as, for example, the modern
wrestling card that always includes at least one "dirty" bout.
Management hopes thereby to show a genuine contest despite
dishonesty in some respects, in some areas, at some time, in
the history of most mass-entertainment sports. The audience
in turn likes a genuine contest—even if it must be between
player and referee—because it senses a lack of "fair contest"
in big sports.

Second, management itself, in its function prior to the actual
contest, is often committed to unfair practice. Many boxers,

for example (and this is reflected in other popular media), are managed by gangsters.

Third, what management considers as unwarranted violence on the part of spectators is often an effort at participation, however foolish. Audience violence is a response to player violence sponsored by management as a promotional device.

However, even staying within Suehsdorf's reasons for bad sportsmanship—ignorance, complexity, betting, and anxiety to win—and ascribing truth to them, we see an authoritarian formula of consumership. The consumer, according to this formula, must be blamed for the consumption patterns imposed on an entertainment management that itself changed the pattern of the sports. The article suggests two methods for improving the situation: more police in stadiums, more education for sports consumers. Their essential onesidedness is revealed in the fact that the first leads theoretically to a situation where a crowd would be required to keep silent while watching a "fixed" game and the second leads theoretically to a situation where a spectator would spend time in night school learning how the mass-entertainment industries want him to respond to the sports for which he pays.

On the other hand, the sports public often responds with an ugly eagerness to the promotion of sports sadism and masochism. Perhaps it even brings to the sports arena—from the depths of American feeling—a brutishness that reminds us of lynch law, Texan male compulsives, and child-hating antivivisectionists. Slaps on the wrists of venal promoters are less likely to improve conditions than is a change of heart in the public itself. The spectator needs a code.

The Code of the Spectator

These comments on the spectator in sports may remind the reader that the audience of a TV show and the spectator of a sports event have been treated here as if they were members of the same species. Yet aren't they different creatures, in many important senses? And if so, what are the differences? Some answers to this can be suggested by considering the different standards of spectatorial perception that are associated with audiences for fictions (movies and TV), audiences for contests (a wrestling match), and audiences for performances (popular singers).

It is well known that a content-analysis of the characters, actions, symbols, and meanings of the products of popular culture, such as the movie, does not tell us what the "real life" of the audience is. In fact, the characters, actions, symbols, and meanings that occur in movies are there *because* they do not exist in real life. Comparisons between actuality and fiction ought to be made. We are beginning to realize that such comparisons are constantly being applied to a wide range of symbolic activities and that the so-called problem of "movie realism" is only a special case of a general question.

Suppose we were to set up a scale of entertainment products ranging from those products in which realism is an issue only in a minor degree, such as music, to those in which it is an issue to a major degree, say movies. Discussions of realism in music tend to be discussions between disputants who disagree with each other about the degree to which they hear, or permit, progammatic elements in their favorite music. Most contributors to it appear to be aware of the ambiguities involved. Discussions of realism in movies, on the other hand, often tend to be arguments between disputants who, while they define social reality differently, agree in thinking that the attribution of some such realism to any and all movies is the best way of beginning to criticize them. Between music and movies, however, there is a range of products for which realism is also applied as a standard.

Closest to the movies in this respect is the field of sports. The TV broadcasting of boxing and wrestling induces a heavy investment of audience attitudes centered on criteria of realism. The realism in these exhibitions is expressed in the notion that, ideally, the contest enacted and portrayed should be a real contest with fair rules. In general, attitudes toward the reality of the contest become, for the audience, the test of different levels of competence in viewing the contest. The viewer who is unaware that the wrestler dramatizes his triumphs and despairs as a part of the box-office appeal is dismissed as unsophisticated by the audience-in-the-know. At the same time, other sports tend to be arranged in a rank order according to the general public belief as to the possibility of the "fix." Wrestling appears to occupy the bottom of this rank order, and probably professional baseball, if we disregard the factor of the farm system, appears to occupy the top of the rank order. Horse racing appears to fall in between these two, along with other major professional sports.

Wrestling is an especially interesting example of the public's problems in search of realism. Because the public believes that wrestling is often "fixed," it protects itself from cynicism about the matter by preferring to view the sport as drama rather than as a contest. It is willing to give up the sense of pure competition between equalized or handicapped contestants in order to pay attention to a drama of alternative scenes of dominance and submission. One gets the idea that audience interest is concentrated not so much on the indeterminant moments of the contest, in which neither contestant is ahead, as on the moments in which one contestant is very much ahead. The price paid for this view of the sport is that the audience loses competence in some other sense. Strictly speaking, it loses competence in the judgment of the real hurts suffered by real wrestlers in their stunt-man approach to a spectacle performance of fictional violence.

The question might be asked whether a plainly fictional contest whose major rule is to have the rules broken constitutes a problem in realism for the audience. Apparently it does. Conversations about wrestling seem to involve two claims on the part of the participants: (1) the claim that they can recognize situations when the "fix" is upset by the "real" and (2) the claim that they can distinguish a normal amount of villainous rule-breaking from an abnormal and indecent amount of villainous rule-breaking. The first claim, that the "fix" can be distinguished from the "real," is clearly untenable. The same audience cannot pretend to itself at one and the same time that wrestlers are great actors in their line—and not great actors. Probably social perception of wrestling works the other way, that most injured wrestlers leave the ring with injuries unperceived by the audience. The second claim, that there is a line separating "too much" from "enough" rule-breaking, is a highly tenable claim. Audiences do develop keen discriminations of this sort; and in this respect the audience' "realism" is at its height.

Given the etiquette of any sport, the audience is involved in the competitive state of the struggle and the fairness or unfairness of the application of the rules. The audience claims to know a practical, if not formal, norm. With both movies and sports events, the audience possesses a practical norm which it resents being flouted by the demands of fiction.

The problem of realism has been approached in terms of realism in fiction and realism in contests that have become fictions. We can generalize the problem of realism to make it include the realism of performance. Thus, most cases of ordinary people calling a movie unrealistic center about the acting. Story structure is not really perceived at all; the question is whether, given the story situation, the characters behave as expected or desired.

It is important to the popular audience to feel competent in the judgment of singers. In recent years, the performances of popular singers have been described as being "sincere" or "commercial." In this polarity, "sincere" may mean any one or all of the following: (1) The singer reflects in artistic performance well-known biographical aspects of himself. (2) The singer dramatizes a widely diffused social role. (3) The singer identifies with the audience. (4) The singer is self-stimulated by his own performance to such a degree that he becomes a person making a true statement. (5) The singer employs a new style that, because of its apparent informality or its intensity, achieves the appearance of personalization. (The artist appears to dominate convention and make it his own.) Claims to this sort of competence on the part of audiences are often challenged on the ground that they are naïve. The audience, it is said, mistakes the well-known capacity of the skilful artist to use the most calculated and impersonal means to achieve "personal" effects.

Such an attack on the competence of the audience holds up quite well when it is applied to biographical reflection, role dramatization, or audience identification. By the same token, it does not hold up well if the audience claims to perceive sincerity or some other aspect of realism in cases of self-stimulation or stylistic innovation. Even to want to perceive the self-stimulation of a performing artist is to be in a position of considerable familiarity with his routine work. Such familiarity may be sufficient training (it is certainly the pertinent training) for recognizing moments when a performing entertainer, stimulated by face-to-face contact with his audience, also stimulates himself to new levels of dramatic directness in his handling of expression. Again, when a performer introduces a new expressive style, the audience that calls it real or sincere may be simply making a semantic error. Seeing the inhibitions of an older style fall away, it does not yet perceive the inhibitions of the new style. This recognition does not occur until the new expressive style has been present long enough to expose its own stereotypes.

The basic audience claim to competence in the judgment of a popular singer's performance is a claim that the audience perceives the artist's relation to himself when stimulated by the live audience and that the audience recognizes a shift in expressive styles at the moment the artist is making one of these styles his own. Both claims are reasonable, and in structure

they resemble the claims made by all audiences in the performance of all the arts. On the other hand, the popular audience
often fails to sort its claims of competence out. Its aesthetic
theory is perhaps worse than its aesthetic practice. The meas-
ure of competence of the audience for a popular singer might
be said to consist, then, of its capacity to outgrow biographical,
role-identification theories of the "realism" of singer performances and to concentrate on its other intuitions about such
"realism." In general, popular intuition of realism in performance of popular music has outgrown biographical, role-identification theories in the last twenty years or so.

It is true that young fan groups usually repeat all these critical stages in their growth. A new singing star, as he develops a
fan group, becomes first an object of biographical interest. (It
may be important that he is an Italian from Bridgeport and
that in high school he couldn't sing a note.) At a second level
it may become more widely felt that his biographical success
is in some sense representative. At a third level the singing
performer may appear to interact with his audience on the
basis of a common though implicit recognition of these images.
(Frank Sinatra became, at one stage of his career, almost over-
skilled in telegraphing to his audience what he thought his
audience was about to expect from him.) At a fourth level,
the audience discriminates enough to perceive when the performer is "on" and when he is "off" and at this point begins
to achieve real competence in criticism. It is only a step from
this level to the perception that a singer's appeal is bound up
in his showmanlike control of a new expressive style.

The so-called problem of realism in popular culture has been
generalized here to include fictions, contests, and performances. It is suggested that each of these forms of entertainment
has a problem of realism and that, although each of these so-
called problems of realism is stated by the audience to itself
in different terms, they have deep common elements. The
question is how to define these common elements more exactly.

The answer lies partly in the act of self-reference achieved by the spectator, such an act shaping the response whether he is seeing a movie, watching a game, or listening to a singer. The *kind* of self-reference varies from form to form, and to achieve the appropriate self-reference for each, not confusing it with the others, would be the basis of a spectator's code. The self-reference in the proto-critical movie audience is best expressed in terms of Nelson Foote's assertion that some, if not all, leisure activities depend for their quality on "empathy without loss of integrity." If this rule applies to all leisure, it applies especially well to movie and TV spectatorship, where the popular audience' ideas of realism appear to rise from just such a concern. The self-reference in the wrestling audience is best expressed in terms of David Riesman's assertion that some, if not all, leisure activities depend for their quality on a deliberate decision to sustain ambiguity, to test one's tolerance for ambiguity. The self-reference in the singer's audience is best expressed in terms of John Seeley's notion that leisure activities include "the reduction of self-induced tension."

This is not to suggest that an appropriate ethos for the American spectator has now been worked out. Such an ethos clearly involves more fields than movies, popular singing, and sports, issues other than repressed anxieties about commitment and competition. It relates to the theme often pounded by the European, that the American lacks a certain amount of privacy from *himself*, because he insists on interpreting the Socratic "Know Thyself" in pragmatic terms. American spectatorial tension may be strong because it is a special instance of the general case. The American of the twentieth century is an inveterate and compulsive spectator of himself. And the fact that the mass media have generally been occupied with an extensive attempt to teach people how to behave as spectators suggests that anxiety is still strongly connected with the role.

CHAPTER SEVEN

The Plastic Machines

Three Portraits at the Wheel

What do people do when they are not satisfied with the movies and TV and when they react against merely spectatorial relationships to the world of sport? They make things, or they participate in some sort of performance or contest themselves. This might be the place, therefore, to reconsider such things as the little-theater movement in the United States or the rise of the amateur musical performing groups to numbers unheard of a generation ago. However, these developments have been studied before; they are not essentially new; and they are not fully popular. To speak in terms of the mass culture and its audience competency, it would be more germane to find, if we could, an activity which involves a wide range of economic groups, which hooks into the major daily consumption patterns of the nation, and which has had a powerful amateur influence on the professionals in its own field. In the past twenty years, hardly any activity of this sort is so worthy of notice as hot-rodding, with its manifold implications for the place of the auto and automotive craftsmanship in American life. Here, then, is a case study of a group of Participative Purists.

Almost everyone now looks at the auto industry as Thorstein Veblen would have looked at it; we all enjoy our spoofs at conspicuous expenditures in chrome decor. And when we think of the producers of autos, we think of a group of businessmen who are pre-eminent the world over as representatives of Veblen's dictum that "men everywhere seek to *do* something." The fiery pragmatism of Ford and Kettering are recent enough examples; and there was the Detroit auto engineer of the 1920's who used to say to his tippling friends when they got tired of just talking cars, "Let's go out and *do* something, even if it's not good." The behavior of the auto producer and his dealers and salesmen often confirms Veblen's assertion that business is a process not so much of "exchange" as of intelligent "coercion" of material and personnel.

We pay somewhat less attention to the auto as the vehicle of those "instincts" of aggression and workmanship that Veblen saw as the biological masters of the industrial society. Yet the building of the auto industry was a competitive battle royal on a Darwinian scale: fifteen hundred companies folded or were merged to permit a few to survive. Today, the industry affords us a good look at those contrasting types of capital enterprise (Ford, the creation of a production man; General Motors, the creation of Durant, a finance man) that Veblen emphasized in his portraiture of entrepreneurial types. General Motors, Ford, and Chrysler now resemble each other more and more, of course, being unable to retain their old individuality in the face of a competitive struggle—the struggle to keep up with the taste of the market.

After World War II, the news was that the auto wars were over for a while and that this great semimonopolistic industry had made a kind of peace—indeed a very forward-looking, if not inflationary, peace with the United Auto Workers and its assembled trades. In Ford, the house cleaning was dramatic;

the bullroaring foremen of the days of Harry Bennett were checked; the death of Henry Ford himself made way for a new image of the Company. Some of the old fire and iron and blood had gone out of the industry, and no one was sorry to see it go. By 1947 labor had organized its countermanagement aggressions so well that it had the slowdown as a weapon in addition to the strike vote; in that year the forgotten man of the industry was not the assembly-line worker but the foreman, who lived as a buffer between higher management and the labor force. With increased labor control over assembly-line speed and time-study criteria—including the problem of standard rate-setting—the industry seemed well on its way to the rational pacification that Veblen spoke of as an industrial outcome of man's close relation to the machine. However, contrary to Veblen's idea, modern industry, like many others in our high-wage economy, appeared at times to be substituting "overcapitalization" of equipment and traces of redundance in the labor force for the old-time "industrial reserve army" labor practices.

Production practices in the industry after World War II brought other changes: the assembly line was increasingly rationalized as customers of the postwar years showed a new interest in high-compression power plants. The producers later gave a variety of reasons for this development. One of them was a straight sales-appeal rationale to the effect that owners wanted more power as well as sleeker design; another reason tended to be expressed in functional terms, when it was argued that modern thru-highway driving required fast acceleration as a safety factor, particularly in passing. This was not well supported by research, which tends to show that misuse or non-use of the rear-view mirror is the crux of passing faults in American highway driving; but it was not an unconvincing argument.

The demand for higher power, plus the introduction of a variety of semicybernetic controls on the modern car, had two immediate effects on the auto's relation to auto workmanship.

First, it overtaxed the older interchangeable-parts technique of assembly and ultimately made necessary the introduction of new quality control in the factory: this change took even more of the workman's control over the product away from him than he had lost before. Second, it produced a car so complex that it made most drivers finally give up any idea they may ever have had of doing some tinkering with the car themselves.

What, then, has happened to the "instinct" of workmanship that the factory worker used to be able to put into the car in the earlier days of auto-building? What has happened to the amateur or leisure interest in car-tinkering? How do these happenings tie in with other changes in the style of producing, marketing, and consuming cars? To look at the production managers first, it became clear by 1950 that some of the old-time "enterprise play" had gone out of the industry; instead of being a game with many firms as players, it was a game along "oligopolistic" lines of bargaining. The Big Three played at going along with such independents as Studebaker and Nash; and one of the postwar rules of the game seems to have been the semiconscious decision to "allow" the second independent, Studebaker, under Paul Hoffman, to be the first American car-maker to merchandise a new postwar design. This took the form of winking at the preferential supply of allocated materials assigned to independents during the demobilization period. The Big Three and the independents together played a fairly tight game, too, with their suppliers, engaging in a variety of strategic moves tending toward extended control over such materials as rubber, chrome, steel, and special parts.

So far as the workers were concerned, the auto industry had become something of a model in labor relations by 1947, and many an auto worker left his plant at the end of the week with enough energy and overtime to have a business of his own or to become a moneyed hobbyist of the boat-building or plane-flying variety. By and large, the auto worker had become a "semicontractor" who was paid a standard-of-living wage

and promised fringe benefits, in both the present and the future, in part payment for his mechanized withdrawal of emotion and efficiency from the auto plant itself. At least some
auto workers ran through the day's work of eight hours in five
hours, like a football player who is anxious to get the practice over; and their emotional commitment to the final product
was minor. They had their eyes, justifiably enough, on such
matters as the cost-of-living proviso in contracts. Except a·
top levels of plant management and control, the virtues of the
mechanical man had been built into the machines and the pro
duction plan.

Where, then, was the auto still the object of what Vebler
called a "conscientious input of efficiency"? It appeared to be
such an object in two different spheres of American life where
auto construction and maintenance were still personalized
One was the shop of the garage mechanic, who benefited in
terms of an increased demand for his skill because of the in
creasing complexity of the auto. Another was in the shop o
the leisure auto tinkerer: sometime between 1920 and 1945
roughly, the auto had passed through a stage of its existence
symbolized by the comic strip "Gasoline Alley." As auto, i
had lost much of its old novelty as transportation; in order to
retain glamor it had to become, in differentiated forms, a kind
of daily apparel. As such, it could be new and expensive (th
Lincoln Continental) or old and expensive (the antique Olds
mobile) or personally rebuilt (the hot rod) or imported and
sporting (the small sports car). It became clear by 1950 tha
one of the new areas in which the auto was being glamorized b
"marginal differentiation" in consumership was worth a close
examination—not only for what was happening but for the wa
in which the mass media, especially the press, were reportin
the events.

It is not easy to sort out the relations between the mass me
dia and the circle of activities of the various mass-media au
diences; but we may analyze a mass-media attitude toward a

automotive hobby, with the idea of showing merely a few of the reflexes that join or fail to join a particular leisure-interest group with its imagery in the press. Now, in the first place, a hobby can be defined in a number of different ways. One definition begins by invoking Veblen's "instinct of workmanship," and his belief that this "instinct," because it tends to be rationalized and overrationalized, or deflected and contaminated, or simply underemployed, expresses itself in non-pecuniary forms. We need not discuss the validity of Veblen's instinct theory or quibble with his vocabulary to accept the idea that our industrial culture is full of deflected artisanship. The quasi-technical hobby and the hot-rodder are often explained as a defensive response to this deflection; and this leads to the notion that we can make a rough distinction between the consumership hobby and the production hobby. Some people and groups express through their hobbies a desire to polish and modify the forms of gadgets that already exist; thus, the collecting and refinishing of antique furniture is often a consumership hobby. On the other hand, the collecting, cutting, and mounting of semiprecious stones found in their natural settings might be termed a productive hobby—bearing in mind that these classifications would prove brittle under strain. Perhaps the hot-rodders deserve to be called the most passionately original and energetic production hobbyists of recent years.

The mass media can usually be depended on to notice and report variations in the customary use of such a commodity as the automobile; and in 1948 the mass media reported three interesting and distinct types of the hobbyism of the auto. *Life*, late in 1948, reported on what was then described as the "West Coast" craze for the small, British-made MG car. The little two-seater cost something over $2,000 and did not possess the power of American cars; as an attractive little speedster it had developed an audience adept in the ways of marginal differentiation. The interesting thing about the California "fans" for the MG is that many of them felt a strong sense of community and that they organized this interest into a voluntary "fan" association. The group went on week-end jaunts to the mountains to enact their rituals with all due ceremonial circumstance. A high point of the day came when the owners reached under the hood to tune up their cars for the return trip, compare notes on engine power, and go through all the motions of Participative Purism attached to a technological fandom.

A second variation in the consumership of the auto was stereotyped by the media in a comic strip. Beginning in 1949, the comic strip "Smilin' Jack," a strip that emphasizes airplanes and pilots, introduced a new character. His name was Hot Rod Happy, and he was pictured as an adolescent of seventeen or so who drove around in a hot rod of his own creation. Within a few days after his introduction into the strip, we were told that his old fisherman father was dying and that Hot Rod Happy was more interested in his cut-down car than in his father's illness. The father died, but before dying he told Hot Rod Happy that he, Hot Rod, had a sister. The sister, Hot Rod learns, is the bride-to-be of the famous aviator Smilin' Jack. Without a tear for the dead, Hot Rod Happy is off to attach himself to the famous flier; on his way he outruns the cops with his self-made car. At this stage of the continuity, the profile of Hot Rod Happy was clear: the reader was being given a comic-strip version of the semidelinquent of the highways, the kid who is riding for a fall. Later, the cartoonist showed the same character integrating himself in a variety of adventures in which his passion for cars became a part of a responsible stance in the world.

A third variation in car consumption reflected by the media in the late 1940's was represented by a comic-strip adolescent character who drove a car that looked like an MG, or pocket-sized Continental roadster, in a comic strip known as "The Ripples." He was a photographer, and the little car was definitely associated with a Bohemian way of life.

Each of the three early appearances of the small or unconventional car in the mass media reported or emphasized a special taste. In the case of the MG the small-car owner was one of many bonded together in a community of interests; in the case of Hot Rod Happy the small-car consumer was a "crazy, mixed-up kid"; in "The Ripples" the small-car owner was what Russell Lynes has called an "upper Bohemian." The three images seemed to constitute a scale that showed a three-part range of relatedness to the car: the Bohemian was distant from the car as machine; the MG fans were much closer; and Hot Rod Happy was so close to it that he was almost an inventor. Notice that Hot Rod Happy was the "worst" of all these characters. Apparently, there was some association between juvenile delinquency and the ability to revolutionize the design of the car as it came from the factory. Zack Mosley, creator of "Smilin' Jack" soon received protesting letters from hot-rod associations that had made their peace with the state police and signed pledges to be law-abiding hot-rod fanciers. His subsequent modulation of his hero into a mood of reform did not stop letters to the newspapers. Attacks upon the recklessness of hot-rod youth were often coupled with the implicit notion that their cars were dangerous because they were unconventional. Not a few people seemed to feel, without quite saying so, that the duty of young Americans was to buy cars, not to rebuild them. To rebuild a car, it appeared, was an attack on the American way.

Images of Competence

A general early public image of the hot-rodder is crytallized in a statement made in 1950 by Thomas W. Ryan, director of the New York Division of Safety. "Possession of the 'hot rod' car is presumptive evidence of an intent to speed," he said. "Speed is Public Enemy No. 1 of the highways. It is obvious that a driver of a 'hot rod' car has an irresistible temptation to 'step on it' and accordingly operate the vehicle in a reckless manner endangering human life. It also shows a deliberate and premeditated idea to violate the law. These vehicles are largely improvised by home mechanics and are capable of high speed and dangerous maneuverability. They have therefore become a serious menace to the safe movement of traffic. The operators of these cars are confused into believing that driving is a competitive sport. They have a feeling of superiority in recklessly darting in and out of traffic in their attempt to out-speed other cars, on the road. . . ."

In an article for the *American Quarterly* Eugene Balsley, a former hot-rodder turned reporter on the fad, showed that the hot-rodder's picture of himself was quite different. He reported that in a letter to the creator of Hot Rod Happy, protesting the cartoonist's picture of the hot-rodder, a hot-rod organization wrote: "A hot rod accident or incident is newsworthy, while an accident involving ordinary çars is so common that it is usually not newspaper-worthy. We wonder whether you appreciate the real contribution that the hot rod industry, for it is an industry, has made to automotive transportation. The automotive industry has the equivalent of a million dollar experimental laboratory in the hot rod industry from which they can get valuable technical information free of any expense or risk of reputation. . . ."

By 1951 or so, *Hot Rod Magazine,* with a claimed circulation of 200,000, devoted many of its editorials to presenting its own picture of the hot-rod car and driver: "A real hot rod is a car that is lending itself to experimental development for the betterment of safety, operation, and performance, not merely a stripped-down or highly decorated car of any make, type or description, or one driven by a teenager. As to the menace or nuisance element, very few hot rod enthusiasts want to risk their specialized equipment for use as battering rams."

Balsley documented the degree to which the hot-rodder and his friends were highly articulate in their criticism of the Detroit automobile, with scorn for "the Detroit solution of a problem in transportation, engineering, esthetics." Hot-rodders asserted that Detroit's mass-production car was uneconomical, unsafe at modern road speeds, and uglier than it had any right to be; they added that it was too costly, too heavy, and too complicated by class and status symbolism to be a good car. The hot-rodder's credo, that driving should not be so effortless that one forgets one is driving until after the crash, was another ground for rejecting the Detroit car.

"When the hot rodder rebuilds a Detroit car to his own design," wrote Balsley, "he is aiming to create a car which is a magical and vibrant thing. Yet, back of his dream design we can see the workings of the practical engineering standards that dominate the hot-rod culture. There are sound reasons for the hot-rod builder's selection and rejection of various components of the Detroit car. Any given car, when rebuilt by a hot rodder, can be loosely assigned to one of four classes of design. . . .

"Cars rebuilt by means of the simplest changes can be classed in the fourth rank. The owner in this category changes only the exterior of the body. He is, unfortunately, aided by the countless manufacturers of doll-up accessories, who provide such mechanically useless items as cutout mufflers, 'supercharger pipes,' and the ubiquitous Buick-like ventilator ports that do not ventilate. . . .

"Transformation in cars of the next higher rank, the third, are dictated by consideration of function, although ornamentation may still be used. While in cars of the lowest category the engine remains substantially unaltered, the engines of next-higher rank cars are changed in order to increase horse-power and acceleration. . . .

"When we move up to the second highest rank, we cross the line into the true mysteries. The hot rodder in the second rank strips his car of all chromium and ornaments. He lowers the body of the car, often as much as ten inches, to increase roadability and safety. He stresses clean lines, lightness, simplicity, and gasoline economy in his design. He may not change the chassis, but he will surely add disc or hydraulic brakes if needed. He has failed in his avowed objective if the car is poorly constructed, or if it is not safer, better looking, and more efficient than ordinary cars. His car is a pleasure car, and all the changes he makes are practical for everyday road use. If he happens to be interested in competition he is likely to drive against time at the dry lakes outside Los Angeles, or at the various national meets. Generally, however, a great deal of his time is spent talking about performance figures with his cronies at the garage or at his hot-rod club; dry-lake racing tends to force him toward ownership of a top rank car.

"What are the cars of the top rank? They are super-stream-lined, often made of surplus aircraft wing-tanks, and will run only at top speed. They can be started only if they are pushed, one of the many reasons why they cannot be run on the high-way. They are of interest in the hot-rod complex mainly be-cause their owners are the designers and the innovators in the hot-rod field. Many automotive manufacturers, knowing the excellence of the timing apparatus at the lakes, time their own test model there."

Bonneville Salt Flats, Utah, sees hundreds of hot-rodders fussing around trying to gap spark plugs and adjust carburetors in the early mornings of August, at the annual meet. The em-phasis there is on speed, power, and streamlining, on a white salt desert that draws hundreds of cars from all over America. This display of engineering skill and aerodynamic ingenuity, however, is only one side of the activity; the idea of selling individualization in body design by rebuilding from originally disparate parts has become a commercial motive of the "body shops."

In such shops, where customers and operators speak with a critical vocabulary all their own, ornaments and chrome are removed from Detroit cars. The man with money who is will-ing to spend it to make his new car a different car drives away with a "custom" model. And the young man with an old car and little money likewise gets a "personal" model with lines unlike those of other cars on the road. At this point, of course, when buyer criticism of standardization is more passive, the car-rebuilding impulse passes beyond the Horatian desire to express a mood of "simplicity in elegance" and becomes something else—an exercise in what David Riesman identifies as marginal differentiation.

Rebels with a Cause

According to a Twentieth Century Fund study of national expenditure habits, hobbies fell off in percentage rank, as compared with spectator sports, in the period between 1900 and 1929; they began to reverse this trend only in the 1940's. How do the hot-rodders fit in? In the first place, we must recall the historical depth of the American adolescent's interest in car-tinkering; it goes back certainly to the appearance of the Model T Ford, a car that supplied the United States, within five years or so after its first appearance, with a large backlog of cheap and repairable vehicles. Furthermore, there is much evidence that hot-rodding has involved boys of widely varying economic and social backgrounds; and there are indications that it is relaxedly interethnic. The rising costs of hot-rod-car rebuilding may have introduced recent changes, but it is a good guess that hot-rodding still remains in the hands of young men who can plan to spend no more than about $1,200 on a car over a period of three years or so. It is certain that in the 1940's and 1950's the participants in the dry-lake races to some extent engaged in a cross-class conversation, the wide range of classifications, from high-cost to low-cost cars making that possible. The building of hot rods calls on the skills of boys who have had some automotive-school training and garage experience, thus tending to draw non-college kids into the field; and many of the hot rods are built by teams in which there appears to be a division of labor among individuals drawn from different ethnic and social classes as well as from different skill ranks of adolescent society.

We might ask, Are the hot-rodders to be termed "competents" in leisure? Did some of the media resentment-image of the hot-rodders arise from envy of their felt competence and originality, this being rationalized in the form of objections to "delinquency"? To what extent has hot-rodding already increased its standards of competence to a degree shutting out amateur ambitions and urges? To what extent has this raising of competence been connected with the prospects and threat of professionalization, for designers, drivers, and others? How many hot-rodders are more than casually conscious of their function as "commodity critics" of Detroit? What effect on Detroit auto-building can be credited to the hot-rod movements from the end of World War II? Has the increasing organization and socialization of the sport had any reciprocal effects on its followers?

The leisure competence of the hot-rodders has been so perceptible in terms of their products and their race meets, as at Bonneville, that one might be tempted to let a favorable case for the fad rest on the excitement that goes with these gasoline fiestas. The races are proof enough that at least some of the adult sentiment directed against the hot-rodder as lawbreaker was based on a rather limited definition of the type or on a selective attention to some of the types rather than the others. It seems highly probable that at least some of the sour public responses to the breed, stated in terms of attack upon their lawbreaking, were based on a vaguely sensed envy of the hot-rodder's morale and an even more vaguely felt anxiety about the hot-rodder's satirization of the Detroit car.

The degree to which the hot-rodders have been critical of the commercial-car market in the United States is hard to determine. In the sense that they revolted against the soft-sprung "status car" obligatory for most adults in the American social system, they revolted not so much against the car as against the older generation and its image of the car. On the other hand, if we scan the entire consumer-goods market in the period 1946–56, the scene provides us with no other so deeply

felt, widely powerful, and economically penetrating revolution
in style organized by the consumers themselves. With every
other commodity, in every other market, changes in style have
been brought about by research and promotion campaigns; and
the public has had its choice of a variety of new products
within a broad range of similar style. The hot-rod movement
is unique in the history of the market and in the history of
"organized" consumers in the last twenty years.

The craftsmanlike revolt that sought technological and artistic integrity and individualization in cars began to change even
before 1950, however. The field became more commercialized
and respectable; and as it drew greater and greater numbers
in, it ceased to be the possession of a passionately different few
and became an activity demanding such a high degree of institutional organization that it began to look overorganized. It
is possible that the same sort of youth who would have gone
into it in 1946 would not go near it today.

Lee Bramson has analyzed the magazines of the hot-rodders,
with special attention to the letters to the editor. He writes:

"In California, a new level of competence and organization
was introduced around 1950 or so, by the establishment of
diplomatic relations between the citizens of the locality and
the hot rod club. This was achieved in most cases by a conference with the police officials concerning minimum requirements for the hot rod, which inevitably resulted in some sort
of standardization. Also specific areas were made available, as
in the case of the Dry Lakes, where the hot rodders were allowed free rein. . . . These consolidations imparted a still higher
degree of standardization to the hot rod group. . . .

"It was at the beginning of such developments that an interesting note of conflict appeared on the scene. Thus far *Hot
Rod Magazine* had served to reflect the attitudes, satisfy the
desires, and at the same time crystallize the self-concept of the
hot rodder. By publishing much data on the results of competition and comparisons of performance, timing, construction,

etc., they had played a great part in the increase of standardization; they had a very large circulation (200,000). A counterattack took the form of letters of protest from readers concerning the increasing amount of space that the magazine had been devoting to club news. The protest demanded that more space be allotted to cars, details, specifications, plans; in short, as one reader put it, 'CARS, CARS, CARS! NOT CLUBS!' "

Bramson's analysis uncovers new difficulties in the way of the individualistic hot-rodder. For one thing, the activity is not only regularized in California today but approved by a large section of the public. For another, prize money and other professional rewards in the sport are increasing; it is far more difficult now than in 1946 for a hot-rodder to know whether he is in the game for fun or for business. The sport has reached the point at which almost all respected competence is at a semiprofessional level, requiring greater investments of money and a compulsive attitude toward the achievement of a high-status car.

What effects on Detroit auto-building can be credited to the hot-rod movement from the end of World War II? The question, put in this form, is important to our general theme for several reasons. If hot-rodding has had any influence at all, then there is ground for believing that the large rationalized industry of auto-building in the United States no longer supplies all of its creative impulse from inside the industry. If so, there is ground for believing that at least some of its future technical advances will depend on amateur criticism and invention; and this, in turn, warns that this may also be true in other fields of American industry, the building trade and the furniture trade, for example.

One answer to the question of hot-rod influence on Detroit is contained in an article in *Business Week*, March 22, 1952, which also reported that the circulation of *Hot Rod Magazine* had climbed to half a million and parts sales to $50 million. At the conclusion of his article, the *Business Week* reporter remarked: "The hot rod movement has developed enough so that Detroit has begun to pay a lot more attention to it. More and more engineers from the big companies are turning up at hot rod races."

These claims for direct influence must be assessed rather carefully, to be sure. Publicity coming from Detroit after V-E Day was already mentioning new high-compression motors, dual carburetion, and dual exhaust systems. Current and continuous change in the American highway system, in the quality of automobile fuel, and in metallurgy all have an influence on car design that affects amateur and industrial design alike. It may be that the claim of technological influence by hot-rodders on Detroit is partial and marginal, and perhaps hot-rodders are most influential where they try out features that would otherwise be years slower in acceptance. From that point of view, the usefulness of the hot-rodder to Detroit lies more in the field of consumption pioneering than in technological advance. The reports of Balsley and Bramson, however, return us logically to some of the issues already emphasized in reference to mass media and to sports. It should be clear to all of us in 1957 that a rich industrial society can provide an enormous number of toys for people of any age, and these toys can be used in a variety of ways. Just as young people use sports as a way of grasping at the latent meaning of folkway in the United States, they use the cast-off cars of a rich economy to play a quasi-adult game with them. The game is at first a revolt against the market place and the rhetoric of advertising; later it becomes a group process richly invested with public values, even at the expense of the individualism with which it began.

A Salon of the Refused

It is important to observe that the cult in its earliest postwar stage embraced a code of naturalism—a holy war for the dominance of "function" in design. Clearly, this was one of the high points of postwar youth activity. It was the only large-scale evidence that many young people were committed to preserving in some fashion the aesthetic legacy of Thoreau, the Yankee shipbuilders, Louis Sullivan, and all the rest who have labored at the expression of what John Kouwenhoven calls the "American vernacular design." The ranch-style house is another example of postwar vernacular design appealing to a popular group, but it is not such a clear-cut case as the hot rod. The hot-rodders unmistakably constituted a salon of the refused.

It might be said that this integrity of the hot rod provided an escape from the passivity of spectatorship and from failure to meet the tests of "identification without loss of integrity" that trouble the heart of the spectator. So it did, for some, for a while. Then the cult of the hot rod led directly toward interaction with other fans in the contest, the spectacle, and the lessons of performance. Certainly a conviction that there was an ultimate test, in terms of a competence that could be rationally discussed if never calibrated to the last micrometer reading, was a part of their cult. Significantly, the hot-rodders surmised for themselves and for us in their world that we need to transfer more of our motives to machines. Because one must transfer some motives to machines and because one cannot, being human, transfer all of them, it is important to commit to them decisions on which they and not human reactions are most reliable. The notion that this takes place and should take place only in science and applied science is one of the beliefs of the age. It encourages us to believe that being independent of the machine in so many ways makes us independent in all ways. What could be more fatuous than this false claim to autonomy? Perhaps we achieve some independence from the machine only when we demonstrate that not we but the machines are plastic in our hands.

The members of this group of Participative Purists began their escape from the conformities of mass consumption, in the consumer-goods market and the mass media alike, with a search for auto individualization. High in their code was a notion of functional realism in the product; it should serve specified consumer wants in a way directly and economically related to the possibilities of technology. It should demonstrate its freedom from the superfluous adjuncts of styling-for-obsolescence practiced by the auto industry to outdate older models. It should demonstrate its freedom from the marginal differentiations employed by the industrial auto-maker to distinguish "lines" of cars for different income groups and different social styles of life.

The group succeeded in these aims only by erecting new rules of the game; and the new rules, at their upper levels, began to subvert the original amateur impulse and install the professional standard in its place. The product returned to the industrial and conformist market just as the fad widened its appeal enough to swamp the self-defined separateness of its founders. The fad became less important for providing new standards of the economic process of consumption than for providing the rules of a game. Hot-rodding lost some of its prestige as a revolt of young commodity critics aiming at an effect on society beyond their own ranks, and it acquired another kind of glamor as a partly fictional construct in which participants delighted in gratuitously holding over themselves the rules of a game rather than social life itself. This reappearance of the non-practical coincided with the fad's reintegration into the automobile culture as a publicly approved activity; and the hot-rodders had ceased to resemble industrial revolutionaries so much as they resembled yachtsmen. The return of the explicitly playful and vicarious note brought losses as well as gains.

Meanwhile, in the course of the fad's expansion the mass media remained impervious to these considerations and, in conscious or unconscious complicity with the automobile advertisements, gave the hot-rodder a bad name until about the time that Detroit itself had had time to incorporate some of the hot-rodders' mood into its own product. Since there is little likelihood of a new hot-rod movement, we can expect that similar impulses among the young will be expressed in different and unforeseen ways. Lacking such movement, the increasingly monolithic auto industry will seek new ways out of its self-imposed style captivity.

A recent review of automotive market research (*Fortune,* November, 1956) shows that even the most sensitively contrived investigation into the nature of auto sales fails to pick out in advance the trends that will be dominant. This suggests that nothing would be so helpful to styling intelligence in the industry—not to speak of qualitative criticism of design—as small sectors of actual experiment with advance design.

Perhaps voluntary divestment, each of the large companies placing one of its "lines" with an independent design-and-construction group, is the only way left to the automobile industry. As soon as Ford is expanded by the "Edsel" to provide a full price-range parallelism with the General Motors and the Chrysler lines, the basis for the move will be established. Plainly, the auto companies should make an outright gift of 10 per cent of their capital to the youth of California, who would use it for experimental auto design and construction. On the whole, General Motors might have the most to gain from such a move. If it is an industry with a reputation among the young for sloppy design, its stylistic troubles can probably be arrested by a voluntary surrender of some capital to these very youngsters who hold it in poor repute.

Such a cavalier suggestion, however, no matter how much good it might do the manufacturers, is not the point here. For all its faddishness, hot-rodding deserves study as an attempt to discriminate among the values of an industrial culture. We should be more concerned with the pathos of a social movement among young consumers than with the comedy of a muscle-bound industry.

. . . Some let me make you of the water's speeches.

—Dylan Thomas

CHAPTER EIGHT

Children of Thoth

The impact of TV on reading has been widely discussed and rather thoroughly investigated. We know many children spend an average of 3 hours a day with TV and that some watch as long as 27 hours a week; we also know that over 90 per cent of all American children between 8 and 13 read comic strips and comic books regularly. It is guessed that reading drops during a family's first acquaintance with TV and then picks up again afterward. Newspaper circulation has maintained a steady upward trend, and newspaper advertising seems to be growing in dollar amounts about as fast as TV advertising, which now costs advertisers about $1 billion a year, not including the cost of transmission. Over-all magazine circulation has been rising fairly steadily since 1938, although news-stand sales of magazines appeared to be dropping steadily in the 1950's. Paperback books approximately doubled in circulation from 1947 to 1955, from 92 million to about 200 million copies sold per year. It appears that about half the adults of the United States never or rarely buy even a paperback book. This is not surprising in view of the probability that 50 per cent of the college graduates in the United States read less than seven

157

books per year. On the other hand, the decline of book club sales in the total book market is a sign that many readers make more of their own reading decisions.

Reading, along with legitimate theater, is one of the few activities that has been lagging behind the general advance in American leisure expenditure, especially for travel, fishing, home-centered leisure, TV-show budgets, gambling, and juke-box-playing. Its share of the leisure dollar has dropped fast since 1929, probably as the result of the fact that three out of every four books sold are bought by 10 per cent of the United States population, with almost half of that 10 per cent concentrated in New York, Connecticut, and Massachusetts. On the other hand, there is some indication that special-interest reading in connection with the expansion of sales of musical instruments, art materials and garden supplies, and scientific or technical hobbies has been very much on the rise. The boom in musical instruments and art supplies drags readership with it.

Reading tends to be a rather independent variable when considered in relation to the other media. For example, in a borough of New York where TV reached 88 per cent of the inhabitants, library usage had been going up steadily all the time.

However, the fate of the word is increasingly determined by the sort of disc played on the approximately 40 million home record-players. Something approaching 6 or 7 per cent of all the discs are now the carriers of dramatic diction, documentaries of news reports and speeches, fiction and poetry. Some 100 such recordings per year reached the commercial market of 1957, but it is probable that for every commercial disc containing a reading, there is at least one and perhaps more home tape recording. The repetitive hearing of the word spoken by a skilled reader or speaker is rather different in its impact from the spoken word of radio, which was rarely repeated, and if so, rarely for the same audience that heard it the first time. The audio age of language is supplying an inten-

sification of the market for the well-turned word, if not necessarily a rapid broadening of it. Sales of speaking-performance
records appear to be limited to, say, the size of a good FM
audience in a large city like Chicago. This amounts to about
75,000 people in the metropolitan area for the more popular
broadcasts, perhaps as few as 20,000 for the more recondite
programs.

Thus the word is distributed confusingly among the media.
Reading, in particular, is related ambiguously to the audio-
visual media, and it receives a mixture of neglect and esteem.

Readers and Misreaders

Reading is the most protean of leisure pursuits because it
takes on, one by one, the masks of them all. Yet there is no
point in talking about readership, in the terms proposed here,
unless reading is seen in some relation to prior arts of oral
memorization and the later arts of the audio-visual revolution.
Such a view can be established best by comparing the state
of the art of print in a variety of cultures even now extant in
our own world.

The second largest producer of movies in the world is India.
It is also a country where many people still feel and think in
terms of a mythological tradition that arose in the prescientific
era. In Madras, where many Indian movie companies are located, an American visitor recently talked with one of the leading producers. This producer happened to be an energetic man
in his late thirties who was supporting an extended family of
more than twenty-five people. His work, in large part, meant
translating the mythological materials of village thought into
film and TV kinescope footage, with no intermediate steps in
print except a working script. At the same time, this highly
literate Indian had found time to produce numerous books of
verse and fiction, not only in his native language but also in
English. This man, responsible for the transformation of the
materials of an oral tradition into the materials of a cinema

tradition, without book or periodical form lying between the two, is also one of the highly book-minded people of the world.

In our own culture, we are so used to thinking of near-universal literacy *in print* as the precondition of industrial development that even some of our most thoughtful and well-traveled observers miss the point. Thus, Richard Blackmur in recent articles bewails the illiteracy of the Near East and, what is more, the pressure of the mass media into a vacuum of literacy there. He sees little good in a communications development in which the mass media reach the people in a historical sequence different from the sequence in which they reached us—that is, print first, movies and radio-TV last. Why the particular sequence in which we developed our industrialized communications system should be the better one remains more or less unstated.

This is the place to recall an early critique of non-oral communication. In the *Phaedrus,* Plato gave to Socrates the following words, as translated in Jowett's third edition:

"At the Egyptian city of Naucratis, there was a famous old God, whose name was Theuth; the bird which is called the Ibis is sacred to him, and he was the inventor of many arts, such as arithmetic and calculation and geometry and draughts and dice, but his great discovery was the use of letters. Now in those days the God Thamus was the king of the whole country of Egypt; and he dwelt in that great city of Upper Egypt which the Hellenes call Egyptian Thebes, and the god himself is called by them Ammon. To him came Theuth and showed his inventions, desiring that the other Egyptians might be allowed to have the benefit of them; he enumerated them, and Thamus inquired about their several uses, and praised some of them and censured others, as he approved or disapproved of them. It would take a long time to repeat all that Thamus said to Theuth in praise or in blame of the various arts. But when they came to letters, This, said Theuth, will make the Egyptians wiser and give them better memories; it is a specific both for the memory and for the wit. Thamus replied: O most ingenious Theuth, the parent or inventor of an art is not always the best judge of the utility or inutility of his own inventions to the users of them. And in this instance, you who are the father of letters, from a parental love of your own children, have been led to attribute to them a quality which they cannot have; for this discovery of yours will create forgetfulness in the learners' souls, because they will not use their memories; they will trust to external written characters and not remember of themselves. The specific which you have discovered is an aid not to memory, but to reminiscence, and you give your disciples not truth. but the semblance of truth; they will be hearers of many things and will have learned nothing; they will appear to be omniscient and will generally know nothing; they will be tiresome company, having the show of wisdom without the reality."

It is reasonable to interpret the remarks of Thamus to the god now known as Thoth as being, in part, the voice of an oral tradition of communication. Notice that he speaks of readers as being the "hearers" of many things, carrying over as a metaphor for reading the communication process of the earlier, oral tradition. The emphasis here is on the mnemonic aspects of speech versus print. It reminds us that some products of the oral tradition, such as the Homeric epics, were gradually recomposed to make even simpler the ease of memorization that was built into them by the basic devices of poetic meter and stereotyped phrase and epithet.

More than the mnemonic is at stake, however, and this is shown by the later discussion of the spoken word versus the printed word in this dialogue of Plato. At stake is the contextual validity of the written as contrasted with the spoken word. Spoken words were always, in preindustrial society, interchanged within earshot; they were subject therefore to different rules of validity than were words channeled in some other way. Does anthropological literature provide us with any example of preprint culture, in either the present or the past, that felt itself easy in mind when it moved under historical pressure from the mode of oral communications to that of letters, and even of print? It may be doubted.

There is no doubt that Thamus, if he were here today, would consider the movie and the recorder as inventions raising quite as many new problems as to the validity of human utterances as the alphabet itself. Print and other media are to be suspected equally today from the point of view of an oral tradition. This is quite different from the position taken by the print-centered culture of the American newspaper reader, who often damns the oral tradition with the single word "illiteracy" and the cinema tradition with the single word "mendacity." Is such a person likely to be sympathetic to the Indian situation in which print is bypassed as an element of opinion formation while at the same time the oral and the audio-visual traditions are brought into close contact with each other? Such a reader is not even likely to raise the pertinent questions about opinion formation in a situation so radically distinct from his own.

This cross-cultural contrast may help to dramatize some of the cultural pathology of print in our own society. Our own overwhelming use of print has been for the establishment of the market for goods and services; the fourth-class postal regulation is the salient clue to our use of the printing press. The extravagant rhetoric of advertising has finally led to a feeling on the part of many in the reading public that the language used in advertising is to be interpreted by a method different from that applied to all other uses of print. To be used, that is, only by a careful discounting of virtually everything in it except what can be filtered out as valid and relevant through the screens provided by the reader's membership in social groups. Thus, the attitudes taken toward "ad" copy by high-school students are less a function of what the ad says than they are of what the social group of which the student is a member says they say. Vast quantities of advertising and reading are necessary to establish what prove to be only marginal differentiations in the products, consumer images, and sales resulting from the pressure of print. The task of reading these differentiations into the ads—or out of them—is the "discounting" function of the various small groups.

This discounting of print seems to have two diverse effects, variously distributed among audiences exposed to print. One is to encourage the discounting of all print and all communications as such. Another is to encourage readers to polarize commercial and non-commercial print and to attribute to non-commercial communications all of the virtues that seem to be lacking in the commercial communications themselves. Either of these attitudes leads to tension in the readers. One general tension is the feeling of readers that manipulative print outweighs all other kinds and that the massive communication media outweigh the more personal media. To illustrate: it is common for people of some education today to feel that the movies usurp print and that print usurps conversation and, one supposes, that talk usurps contemplation.

These perceptions of the comparative pressures of the various media provide the background for a good many of the viewings-with-alarm of the state of the nation's media. Among all the anxieties about the health of the media, there is a general prejudice in our society to be worried most about the fate of print. This goes along with the assumption that exposure to print is the exposure that may save people, especially young people, from the supposed bad effects of the other media. In recent years this anxiety has reached the point at which a periodical such as the *Saturday Review*, whatever its doubts, is willing to imply its approval of curbs on the reading liberties of the American child. This view is faintly like that of those who are willing to use dubious assessments of the media as grounds for decrease of freedom. How far this feeling can go is suggested by some of the results of Samuel Stouffer's recent investigation (*Communism, Conformity and Civil Liberties*) into a variety of American attitude structures. There we find that many more than 50 per cent of the older people in the United States are willing to support a variety of limitations on civil and academic liberties of speech and of the press. At the same time, from other research, we know that older people read less than all others in the population, while at the same time 45 per cent of all others, during an entire year, read not a single book. Anxiety about misusing print seems to be associated with personal distance from any intensive use of it.

In this example, of course, a lack of liberality toward print goes with the same attitude toward *all* the communications channels. It is fair to ask why the concern for *print* is salient and why, in the previous example, the older age groups in the population were singled out. The answer is that the older people are more used to print as the prestigious vehicle and are less educated than the rest of the population. It follows that a nearly superstitious respect for print is found most highly salient in the part of the population that has the least functional relationship to it, or, indeed, to any of the media. And, if this sounds like an attack on those who are retired and in the postparental stage of their lives, it should not be interpreted merely as such. Similar attitudes are found in some of the middle-aged groups, especially when individuals from these groups are the parents of minors. Recent national discussions of the media involving this population group of parents emphasizes not the polarity of the younger and the older so much as the polarity of the parent and child.

The best recent example of prevalent popular concerns in this area is probably provided by the crusades of Fredric Wertham and Rudolf Flesch. Both these writers have taken advantage of the sense of the "media crisis" distributed among the older and parental groups to suggest shotgun definitions of the problem and its solution. Wertham, without evidence of any weight, associates crime comic books with juvenile delinquency. Flesch, with insufficient regard to personal and cultural differences in students, argues that all children should be taught to read in the same way. Neither of these celebrated witnesses in the public trial of the media criminals could possibly have achieved such publicity if it had not been for some of the factors previously indicated. In short, compulsive piety about print, agitated defense of print versus other media, and differential socialization in the uses of the media by the various age groups must be considered.

The evidence offered during the Wertham controversy indicates fairly clearly that parents most willing to believe dubious definitions of the reading-and-child-liberty problem are also those who have engaged the least in the social act of reading to, and with, their children. The evidence accumulated during the Flesch controversy, is that those who possess the least acquaintance with the linguistic learning process are most vulnerable to pronunciamentos. The clear fact that both these men are genuinely sensitive to real problems and that, indeed, some of their suspicions may well be factually true despite weakness in their documentations does not contradict the general point being suggested here. A variety of highly dubious assumptions about the uses of the media are very likely to creep into public discussions sparked by observers who ignore the real cross-cultural complexities of the media.

The development of mass print and the audio-visual techniques has sensitized us to the supposed effects of these techniques on the public at large. The chief charges against the big media by the mobile middle-class man is that they are stereotyped and mendacious. The chief charge of the somewhat more sophisticated observer is that their "overcommunications" generate a feeling of helplessness on the part of the audience that wishes to be selective in its reception of messages.

It may strike us as strange that those who attack the saturation of the mass media are so infrequently heard from when it comes to the saturation of learned print. Perhaps they feel that to be saturated by entertainment is worse than to be saturated by monographs and other messages emanating from the world of the learned. The librarian, to be sure, feels a special responsibility to the products of the learned world and protests little about their vast multiplication. But he begins by accepting the world of learned print and does not stand in a position in which he can defend himself from its irrationalities. Someone, somewhere, should speak for him, and speak in terms that emphasize the organized idiocy, not of the saturation from all the big media across the media board, but of the saturation from the academic world alone. The causes and effects of media saturation and academic saturation may not be the same, but the disadvantages of bulk may surely be compared.

More and more young people must be withdrawn from the labor force, on the one hand, and, on the other, free educational opportunity must be universalized for greater and greater percentages of the young. Keeping people out of the labor force longer is co-ordinated with entering them into the labor force at a more specialized level later. A major result of this is that education has been getting more and more clients all the time, irrespective of its own intellectual development. For educational personnel and for educational publishing, this constitutes an increasing captive audience to be subjected to print and its interpretation. There follows the massive training of teachers and the production of textbooks. Some educators in this situation feel that they must get their licks in early and saturate people with literacy and cultural literacy while they can.

Since reading and discussing reading is the work of the scholarly expositors, it is easy for them to get the idea that all of the dimensions of reading and, indeed, relations to the intellectual fields are work-minded ones. Consider the price that universities have had to pay for the development of the Ph.D. system in the United States in the field of the humanities alone. We hear of Ph.D. students warned away from an interesting topic because it might produce a thesis without enough pages. Can there be any doubt that British humanists have some right on their side when they raise questions about the "trained incapacity" of many American humanists to think in terms of quality rather than quantity? Can there be any doubt that some of the bibliographical glut is the result of an educational and class mobility system in which those who have the least to say are encouraged to make up for this by long-windedness? Can there be any doubt that the glut is connected with a system in which the professional work-minded interests of the scholar-teachers are sometimes put ahead of all other motives.

When such multiplication of print about print goes on, it has the odd effect of reinforcing the old American notion that hard covers bound around pages can make practically any utterance respectable, interesting, and worth looking at. This semisacredness attached to the busy-work of cultural activity is enshrined in the attitudes of those who tell us every day, as Clifton Fadiman and Joseph Wood Krutch do, for example, that we suffer a decline in attention, attention to these serious things in their serious hard-cover forms. Such arguments, considering the richness of the mass media, are somehow like telling Americans to look hard at the fountains of Rome while visiting there. Such notions leave out the fact that most hard-cover books are junk just as most of the fountains of Rome are bric-a-brac. Most of all, they leave out the fact that the great artistic cultures, including that of Renaissance Rome itself, did well to regard the serious arts as in some sense non-serious. What did the Italians do with great paintings? They painted them over when they got tired of them. What did they do at the first appearance of great operas? They gossiped in their boxes. Attention should, if anything, be selective—not a generalized standing at alert.

How far some humanists can stray from a sense of the common usefulness of the tradition they serve is suggested by a comment once made by Irving Babbitt. In decrying a certain intellectual activity, he said it was like the situation found in "teaching poetry to girls." The implication was that both poetry and teaching were degraded by the female audience, an implication that suggests how deeply disrespectful this critic was of some aspects of the work of the humanities. Yet why there should be any value in the learned tradition greater than any truly interested citizen can get out of it, and why there should be anything that the humanist is privileged to do besides playing an honorable part in this process, is far from self-evident. In recent years the contact between the intellectual tradition and the public has been enhanced by the simple fact that there are more serious books in print than can be "used hard," dirtied up in reading, and thrown away. This may have more to do with the promotion of an everyday contact between the general reader and his culture than may scores of expositors like Babbitt. If some humanists are wrong because they have been the last to take a real interest in the leisure uses of the arts, it is partly because they have used their own work interests to betray this value.

A note of confidence in the escape function of literature and literary studies is likely not to be acknowledged in the United States. We believe in art for art's sake, perhaps; but we believe in it with a workmanlike fervor that suggests some other sake is heavily involved as well. Perhaps the failure to acknowledge the escape uses of literature accounts for the heavy hand with which we so often approach it. Three or four generations ago, the serious teacher of the classics enjoyed his work at least partly because it was an escape. The Genteel Tradition, however, hardly allowed for this kind of self-definition. It was imagined that physicists and economists, for example, were hard-working fellows who were anything but escapists; and classicists had to act as if they were of the same breed. The classicists, caught in a race to appear practical, never had a chance to tell their students how much they enjoyed their work as an irresponsibility. By concealing its irresponsibility, they emphasized its practical ends; by emphasizing its practical ends, they raised questions they could not answer. The study of literature has suffered from lack of frivolity ever since.

Words and Pictures

The sense of leisure and frivolity that we miss in the human-istic studies is absent also, but in a peculiar way, from adult criticism of comic strips and comic books that, as pointed out at the beginning of this chapter, are read by 90 per cent of American children eight to thirteen years old. An amazing host of men and women twenty to fifty years older than these chil-dren habitually regard the comics as a direct, immediate, and profound influence on the behavior of the readers. Thus the seriousness with which the comics are inspected approaches a moral imperative, but, at the same time, the inspectors seem to desire an eventual abundance of "good" comics, that is, light, pleasant, gentle, negligible ones. While searching out evil and waiting for deliverance, these critics fail to see that the comics already in existence are often produced as purposeful leisure and received in kind by adult readers raptly engaged in their popular culture. Moreover, the purposeful leisure of the comics is rooted deeply in literature—the printed literature we have been talking about.

There are a number of good reasons for looking more closely at the "social realism" of the comic strips, comic books, and popular children's books. One reason is that while the content of the strips has been much studied, less attention has been paid to the artistic conventions of various kinds employed by their creators. Thus, while many observers prefer to think of the comic strips and books as being generally fantastic, they fail to observe how much the comics have accepted in recent years the conventions and traditions once associated with the literary and artistic movement known as naturalism.

True, the naturalistic movement and its high period are not easy to define. To use an almost overworked bench mark, let us simply say that some of the tendencies present in the work of Zola have re-emerged in the popular arts. Some people de-fine naturalism in literature as a tendency toward the stenographic and documentary, in painting as rivalry with the photograph, and in both literature and graphic art as a willingness to take for granted a materialistic social psychology that expresses itself in terms of a theory of "interests." In this chapter we shall be especially interested in the naturalistic and realistic tendencies that result from the attempt to use pictures in place of words.

In surveying this convention, it is noticeable that naturalistic influences in certain of the popular media and in children's books are the result of a socially downward distribution of fashions. In this sense, much of modern popular culture contains the diffused, reorganized, and to some extent simplified viewpoints of a now aged artistic movement. (It would be unfair, of course, to say that this is all there is to popular culture.) The shift toward social realism in children's books was also, in part, a result of a cheapening of the ideas of John Dewey and in part the result of the Popular Front of the 1930's. Moreover, the shift toward representationalism in the comic strip was largely a result of the motion picture's impact upon artists and their audiences. The 1920's, the period in which the film made its initial impact, happened to be the period during which the older, cruder cartoonist began to lose ground and the new, trained cartoonist began to come into favor. Soon after the early 1920's, we know, the film further increased the social realism of the comic strip by encouraging it to adopt such movie techniques as serialization, continued episodic action, and rapid cutting from scene to scene. Today's comic-viewing eye is an eye trained in part by movie naturalism.

There was no single revolution of comic-strip realism in the years 1900 to 1950 in the United States. There were, on the other hand, a number of changes that can be viewed from one unifying artistic perspective. Some of the major developments are as follows:

1. Skilled draftsmanship was emphasized in the comics following the appearance of the illustrator and advertising artist.

Their conquest of the field, which began in the 1920's and was consolidated in the 1930's, put a premium on representational draftsmanship. Some of the cartoonists who started earlier, as, for example, Bud Fisher, the creator of "Mutt and Jeff," might not have been accepted after competence in draftsmanship was firmly established as a prime requisite in cartooning.

2. The continued-story method of narration became the commonest method.

3. Adolescence and babyhood were represented in the comics where previously almost all the children portrayed were drawn from the six-to-ten-year-old group. The shift to adolescent themes was roughly co-ordinate with the great increase in the number of high-school students in the United States and the resultant rise in normal age at which young people enter the labor market.

4. Current history, as reported on the news pages, was introduced to comic-strip plots. This change was engineered by Milton Caniff, who began "Terry and the Pirates" in 1934, some years after the beginning of illustrative realism. "Terry and the Pirates" did not begin as a China War strip, but it soon became one.

5. Some strips began to provide familial and biographical continuity, as in "Gasoline Alley," with its characters who grew older year by year.

6. Illustrative standards merged with cinematic standards of drawing and narration.

7. Intensive regional and cultural realism appeared, as, for example in the "Li'l Abner" of 1935.

8. The rising status of the women portrayed in the comics brought increased individualization and increased ambivalence of portraiture.

9. Changes in the specifications of social class and class mobility were reflected in the comics.

It appears that draftsmanlike realism in the American comic strip was the result in part of a rationalization of the industry.

In the late 1920's one of the syndicates became interested in exploiting the popularity of the Tarzan books in the comic strip. An advertising agent named Harold Foster was engaged to draw the continuity. The very conditions of the public acceptance of "Tarzan" made it necessary to have the strip drawn by someone who could handle the jungle and animal scenery with some cinematic accuracy of representation. Foster and his successor Rex Maxon turned out a strip that soon became the envy of the syndicate world and encouraged other illustrators and advertising artists to consider the possibilities of combining their draftsmanship with someone else's talent for fiction. The success of the "Tarzan" strip appears to have broken a previous myth of the profession—that the successful cartoonist had to be a popular cultural "genius" of some kind.

"Tarzan," with its glamorously realistic portrait of jungle adventure, came out early in 1929. The first more or less realistically drawn feminine heroine appeared in another strip in the fall of that year. This was also the result of a team collaboration (continuity by J. P. McEvoy and drawing by Striebl) in a strip known then as "Show-Girl," based in part on musical-comedy sources, and known now as "Dixie Dugan." In this strip there was far less passion for documentation of special locale than in "Tarzan" or in the later "Terry and the Pirates," but the important thing is that portrayal was dominated by the realism of illustration and advertising. Dixie Dugan, appropriately enough, was one of the first career girls in the American comic strip.

In succeeding years there were numerous attempts to compete with the illustrative realism of these strips. In 1932, "Wash Tubbs and Captain Easy" appeared in a strip in which Buz Sawyer went beyond the "Tarzan" cinematic perspective and actually manipulated the drawing's viewpoint so that it resembled the viewpoint of the camera eye. Such tendencies had been forecast in the "Minute Movies of Ed Whelan" in the late 1920's, but their possibilities had never been fully realized. "Wash Tubbs," like its "Tarzan" predecessor and some of the following draftsmanlike strips, was a continued story with cliffhanger panels, and thus it broke with deep comic traditions on still another score. The attempts to manipulate the same formula have been legion since the 1930's.

In retrospect, the illustrator and the advertising artist affected the comics by introducing three-dimensional shading into an art which previously had been one of conventionalized line and contour. In turn, these commercial artists had been influenced, at a great distance, by illustrators like Winslow Homer and Frederic Remington, who livened the pages of American magazines in the days before photo-mechanical processes. Some of the skills and the manners of the illustrators were developed under the influence of French poster art, and all the illustrators were influenced by the photograph and later by the movie. In part, their realism was a return to the tradition of Charles Dana Gibson, whose drawings purported to be a social history of the American upper-middle class at the turn of the century.

The appearance of such realism in the comics is probably less interesting than its effects. We can say with some assurance that the growth in the draftsman's competence immediately introduced some correlate changes in content. Thus, in the case of "Tarzan," the draftsmanlike competence made possible a near realistic presentation of the jungle and veldt, and this travelogue exoticism was repeated in "Terry and the Pirates" and the later, and much cruder, "Smilin' Jack." This demanded hours and hours of research on the part of the producers in the *realia* and props of the scene to be portrayed. Thus the comic became research-minded as a consequence of its adventure into illustrative realism. This research-mindedness in both "Tarzan" and "Terry and the Pirates," despite its application to science fiction or picaresque fantasy, had its consequences for the psychological and social portaiture of the Americans in the strips. Thrown into semirealistic contrast with primitives or orientals,

Americans fictionalized in the strips began to develop certain more specific traits of the American. They acquired regional accents, definite social psychologies, and so on.

At the same time, standards of drawing derived from advertising art meant that the artists depended more than before on the folklore of advertising for their characters. "Dixie Dugan" derives from an illustrator's idea of a standard young American chorus girl of the late 1920's. The comics began to pick up some of the social realism of the advertisements and to betray some of the same concerns as the advertisements. Since the advertisement is almost always a message about social mobility, the treatment of social mobility in the comics began to develop at a similar pace. In place of the old comics that had established a fabulously naïve class position for the characters and then held them to it ("Polly and Her Pals," "Abie the Agent," "Jiggs"), the new comic began to treat mobility dynamically. In modern strips, the best examples are perhaps "The Baers" and "Mary Worth." In these strips the problem of social mobility is handled openly and dynamically and in terms of recognized social variables such as income, ethnicity, and sexual role. Compare this with the primitive handling of the social climber theme in George McManus' "Jiggs."

Doubtless the acceptance of social realism in the new comic strip was hastened by the fact that the 1930's deepened anxiety about the basis of society in the United States. Each class felt itself threatened, and each member of each class felt the whole class structure threatened. The comics began to represent in a much more complete way the different phases in the standard social cycle of the model American, and to some extent the documentary ethos of the strip became for its readers, especially children, a guaranty of its validity as social reporting. Thus, while one effect of the shift was to disclose in a more detailed way the class structure of American society, still another effect was to throw naturalistic draftsmanship into the support of *any* picture of social mobility. Belief in the comic strip as a fictional reporter of the society's demands on the individual became more widespread. The comics stopped being a fantastic escape valve for hurried readers; they became a text-book for oppressed social climbers. They became, in the final analysis, a rhetoric of approved social beliefs. And of course they stopped being comic.

Southern Style

One way to dramatize the contrast between the naturalistic tendency and the fantastic tendency in our comics is to compare two strips possessing some similarity in content and theme but varying widely in the artistic formula employed. Let us take two strips that deal, in different artistic conventions, with rural life in the South. One is Al Capp's "Li'l Abner," a product of early New Deal days, in which a certain amount of natural-ism is employed as the basis for caricature, social satire, par-ody, burlesque. The other is Walt Kelly's "Pogo," a strip in which the highly developed fantasy of an animal community is employed as the basis for social satire expressed largely in terms of the fable or parable. "Li'l Abner" is punitive satire on class relations in the United States; "Pogo" is gentle satire on the social politics of the United States. Both make ultimate reference to the social fact of a community of poor folk in the South. Let us compare their symbolic content and examine the ways in which the similarities in content and differences in artistic convention influence the expectations of the audience and enable this audience to ascribe a determinate meaning to the content.

Who is Pogo, what produces him, who are his readers, and what does he mean to them? The strip is a nationally syndi-cated comic that dramatizes the lives of a group of talking ani-mals who have deeply distinctive characteristics and concerns. Perhaps the most important characteristic that they share is that they are all a rural group. If it should be objected that most animals in stories are rural because the country is where most animals live, the objections can be met easily. Animals in earlier strips were characterized as urban regardless of their locale. For example, the cat, the mouse, and the bulldog in "Krazy Kat," although they were projected against a south-western desert locale, were metropolitan characters. The bull-dog was a city cop who leaned against city lampposts, and the desert of the locale was surrealistically equipped with fire hydrants. It is important that the characters of "Pogo" are fully rural folk.

The characters of "Pogo" are the inhabitants of the Okefe-nokee land. They are southern, perhaps because the image of the rural southerner has become the standard American image for the rural man in America in the twentieth century. It is important that these animals live in swampy land and that one of the major characters, Albert the alligator, is a reptile, be-cause this creates a generalized image of a primal world scene— the world of the watery margins from which life came. The swamp locale also serves the purpose of creating a scene of roadless hinterland, backwater seclusion. There is a direct ref-erence from these animals to human beings who are uncitified folk, whose vices and virtues are an aspect of their isolation from the urbanism and urbanity of those who like most to read about them. The rural sociology of "Pogo" is rhythmically dramatized by the appearance and reappearance of a slicker with a different set of values, particularly Mr. Bridgeport, the confidence man and promoter bear.

The economics of Pogoland does not entirely correspond to stereotypes of rural poverty. In "Li'l Abner," for example, we are asked to believe in the existence of a community whose stand-ard of living is so dangerously low that the failure of a turnip crop or the loss of a ham may mean starvation. "Li'l Abner" as a report on rural life was much influenced by the rural disasters of the 1930's. One of its powerful early themes of satire was the relationship between the migrant picker and his labor bosses. By contrast, in Pogoland we see that a little work sustains a standard of living which is generally adequate for all. The appropriateness of this arises, of course, from the character of the animals themselves. They are all able little beasts who evidently spend part of their time collecting stores of food, and they can do it at all times of the year, since they never have to contend with winter. Of course, the struggle for survival in Pogoland is not quite so simple as such a description makes it out to be. The fact is that while Pogo and some of his friends are herbivorous creatures by zoölogical definition, some of the others, including the bear, the tiger, and the alligator, are carnivorous. We shall want to look more closely later at the way in which the economic motivations of these meat-eaters are handled in the story line.

Nevertheless, it is important that these animals are described as living a life in which they possess a certain surplus of goods and leisure time. Otherwise, they would not be able to devote themselves so fully to the activities they engage in: celebrating holidays, having poetry contests, looking for lost children, playing baseball, getting involved in civic controversies over the loyalty of postmen, and running elections for President. Few of the realities that they face are the Aesopian difficulties of getting a living—jumping for grapes, dividing cheese, trapping chickens. The question of economic distribution, it is true, is not absent from their moral struggles with the goldbricking cowbirds, who have a zest for using other people's property, along with an agressive share-the-wealth philosophy. The cowbirds, however, are no great threat to the economic system of Pogoland, even though they do make away with canned goods now and then. Pogo and his compeers live in a land of decent surplus, which frees their energies for the greater goals of furious involvement with each other in the task of finding the right answers to questions of politics, art, science, medicine, and recreation. The threat of leisure is ever present. One of the sequences, "Slightly Holidazed," begins with Bun

Rabbit's assertion that he is going to say to the President: "Put down that piano! An' fix our holiday situation. Every time a man wants to work he got a vacation staring him in the face." One feels that this is not the enforced idleness of a rural community lacking capital and enterprise, like Dogpatch, but the enforced idleness of an economic system that works pretty well.

It is this assumption, we see, that makes it possible for the artist of "Pogo" to achieve his second major reversal of meanings. His first major reversal, the traditional one, is to ask us to believe that animals can act like men; his second one, the one that creates the true Pogo world, is to ask us to believe that these rural animals in these circumstances can act like the people of a small town, a suburb, or a city neighborhood. Given the simplicity of the basic scene, there are few subtleties in social behavior in our urban society that the artist does not exploit. In the book-bound versions of some of the adventures of Pogo the issues range from loyalty checks to political slander, from aesthetic standards to rent-control picketing. In general, the people of Pogoland face these issues with a good deal of naïveté, and it often appears they are going to be exploited by Bridgeport the bear, or Tammany the tiger, or Deacon Mushrat, or by the cowbirds. In the end the "simple people" prevail, and the manipulators and exploiters are discomfited.

Enough has been said here to suggest that the basic political theme of the strips is that the people shall judge and that the people are competent to judge. The threats to liberty and happiness in Pogoland are recognizable in terms of a general American politico-economic mythology. Bridgeport the bear, the Barnumesque figure, is a modern rendition of the confidence man who appeared in America before Herman Melville and Mark Twain wrote books about him. Wearing the garb and using the language of a nineteenth-century swindler, Bridgeport the bear depends heavily on the profile of the late W. C. Fields but displays some knowledge of modern forms of public relations dishonesty. Deacon Mushrat is, of course, the blue-nosed Puritan who was re-introduced to the American public as a symbolic figure when he was employed to symbolize Prohibition in the Rollin Kirby cartoons of the 1920's and 1930's. He is the Paul Pry, the investigator, the self-righteous slander-monger; his pharisaical character is symbolized by the fact that his speech-balloons render themselves in the type face of the old Bible. The cowbirds are Stalinoid birds who make a mock of Marxism by treating larceny as if it were an exemplification of the dictum: "From each according to his capacity, to each according to his needs." It is against such menaces to their political decency that the people of Pogoland are forced to struggle at least half of their waking time.

This suggests strongly that the political ethos which informs the "Pogo" strip is the optimistic ethos of, say, a Lincoln Steffens. We are invited to consider the probability that people are confused by democratic politics and vulnerable to a variety of ills: corruption, authoritarianism, influence-mongering, patronage, and boodling. Forced to organize against these ills, people find it difficult to do so. There is a tendency for every group of men in a democracy to form a splinter party of its own. Crusaders against the same evil, but operating on different principles, trample each other down in the confusion while the pols steal the cupboard bare. Nevertheless, after a crisis of cross-purposes, the steadfast honesty of the people has more staying power than the forces of evil. There is much in "Pogo" to suggest that the ultimate collaboration of these various beasts is imagined somewhat in terms of the collaboration of disparate forces in the American Democratic party. This chaos of strange bedfellows represents in some mythical way the vagaries and subtleties and inner contradictions of the Democratic "caucus" during the later New Deal years.

However, to emphasize the topical political meanings of "Pogo" is to ignore other ranges of meaning that can be found in the strip. One way to evoke those meanings is to remind ourselves that if the political stance of the strip is Democratic and Steffens-like, the literary stance is post-Joycean, and the psychological stance is post-Freudian.

It is no accident that Joyce, in his anthropological and linguistic search for the sources of myth, found Mutt and Jeff quite as interesting as Romulus and Remus or Isis and Osiris. In his later work, he writes as if he believed that the fantasy of the comic strip is another form of the fantasy of the folk tale or the myth. Joyce himself was well steeped in American popular culture and kept written records of the development of American slang, not only in its oral appearances, but also in its recognitions by the media. It is only natural that some sophisticated American cartoonist should exploit in turn some of the artistic devices employed by Joyce to represent the world of myth. The major verbal device in "Pogo" is polyglottism.

The artificial-dialect American speech invented by the artist for general use in "Pogo" is a comic version of rural southern syntax, vocabulary, and pronunciation. ("They sure built that capital awful far up the creek. . . . Figger them folks up there gits outen touch with us ol' mortal critters here at the headwaters?") True, there is no attempt at phonetic accuracy, particularly, for example, in the handling of the vowel values. One guesses that the artist felt that this would be overdoing regionalism. It would certainly make it more difficult for his characters to depart from their basic speech, as they often do, to engage in the creation of new words, to speak in verse, to speak in foreign languages, and to speak in a variety of crypto-languages that can only be called Pogo-Latin, or Okefenokese. The artist's general aim is to introduce every type of semantic and phonetic confusion, but perhaps especially punning and malapropism, into the speech of his characters and to employ the blockages of communication that result from all these private languages as evidences of their neurotically unstable relations with each other. Artistically, the confusion and ambigutiy of the language of the animals is offered to the reader somewhat in the same terms that polyglottism is offered to the reader by Joyce: as the representation of a stream of individual and group consciousness—a consciousness the confused fantasy of which cannot be adequately represented by conventionally ordered speech in one language but only by dipping into the muttered dream language.

It is true, to be sure, that the emphasis on problems of verbal communication in "Pogo" bespeaks a semantic slant in the way in which the artist interprets the ills of mankind. One gets the idea that the artist has been influenced by a variety of studies of communication leading up to the claim that a purification of the world of words would lead to an improvement in the world of things. As Albert says to Pogo during the poetry contest: "I made it up. I made it rhyme. Now I gotta make it mean somethin'?" While Albert is almost self-consciously taking a Dadaist artistic position during this interchange, it is also true that his antisemantic tendencies are constantly with him. In the strip, he stands as one of the greatists of sophists, over the straight-faced Socrates of Pogo. This is not to say that the artist is a faddist for semantics. It is to suggest that in a general framework of animal fable the reduction of communication by way of the zoölogical probabilities such as gesture, cries, scent, and so on, along with the corresponding shift of communication to human language, does much to suggest the predicament of American media-minded culture, in which words are expected to do more and more.

To speak of the influence of Joyce on "Pogo" is perhaps to go too far along what some might consider Jungean lines, placing too much emphasis on the problems of some collective unconscious in Pogoland. That, however, is merely the result of looking at "Pogo" in terms of the employment of certain linguistic devices supplied by the artist. If we turn for a moment from dictional texture to plot, character, and motivation, we see post-Freudian psychology at work in a way that invites us to regard human existence as a series of problems posed to individuals in the psychopathology of everyday life. The prime exemplar of this formula is probably Albert the alligator. Consider what he is and what he does. Zoölogically, Albert is a meat-eating predator, situated among a group of animals who, in real swamp life, would be considered his potential prey. It is true that civilization and its discontents bear more heavily on Albert than they do on many of the others because, while Pogo and the Rabbit and many others have only to forswear fighting with and stealing from their neighbors, Albert has to forswear eating them. His suppressed cannibalism, the capsheaf of all the cannibalistic themes that run through "Pogo," is one of the reasons that he often seems maladjusted in the society of Pogoland. True, he has the substitute gratification of a cigar, which he chews as vigorously in place of flesh as a smoker chews gum when he is trying to give up cigarettes. However, the suppressed tendency to want to eat everyone emerges in Albert's daily life as a proneness toward the accident of swallowing people. The small creatures of "Pogo" have to be careful what trees they fall out of because, by some mischance as powerful as the fate motif in the novels of Hardy, Albert usually by happenstance is underneath them with his mouth open. Albert, of course, remains quite unconscious of the older tendencies; and when he has actually swallowed something or someone, he resents the event as an invasion of his privacy. This sort of parataxis, or fantastical reversal of his basic unconscious relationship to his friends, even convinces some of his friends and swallowees.

The emphasis on problems of oral aggression, as Freud would call them in his references to zone development and fixation, seems appropriate enough to a society of animals who live largely by their teeth. On first glance, this might suggest that the symbolic world of Pogoland is rather a limited one or that oral aggression is made to substitute for all types of strongly motivated human desire for gratification of physical impulse. However, unless this be too eager a reading of some of the episodes, it seems pretty clear that the artist talks the

language of Freudian theories of sexuality in some of the episodes that link Churchy Le Femme the turtle with Mam'selle
Hepzibah, the skunk Chloe of the swampland. The turtle is a
classic figure of anxiety in myth and fable, and the reader is
invited to examine what the artist has made of this possibility
in some of his sequences.

This brief inventory of some of the themes suspended and revolved in "Pogo"—themes that the followers of the comic strip
have certainly recognized from the beginning—is meant to suggest that the thematic development of "Pogo" is made possible,
essentially, by the fabular formula employed by the artist. It
is impossible to imagine "Li'l Abner," for example, developing
the same low-pressure mode of narration on the same subtleties
of social life. The very drawing of "Li'l Abner," in spite of its
qualities of caricature, has the naturalistic heaviness of a Sher-
wood Anderson or a Dreiser, and under its guffaws there is a
nervous pressure of social seriousness and solemnity. The characters of "Li'l Abner" live in a world of clear-cut class and power
structure, in which the energetic neurotics run everybody else
by dint of brass, guile, crime, and paranoia. The strip has never
lost its hurt, serious tone of concern with inequality of social
opportunity, no matter how much the poor and the sick are
made to triumph in the end. Compare the dourness with which
Capp pursues and makes fun of radio and the media and the
lightness with which Kelly seeks out the same satirical prey.

It seems clear, from the interest taken in a *Life* article
through which Capp explained to his readers why he married
Li'l Abner to Daisy Mae, that his strip enjoys a massive popularity. Since he specializes in irritable criticisms of both the
uppermost and the lowest levels of society, one gets a feeling of
class defensiveness in his work, as if he were speaking for a
middle class jammed between extremes of delinquency below
and irresponsibility above. His punitive satire expresses itself
in camp-style boffos about sanitation, food habits, the battle
between the sexes, and the constant clashing of class etiquettes.

All this suggests that it appeals to those elements in us that are in uneasy flight from lower-middle-class cultural definitions, from ruralism, from any and all connections with the other side of the tracks. Although the actual scene is a hillbilly village, there is reason to guess that one of the actual social scenes he has in mind is the lower-middle-class suburb.

By contrast, "Pogo" is certainly the darling of the intellectuals, their La Fontaine of the comic strip. His readers appear to be the kind of people who take a positive enjoyment in being able to read and interpret an "animal" comic strip that even their own sophisticated children cannot always understand. The mock-pastoral genre of "Pogo" certainly represents, for its readers, a tacit claim that the culturally primitive and the psychologically basic patterns of human affairs are not only very fascinating but also within the scope of reader control. Thus, the strip appears to employ whimsy as a means of releasing the recognition of, and then exercising the power of, the irrational. One might add that while in "Li'l Abner" the individual is threatened generally by social disorganization of some sort (turnip famine, idiotic intervention by urban or bureaucratic forces), in "Pogo" the individual tends to be threatened by the runaway character of his own group's impulses toward organization. The class locus, the content of challenge, and the artistic convention employed in each of the strips appear to interrelate.

There is a residue of cuteness and sententiousness in Kelly's manner, part of it the result of the same topical forces that reduce the universality of the other animal fables and tales such as *The Parlement of Foules, Wind in the Willows, Animal Farm,* and so on. Part of it is just cuteness—an undigested habit closely related, probably, to Kelly's training with Disney. This is sometimes accompanied by a kind of egghead self-consciousness. At the end of a sequence, when one of his small friends asks Pogo if he has been elected President, Pogo says: "Well, I dunno . . . I'll go 'long and vote for EVERYBODY in sight . . .

that way we'll get a good one . . . y' know, chile, CRITTERS is nice, but human beans still makes the BEST people." One might be tempted to take this continuity of thought as limp satire on liberal-labor optimism and softheadedness, if one were not sure, on the basis of context, that there is a serious ideological pressure behind the statement and restatement of this hopeful commonplace. Kelly's book publishers, in recent years, have gone far in dressing him up commercially as a "folk-singer" type, a Kin Hubbard of the media-conscious, college-educated set.

Such reservations aside, it remains clear that Kelly's portrait of the social and political gamesmanship of the middle class, as filtered through his swamp scene, is made possible by outright revolt against the habits of illustrator realism in the comic strip. It is the artistic convention—Kelly's symbolism versus the naturalism of, say, "Li'l Abner" that makes the crucial difference. "Pogo" appeals to an audience whose revolt against the sociologese of many of the illustrator strips is in part a matter of class stance.

For more than fifty years now, naturalistic devices have been passed down the social scale to the lower-status sectors of society, while the self-identified elites have turned away from it. Comic-strip changes in style in the period 1920–50 recapitulate, in part, the previous history of literary and artistic style-wars. "Pogo" is a stylistic reaction against the "Li'l Abner" vein in much the same way that Flaubert's whimsical *Bouvard and Pécuchet* provided a counterstatement to his earlier naturalism and in much the same way that the "child's eye" in twentieth-century painting supplanted the "camera eye" of the late nineteenth century. As crucial as the shift in content is the shift in genre.

*Folk crosses formal art . . . when
formal art has become easy and
secular enough to recognize
where folk lies. . . .—Louise Bogan*

CHAPTER NINE

Reactors of the Imagination

The Astronauts

What's play for the man is work for the child. Kids who come home in the late afternoon from ducking ray-gun fire in every interstellar empty lot are almost pleased when they are told that their faces are dirty go wash before dinner. Organized bands of space patrollers, after struggling all day to keep the Seventh-Grade Martians from reaching the water-fountain button (whose touch will blow up the world), are glad to enjoy the overnight truce until next day's recess. These minions of cosmic law and lawlessness have left on the apartment houses a chalk trail that seems to glow at twilight. "This is Planet X and it isn't here." The adepts, exhausted by their playground argument over topics that sound strangely like the theory of limits, have, from sheer fatigue, lost their Moebius strips on the way home. Even a few cowboys and Indians who have not yet learned to trade in their lariats for space suits are glad the day is over. It is time for the children to rest from building the future and time for the adults to begin. The pages of *Arcturus* magazine begin to turn. . . .

In these pages is to be found a product that bears little resemblance to the weird pieces published a generation ago by an editor-publisher named Hugo Gernsback. His publications featured little more than the electronic evaporation of monsters and blondes. Today the readership of a magazine such as *Astounding Science Fiction* includes about 47 per cent college graduates, a percentage much higher than in the total United States population and in most magazine readership. About one out of four of its readers belongs to the engineering occupations, with chemical and electrical engineers leading the list; teachers, executives, and mechanical and building tradesmen are among the other frequent readers of the magazine. Three out of four of its readers are under thirty-five years of age, and their average monthly income is roughly twice as high as the average income of the employed person in the United States. What are they finding in their favorite genre? First of all, it seems, a sort of cosmology.

The Egyptians were fond of referring to the Nile Valley as "the world" and felt that the sun's efforts were patriotically Egyptian. The Yurok Indians of the west coast of North America imagined the universe to be an economy-size version of the Columbia Valley. They also imagined, in order to get some Yuroks into the picture, that both the Columbia Valley and the cosmos were built on the model of man's physiology. The salmon descending and ascending the visceral river in their annual migration sometimes seemed a symbol, as well as a fact, in the nutritional system of the world; and they sometimes seemed a symbol, as well as a fact, in the sexual system of the world. No one thinks it strange that in our world of split atoms, non-Euclidean geometries, and dynamic psychologies we feel a queasy affinity for the farthest spaces and the most distant pasts and futures. Nor that a group of rather entertaining writers are busy populating these unstaked areas of possibility with human and non-human creatures.

It may be that science-fiction writers are special kinds of

people. It is noticeable that although many women write detective stories, and write them very well, almost all science-fiction writers are men. Someone has said that women will always be a little more interested in whodunits than in far planets. And when the talk moves from movies and mobiles to space opera, the women's faces do not light up. Is it possible that they don't want the science, don't need the fantasy, and are already more accomplished in the possibilities of fiction? Perhaps science fiction is essentially a boys' dormitory commodity, like the western story, and is produced most congenially by men. In any event, whatever science-fiction writers are like as social animals rather than as writers, the purpose of this chapter is to emphasize neither the writers nor the readers of the product but the product itself.

Science-fiction, if we hyphenate it for a moment, reminds us that the worlds of wish and the worlds of matter—if that separation is still viable—have been married in other ways before. Some people think that John Donne wrote a kind of science-poetry. Other people will tell you that Jonathan Edwards tried to write a kind of science-theology. And the historian Leopold von Ranke claimed that he was writing science-history. Considering the intellectual ambitions involved in those undertakings, why shouldn't someone named Murray Leinster or Fritz Leiber write science-fiction? Considering the names that have been associated with the very approaches of science-fiction itself—Plato, Lucian, More, and the mythmakers who thought of Daedalus and Icarus—why shouldn't science-fiction writers of today be read respectfully?

The sample of science fiction discussed in this chapter is significant for several reasons. First, it permits us to test more concretely the guess (shared by the author and Seymour Krim) that current science fiction is a late and crucial reincarnation of the great literary tradition of naturalism—perhaps its last stand. Second, it permits us to see how science fiction, apart from naturalism, contains some of the fantasy that has been driven out of other forms. The heroic quests and confrontations that previous generations found in detective fiction now seem to be found in science fiction. Finally, it helps us to identify science fiction as a vehicle for the apt exposition of utopian and anti-utopian attitudes toward society. Perhaps themes debased from higher forms may be discovered in the folk literature of the pulps.

It is true enough that some of our past pioneers in science fiction missed the rocket after having bought tickets. In *The Tempest* Shakespeare toyed with teleportation and sleep-teaching but settled for a story about a duke in five acts of blank verse. Milton in *Paradise Lost* displayed a Clausewitzian grasp of war in space but left the manual of tactics to the authors of *Space Cadets*. Perhaps these references seem to beg the question: What is science fiction? They are not meant to. One way to define it is to make it include much of the "marvelous" that survives into an age of rationality after an age of myth; and by these lights the Alexandrian romancers who followed Euripides and made some of the naïve wonders of mythology at home in the cosmopolitan environment, by converting them, skeptically enough, into the apparatus of adventure stories, were forerunners of science fiction.

A Sample of Universes

Is science fiction merely fantasy masked by self-conscious "realism about the future"? Is it utopianism disguised as a prophecy of doom? Is it the only kind of literature displayed in country drugstores in which young readers are invited to cast off their ethnocentrism and consider the possibility that there are alternative hypotheses about human nature and society? Does it lack manifest sexuality because so much latent sexuality is stored in it? Is it self-concealing secularization of essentially "religious" concerns? Does its current popularity coincide in more than an accidental way with the shortage of physicists, chemists, and engineers? Is it an advance view of the consumer-goods and personality market of the future, and, as such, does it function for its technologically intense readers as a kind of cross-my-fingers prayer about the spiritual presumption that goes into invention? Is it a literary genre that should be associated with the hard-boiled detective story, the realistic children's story, and *True Comics?* And are these all after-products generated by the shattering of the aesthetic atom of naturalism in the cyclotron of popular culture?

Science-fiction writers are careful to expound the physical, social, and psychological principles on which their imaginary kingdoms in space and time are based. Different worlds, different principles. We should take the same precautions when entering the universe of criticism of science fiction. Our voyage cannot carry us through that universe; therefore let us examine the work of two of its prominent citizens, Fredric Brown and Ray Bradbury. Where Brown is deft and clear with plot, Bradbury is potent in the invention of situation and theme.

To speak first of their similarities, it is important to say that in their diction—and diction is the point of first contact between the reader and the writer—they are both smooth workmen. Brown writes in the linotypical fashion of the better pulp writer, knocking out sizable slugs of phrases and clauses in the idiomatic vocabulary of a newspaper feature writer. He is anxious to get there, clearly and quickly, and he does get there. Bradbury writes in the manner of a man who, when he has completed a sentence, stands back to take in the view of it. He has a chromatic vocabulary of adjectives of color and texture and light that give to his space scenes the oddly appropriate effect of being painted in luminescent pigment. He is anxious to set a visual scene with symbolic overtones as a basis for his narrative effects. As in most science-fiction stories, the prose surface wrought by Brown and Bradbury is not employed to any great degree to achieve understatement or overstatement, types of irony, or other counterpoints between matter and manner.

This is not to say that science fiction lacks the technique to shift narrative viewpoint within a given story, but there seems to be a tendency on the part of science-fiction writers to standardize on third-person modes of narration. In the nineteenth century, science fiction was often presented, as in Poe, in the form of a story related by a first-person narrator. At least part of the intended effect was to exploit the journalistic documentary "I-was-there" quality of such a narrative. In a few earlier instances, the "I" narrative was plainly intended to hoax people into thinking that the story was not fiction but journalistic truth. It is understandable that present-day science-fiction writers should lean over backward to avoid such mechanisms. They prefer not to exploit these spurious claims to realism. On the other hand, the distrust of the "I" narrator probably reduces the technical armory of science-fiction writers. Certain fictional effects that could contribute to science fiction depend absolutely on the ambiguities about reality and illusion created for the reader by having the story recounted by an "I" narrator with a gradually disclosed viewpoint and system of knowledge. This is evident enough in some of the "fantasy" of Henry James.

Bradbury generally rests his story on the premise of interplanetary travel and, in many cases, on the possibility of hallucination or other interferences with mental process by some marvelous means. He writes about people who seem to come from a wide range of social classes; and he writes a great share of his stories about people who, while they might come from either the upper-middle or lower-upper class, do not clearly belong to either of the two. His characters are generally engaged in responding to some highly defined problem of group relations, such as racial conflict, industrial teamwork, class differences. Most of his characters are shown in some sort of antagonism toward each other. These characters are generally presented in stories that emphasize tragic, macabre, sardonic, or even allegorical formulations. The major principle of organization that he employs is to focus the reader's attention on a character and the consequences of a character's orientation. Somewhat less often, he appeals to the reader's interest in the ideas of the characters. A frequent focus in his work is the tension between parents and children. Here are some of Bradbury's tales.

Parents, alarmed at the African scenes conjured up in the "mentalistic" nursery of their children, who think that life in their automatized house should consist of nothing but nursery fantasy, decide to close the house and go back to normal living. The children beg for a final "three-dimension fantasy" in their nursery. When a friend of the family comes, they have already fed their parents to the lions they have learned how to materialize out of their nursery walls.

Rocket men, scattered out of a broken rocket in space, keep talking to and baiting each other via radio while they are whirled away from each other in their space suits, heading toward different deaths. Hollis, the one who was captain and is falling toward earth, hears the others killed or cut off or taken away by meteor swarms. He wonders if anyone will see him when he reaches earth's atmosphere. A boy in the country sees a "falling star." Says his mother: "Make a wish."

Braling, a gentleman who has had a marionette of himself made so that he can leave the marionette with his wife while he runs off to Rio for a vacation, tells his friend Smith about these wonderful duplicates that can be bought for only $10,000. Smith, planning to have one made, comes home only to discover that his sleeping wife goes tick-tick-tick. At the same time, Braling returns to his house only to find that his marionette, Braling Two, has fallen in love with Mrs. Braling. Braling Two packs Braling One away in the marionette box and leaves for Rio with Mrs. Braling.

The wife and son of a spaceman, after his last fatal trip, sleep all day and walk only in the rain--because he died by falling into the sun.

Fredric Brown writes about people who give evidence of belonging to what C. Wright Mills calls the "New Middle Class." By this term, Mills means the salesmen, teachers, professionals, and specialists in our society who comprise a skilled group—the white-collar class from its lower to its higher levels, and especially the salaried groups with relatively intense occupational training. These characters in Brown's work are generally to be found in situations involving interplanetary travel or some sort of body-mind problem. They show a great deal of solidarity with each other, but their dominating emotional tone is one of hostility toward, and uncertainty about, each other. Brown's characters are assigned class status by their occupation, which is always noted. By contrast, Bradbury gives away the social status of his characters, not by occupation, which is rarely referred to except in the case of space pilots, but by significant details revealing the life-style, ideology, type of home maintained, and attitudes toward children. Brown's handling of tone ranges from a dominantly sardonic toward a comic and farcical treatment. Where he is satirical, his satire is lighter and less punitive than Bradbury's. His major formal appeal to the reader is that he generally gives his audience a complicated plot of some sort and generally succeeds in providing a tidy denouement. Here are some of Brown's yarns.

Astronomers of 1987 discover that the stars are developing a "proper motion" faster than the speed of light and that all the old constellations, such as the Big Dipper, are going out of business. The stars suddenly spell "Snively's Soap." It is later discovered that this apparent shift of the stars' position has been electronically contrived by a soap millionaire whose sales went up 915 per cent during the period before his apparatus was smashed and the appearance of the constellations returned to normal.

The last man on earth waits for a knock on the door of his dwelling, knowing in advance that it will be, if she has decided to come back and do some repopulating, the last girl.

Napoleon's psyche, rediscovering itself in the body of an American newspaper reporter, keeps itself a secret which is never challenged until the day the reporter is asked to enter an insane asylum to make a special investigation under the disguise of a madman who *thinks* he is Napoleon. The reporter cannot figure out whether his employer thinks he is Napoleon or whether, indeed, he is or not. An extra-planetary voice reassures him that he is and that this knowledge will, of course, make him regarded as a madman. He goes mad, receives shock treatment, forgets he is Napoleon, and is released from the asylum as his reporter self. His delusion that he was the reporter squared with the delusions of all the others around him at the office and in the asylum.

The work of Brown and Bradbury generally delivers shock in reasonable proportions. The major differences between the two authors can be suggested by saying that Bradbury often tries to deliver catharsis in place of shock and fails, while Brown, rarely trying to deliver catharsis, sometimes does so. One reason is that many of Bradbury's stories have a quasi-tragic framework suggesting to readers that they ought to be judged with some of the attention that a "serious" craftsman of the short story sometimes calls for. The trouble is that they cannot stand that test, and one feels that it would be more comfortable if they were not in that predicament. Brown's stories, on the other hand, ask to be taken as comedy of stereotypical types of character and are sometimes sustained by brilliant plotting. When these two elements come together, as in his story of the criminologist who protects criminals from the lie detector by a hypnosis-amnesia which also then deprives them of their criminal drive, "Crisis, 1999," the results are truly comic; and the effect on the reader is a sense of emotional relief and resolution proportionate to his emotional commitment to the yarn.

The suggestion here is that Bradbury, looking more often toward the higher seriousness, aims at a star he cannot reach, while Brown, who is content with a jitney to the moon, sets himself a somewhat more attainable goal. Still another way of suggesting this, in literary terms, is to notice that Bradbury attempts to use a wide range of genres (tragedy, social realism, comedy, parable, the macabre, the sardonic) and therefore invites comparison with those who have been specialists and masters in each of these fields. Brown, on the other hand, sticks to a narrower and shallower range of genres (emphasizing the comic, the farcical, the slapstick, and the facetious) and essentially invites comparison with other popular writers. Both Brown and Bradbury, like other science-fiction writers, find that the plasticity of scene and character in science fiction is a burden on, as well as a spur to, fictional invention.

The Disappearing Act

We should remind ourselves here that it may be necessary in theoretical physics to hold, as Bohr suggests, two contradictory but complementary notions of the same process. Analogies to this exist in literary criticism. Notice that the comments above are haunted by a similar air of paradox. At times they seem to suggest that the stories by these two writers are, by and large, comparable because they are in the same "form." They are all "stories." They are, as some scientists say it, isomorphic. At times, however, the foregoing comments take care to suggest that the stories of these two writers are distinct from each other, individually and en masse, because they appeal to different principles of form. Some are "parables," and others are "comic," and one of the writers is distinct from the other in the frequency of his appeal to such subforms. In this light, the work of these two men is, as the scientists say it, allomorphic. Perhaps the two writers use distinct forms to embody distinctly different intentions; and perhaps the foregoing remarks favor Brown's intentions at the expense of Bradbury's.

Suppose then, alternatively, we set us a different set of expectations. We assume, for example, that science fiction is a folk-tale type and that it takes as its hero a specific kind of man, the type called Faustian. In his American-engineer form, as a stereotype, he is the man who loves the world as an object of inquiry. He is surrounded by other types, the Natural Man (Tarzan, for example), the Tyrant, the Woman (outdoor, dangerous, or little), and others. Assume also that the characteristic actions and passions of these types are myths generated by our own culture and psychology. For example, you might consider the theory that the emphasis on teleportations, hallucinations, and hallucinations materialized is connected with the American Fantasy of Disappearance from Society. (Vanishing was what many young children wanted most, according to their answers some years ago to the questions asked about their wishes by an inquiring psychologist. Vanishing has become a theme in journalistic literature, as is Geoffrey Hellman's "How To Disappear for an Hour.")

Suppose also that you attribute this theme to a tendency on the part of Americans to sense themselves pressured into social conformity so that it satisfies them to involve themselves in fantasies of beating the world by vanishing from it. Suppose further you assume that these themes, along with others, are built into American child-rearing so that they are widespread foci of familial anxiety. Then, in comparing Bradbury and Brown, you might well prefer Bradbury on the ground that he is a symbolic psychologist, sociologist, and moralist for the current scene. You would argue for Bradbury's greater interest on the ground that although he uses the form of a "story," he achieves interest because he is actually making an "argument" and writing "symbolic history." To people who argue that his effects are mere shock, you answer, "Yes, the shock of a kind of recognition of a truth."

With this critical alternative in mind, we would be forced, finally, to the suspicion that, besides catharsis and shock, other effects may be attained by science fiction of some sorts. We would begin to suspect that some fiction, much as it seems to invite us to enjoy an extended suspicion of belief, appeals to us as a morality play, an allegory, a parable. We would notice, too, that the development of the story is often such that it creates a spectral dialogue between the reader and the writer and between both of those and the characters; and this spectral dialogue, although it may change its terms as it goes along, is asking for a definition of the real. "Is this watch controlled by a troll?" asks one character. The other answers: "What a question! What would it be like to know what it would be *like* to have a watch controlled by a troll?"

It may be that with Bradbury the question is little more than "What profits a natural man if he developeth a technology?" To this question the rejoinders can be made: "What is a natural man? What is technology? Isn't the very concept of a natural man a cultural product, like a technology?" The difficulty is that these rejoinders are not anticipated by the texture of Bradbury's work. Nevertheless, the current run of American science fiction is often implicitly, and not necessarily incorrectly, theological. Indeed, it often reminds us, perhaps much more than it intends to, of the reaction against modern life and industrialism found, for example, in Edgar Allan Poe.

The Haunted Palace

"Man," wrote Poe, "because he could not but acknowledge the majesty of Nature, fell into childish exultation at his acquired and still increasing dominion over her elements. Even while he stalked a God in his own fancy, an infantile imbecility came over him. . . . Meantime, huge smoking cities rose, innumerable. . . ." For Poe, Nature, in some Wordsworthian sense, is a palace haunted by the evil possibilities of applied science and industrialism. He was one of the first to touch on a theme that became tremendously important to mass culture: the Faustian theme of the irrationality of too intensely applied reason. As Americans shifted their attention from the business-man to the scientist as the promoter of social change, science as a devil was diffused down the class scale into the mass-culture horror story. Poe's reaction against the inhumanity of industrialism expressed for his generation a conservatism akin to Ray Bradbury's in our day.

Poe's contribution to a popular American image of science was considerable, and it is necessary to get some sense of his own concept of science. His stories appear to group themselves into classes. First, there are the stories of scientific wonders, such as the transmutation of gold in "Von Kempelen's Discovery"; second, there are the stories of criminological reasoning, as in "The Purloined Letter." Each of these types has its own rules of construction and its own characteristic manner or mood. All of them, including the stories of criminological detection, are shrewdly constructed machines for extracting a thrill out of the macabre aspects of scientific activity.

The more one considers Poe's stories of detection, the more one is likely to notice two important elements of these stories that depend on the rise of an industrial and urban order and that anticipate modern science-fiction rather than detective-story themes. The first is the tendency of the later Industrial Revolution to make every state a police state in a sense that it did not approach this form before. We tend to forget that private police have grown about as fast, sometimes faster, than public police in the Western industrial community. In this sense, the disinterested amateur in detection, created originally by Poe and then developed in the portraits of Sergeant Cuff by Wilkie Collins and of Sherlock Holmes by Conan Doyle, is in part a sublimation of the private police of industrial societies. The fact that the private detective is often a knight-errant or a Robin Hood does not detract from his private-force identification with the Pinkertons.

The crux here is that the detection of crime, in an industrial state, becomes a part of the general industrial discipline and develops an appropriately scientific method: the object of the detective is to know more about the city, from a certain point of view, than anyone else. The difficulties of early urban policing are suggested in "The Murders in the Rue Morgue"; French police find it impossible to imagine what actually happened: that the killer was an ape brought off a ship by a sailor. The ape's presence in Paris might be said to represent the sheer improbability of many patterns of crime that appeared in the stages of early industrialization. The bureaucratization of the police in the nineteenth century was a result of the recognition that law and lawlessness were engaged in working out new relationships with each other: easygoing relations between sheriffs and robbers were disrupted by big-city life, and middle-class demands for property protection brought about a new division of labor in which whole new classes of fences and stoolpigeons arose, just as new classes of police officials appeared.

It will help us to see the "anti-utopian" theme in Poe if we recall that large-city life in the United States presents problems in law enforcement different from the problems of the small community, especially the Puritan community, where public opinion was strong enough to be far stronger than the law. The emphasis on punishment rather than detection in the criminological thinking of the Colonial statute books has a double meaning: it means, on the one hand, that detection was easy; on the other, that the very conditions of private snooping, gossip, and word-of-mouth policing in the community built up such a strong pressure that the emotional process of punishment itself became highly charged for the punishers. If an individual reacted so strongly against such a tight web of the mores that he became criminal, what punishment could be heavy enough for him? Scientific law enforcement, appearing in a period when the mores were breaking up under the impact of city life, correlated with a liberalizing change in attitude toward punishment, since it shifted its focus away from punishment in order to focus the better on the detection and the deterrence of crime.

The texture of Poe's fiction often suggests that he was aware of changes like this going on in the United States of his time. The citizen whose attitudes are dominated by the customary law of the personalized country or small town wants the law of both country and city to think in terms of moralities and punishment; the police of the impersonalized city, faced with a breakdown of customary behavior, want to think about it in terms of information and control. In our own history, the moralizing of the countryside, culminating in the Prohibition laws of the 1920's, produced a situation in which the police were forced to act against the very social nature of the city. This, in turn, brings about a breakdown of the city law-enforcement fabric, which in turn is blamed upon the city by the moralists and the country folk. Poe's narratives of crime detection hint at the literary discovery of the law-man so rationalistically interested in the motivation for crime as an element in his pattern of detection that he can, in cosmopolitan fashion, leave obsessions with moralizing and with punishment behind him.

Poe's amateur detective, to be sure, also appears on the scene because the failure of the official police to solve their problems is an aspect of the emotional blocks in their administration which result either from their implication in the crime itself or from their sociopsychological obtuseness. Correspondingly, the success of the amateur detective is an aspect of his clinical disinterestedness in the scene: he is able to uncover the sources of wrongdoing in the industrialized society in a methodical and objective way because, as a gentleman of the older social order, he has not acquired the cultural pattern of the new society, and he can therefore look objectively at its culturally patterned vices and virtues. We have seen the degree to which this clinical aspect of the detective has been developed as a white-collar trait of modern legal bureaucracy in the Jack Webb portrait of Joe Friday.

As we see now, Poe's criminological yarns show a concern for the way in which the scientific method, especially in psychology and secondarily in sociology, begins to assert itself as a mode of social control. The ratiocinative genius of the gentleman specialist is necessary, in the new urban and industrial order, to pierce the web of criminal circumstance. Criminals are defined as superindividuals let loose in an anomic society; they can be caught up with only by a Cartesian mentality that can identify with the "mechanisms" of their aberrant humanity. Deviance is fundamentally systematic—"Vice and virtue are products like vitriol and sugar," Taine said—and it can be controlled, not by feudal bailiffs and sheriffs, but by men wise in the ways of modernity.

In all of this we see Poe employing the generalized scene of the big city and the impersonal society in a way that resembles some current science-fiction writers' use of an imaginary Martian landscape and its "controlled society." Thus the link between current science fiction, which emphasizes manipulation of individuals by a new social pattern and its managers, and the fiction of Poe is a link that connects more strongly with his detective fiction than with his exercises in fantasy. It is his detective fiction that expresses disillusionment with a technological society. He has had a long-run influence on the more popular mass-cultural forms of American fiction.

Dreamwork

Poe's almost mechanical and obsessive conservatism is a reminder that one's general point of view toward life may occasionally interrupt the enjoyment of a science-fiction adventure. If you are not especially Kantian in your views, you may get tired of all the excitement in science fiction over the split between the theoretical and the practical reason. If you are not a monist, you may get tired of the reduction of the cosmos to physicalistic models. If you are aware of some of the problems of the behaviorist, you may get tired of the stimulus-response simplicities of some of science fiction's neo-mentalistic creatures. If you reject Descartes, you may be bored by the mind-body dichotomist. If you follow Wittgenstein into his later phase, you may find that his "book with the blue covers" (as I heard a positivist say) "contains more universes than a science fiction convention." It seems fair to say that science fiction is as philosophically sophisticated as semantics, which isn't much, and as culturally sophisticated as Herbert Spencer or technocracy, which never was much. At the same time, this may be of no relevance at all to the scientist reader of science fiction who, working from non-verbal models of behavior in a way that other readers do not, finds symbolic structures in science fiction that others of us do not find at all. The average reader of science fiction is of course merely revealing his taste for cosmic cowboy thrillers. What he shares with more sophisticated readers is not ideology but fantasy.

The fantasy theme, therefore, raises again the question suggested by Rosalie Moore and Anthony Boucher: Why is it that the *same* stories will sell better, and perhaps even be enjoyed more, if they are bound in a cover presenting neo-technological fantasy scenes rather than any other kind of fantasy scenes? For one pervasive reason, we might guess. The dream content of the science-fiction story is expressed in manifest symbols that are the stock-in-trade of the daydreams of the scientist. When the scientist carries out some of the same dreamwork that the rest of us carry out by representation of landscapes, blondes, tones, and colors, he is representing similar fantasies in new cosmogonies, fancies about biological mutation, and so on. In this manner the twentieth-century scientist wraps up his play in his work; and his influence is such that the style of his dreamwork becomes an acceptable stylistic norm for the dreamwork of many other people.

Just those considerations may make it appropriate for the fan to read science fiction as symbolic journalism of today's world, as prophecy, as occupational guidance, as social theory—

as the dialogue of the hypnotic master criminal, Nature, with the somewhat less masterful, telepathist-detective, Man. A general debate about the status of good, evil, culture, history, progress, psyche, and human freedom is as native to science fiction as rectilinear motion was to the atoms of Democritus. Correspondingly, it compels people to debate whether it is pessimistic or optimistic. Pessimistic or optimistic about what?

Pessimism about human society as a whole, toward which American science fiction tends, may seem to be less gloomy than doubt about the nature of man as such, toward which it does not tend. Pessimism about the values of a specific cultural setting, limited in time and place, toward which science fiction tends, is less threatening than pessimism about the nature of culture itself, a formula toward which it does not tend. Pessimism about rational intervention in historical change, toward which science fiction often tends, is less oppressive than doubts about the very nature of history itself, toward which it does not tend. In their choice of Noble Lies, Americans betray their very hopes in a willingness to include an indeterminate Tomorrow within the scope of their despairs.

CHAPTER TEN

A Taste of Abundance

A Brand of Magic

Total advertising budgets in the United States recently approached the $10 billion mark, with newspaper advertisements accounting for about $3 billion, TV $1 billion, magazines $757 million, and radio about $500 million. Advertising expenditures have grown faster than the total productivity of the economy as a whole since 1952, something that might be expected during a period when the buyer's market seemed to be reappearing. There has been more advertising indoors than outdoors: national TV in 1955 took in about 48 per cent of all the new money for advertising that entered the market during the year, while outdoor advertising showed the lowest percentage growth of all major media.

None of this means that advertising men can always prove a direct relationship between sales and advertising. There is no way to make all the market factors other than advertising stand still for observation. It is true that a mail-order specialist who does not show a picture of a tie rack in the magazine space he buys will not sell the object; but beyond this, advertising men argue approximately and probably spuriously about ads causing sales.

Nevertheless, we know advertising's influence. A perceptive writer on the mass media, Marshall McLuhan, renews an old charge when he says: ". . . Modern advertising is a form of magic ('kissing sweet in five seconds'), and it employs all the techniques of symbolist art . . . The sorry scheme of things as they are is forever being remolded nearer to the heart's desire . . . National brands of commodities have a way of becoming a totemistic institution."

Certainly, some sorcery is the result of advertising, and the very indirectness of the persuasion proffered, not by another person face-to-face, but by a corporation through the vicariousness of the media images, adds to the mystery of the spell. Rapid and pervasive communication adds a problematic dimension to human experience. There has always been an advertising man, but in the past his craft was technologically limited by the absence of duplicating techniques and by illiteracy and iconographic traditions; it subsisted in the monumental and the word-of-mouth, for the sake of highly localized markets. Today, advertising seems a natural outgrowth of the mass-communications world; and the media world of prefabricated experience, fetched from the remote, both influences and is influenced by its use as a contact with a market.

For a long time in American advertising, the emphasis was on the saturation of the potential market, both by shotgun and by musket methods of aim. More recently, advertising research has come to be interested, like the opinion research it helped to inspire, in the telescopic sights provided by the quantitative studies of communication. When it asks what leads to persuasion, to opinion change, to attitude change, it asks the social sciences for both data and generalizations. It is relevant for advertising, as it is for many other fields of persuasion, to learn that all messages tend to reach those who have already received them and not to reach those who have not already received them.

The curiosity of the advertiser about human motivations is sometimes regarded as a shameless affair carried out largely for the purpose of detecting human vulnerability to certain habits for the purpose of "hooking" the consumer regardless of his own good health or happiness. So, often enough, it is; the institutional advertisements of the distillers, emphasizing their contribution to inorganic chemistry, plastics, and what not, must make hard reading for people taking the cure. On the other hand, there is no harm in a curiosity that avows an interest in people's "needs" as contrasted with their "economic wants"; and advertising was long accused of being more interested in confirming the latter than in learning about the former. What is more, there are basic questions about the new drive for motivation research that go unnoticed if it is viewed too cynically as a search for human weakness. Looking at it that way, one too often fails to notice, as Robert Colborn of *Business Week* pointed out, that the burden of results from motivation research so far seems to add up to a rather sunny view of human nature. Why should this be so? And what effect does it have as a by-product of the method?

Advertising's fascination with research has sparked from time to time a lively discussion of the role that the "creative" and the "scientific" should play in the making of the trade's policy and the deployment of its personnel. The discussion contains semantic traps, since the self-titled creative man is often a plodder in his specialty and the scientifically trained researcher may well be a man who rationalizes with mountains of methods a contribution to the conference table that has its real root in his empathy and intuition. What seems certain is the gradual amazement of the advertising business at its milk-and-honey postwar market and its increasing devotion to ways that are deep. The results are sometimes as visible as a January tan; for advertising is always sending messages to itself—through advertisements.

While admitting Marshall McLuhan's ascription of totemic magic to the advertisements, one might see advertising content and imagery as composing a sorcery of a special kind. The Neolithic hunter, we are told, sometimes inscribed on the walls of his cave the pictures of the game he hoped to kill; just so, pictorial presentations in advertising have always presented an idealized scene of consumer acceptance. Recently that scene has taken on new characteristics: more than ever before, the scene of consumer acceptance pictured in the advertisement features a group of people with defined social characteristics in a relationship to each other that has been modeled on research into veritable groups of consumers. The total population of the ads, in various ages, sexes, classes, and roles, is not a one-to-one duplication of the social structure of the United States, but the correspondence is closer than it used to be. This picture of the consumer-acceptance scene represents, in an idealized way, the hopes of the advertiser and his agent and figures as one of many instances in the development of a new market "realism" in advertising. Perhaps this realism was much encouraged by the fad for the comic-book style of advertising fashionable for a while, a style whose dialogue "balloons" enforced great particularity of characterization of the persons appearing in the advertisement; but research itself had a powerful hand in the development.

Such burgeonings can be interpreted also as representing a sort of wishful attitude toward the relation between the mass-broadcast message originated by the advertiser and the momentum he hopes it will pick up in the field of marketing force generated by word-of-mouth propulsion. To present the product as being talked about by persons who look like the chosen market seems the first step toward having it talked about there, in fact. This, however, introduces a new degree of pretension into the advertiser's tone and touch; it involves him more and more in making both explicit and implicit statements about all the other kinds of things in his "picture" over and beyond his product itself. He becomes, at the extreme, a documentarist of the social scene, as interested in telling people what they are and what they are culturally entitled to buy as he is in whether they have the cash for it or in his own products as a candidate for the purchase.

The race for subtle consumer definition, as contrasted with assertive product definition, may lead the advertising man to overreach himself and to begin to say things that vex some members of his audience even while reaching others. A burnished example was advertising's plunge into an aggressive concern with health and hygiene, beginning in the 1930's or so. This seems to have led many to reject advertising en masse as being too nosey for its own good and as attempting to explain to the public a lot of things that real medical men in real white coats had a better right to explain. Every move toward explicit and specific picturization of the consumer-acceptance situation contains its dangers, even when backed by the most innocent research.

It is true that the very nature of the commodity itself does much to determine how far the advertiser goes in this direction. Each of the categories of food, transportation, clothing, housing, and personal care, to name major types of commodities, establishes a distinct tradition for itself in advertising imagery; and the goods whose use-span and wear-span are close to their style-span (like nylon stockings) are distinct in their advertising imagery from goods whose use-span may be much shorter (as in cars and TV sets) than their wear-span. Again, it is almost a tradition of the soap and food industries that the master-of-ceremonies who plugs for them should kid the sponsor and the product as a balm to the morale of their supposedly inferior-feeling, middle-aged female audiences. It is a tradition of car advertising, increasingly so, that the potential customer should be told that he is "now good enough" to graduate himself to a Cadillac. A hard and fast rule of advertising, known as the Seesaw Effect, says that when the scale of claims made for the customer goes up, the claim for the product goes down, and vice versa.

Despite commodity determination of the advertising claim, there are general tendencies in the pitch for all commodities which have spoken strongly, in the last decade, of the advertiser's desire to get close to his consumer. Besides the increasing stress on consumers pictured in socially definite situations (attempts to "get into the conversation"), we find two other phenomena. One is increased effort by both product differentiation and its associated advertising to build new ranges of sensuous appeal; the other is a new-found resolve to emphasize the visual and the operational over the verbal. Since the first of these is closely related to the way in which consumer appeal is thought to play back through advertising sensitivity into the field of industrial design and packaging, it is of considerably wider interest than advertising considered as blandishment by way of the media.

To take just one example as representative of a far-reaching development, it is interesting to see how consistently recent design and advertising have attempted to widen the sensuous range of product appeal to include greater variety in the tactile and kinesthetic, as contrasted with the visual, aspect of products. Very early mass-production method concealed its blemishes (as in the cast-iron stove) by providing a superfluous décor that concealed the roughnesses of•fabrication; later it retained décor by inertia even though mass production mastered smooth surfaces and perfect joints. Still later, in a functionalist phase, it could emphasize the uncanny flawlessness demanded of technique by offering design shorn of surface elaboration. Today, with freedom to acquire either the "smooth" or the "rough," the deliberately "rough" can become a tactile desideratum in metal finishes, wood finishes, textiles, and other goods. This may be alloyed, for the purist, by the instances in which the machine too plainly imitates the blemishes of the hand-made style; but regardless of this, the cultural range is widened, and design makes much of it.

Something similar has occurred in the range of the solicitations offered to the kinesthetic or self-muscular, balancing, and related senses. It seems that seating, including automobile seating, provides one of the best examples. Before the influence of "modern" in the furniture field, seating was class-typed and style-typed, with a school-desk seat at one extreme of the rank order and the overstuffed chair at the other. A group of designers set out to persuade us that sitting is something one should be neither too much nor too little aware of—that we should be allowed to *know* that we are sitting while doing so. The desk seat tortured us out of that sensation, and the overstuffed chair bribed us out of it; what we needed was the chair that was a chair, a sitting machine. They have succeeded in their campaign, and doubtless their concern for the consumer's privilege of seeking a meaningful contact with his buttocks is the banner of a new luxury as contrasted with the old. The new functionalism in household living along these lines seems an appropriate tribute to America's three-hundred-year search for the floor—the unwound, country-storefront hunkering, cat-stretching, 100 per cent American relaxing and seat-sneaking that we have always yearned for as a riposte to European starchiness of posture. We can culturally afford to have the plainness now because we once proved that our pocketbooks could afford the plush. The slogan of the new realism in the décor of consumer hard goods is "Non-Luxury You Can Afford"—or even better, "A Non-Luxury You Can Afford To Finish Yourself To Show How Long Your Week Ends Are."

The Self-sold Consumer

The sharpened focus, in design and advertising, on the "operational" appeal of the commodity, which reaches an extreme in do-it-yourself commodities, is one of the most fascinating recent fashions in the American market. It is not, at first view, congruent with widespread claims for the automatization of, for example, many consumer hard goods. Is there more or less operational appeal in the new automatic range or the new power-steering, as compared with the old range or the old steering? Plainly there is less, in the sense that appeals to the user's sense of direct participation in the working of the commodity. Yet it is not illogical that as some processes, goods, and services in everyday consumer use are automatized and rationalized, other processes, goods, and services acquire a magnetism because they are not so. The guilt-inducing simplicity of premixed cake flour can be countered by the elaboration of the cake itself. Today, advertising is very much in the business of supplying with one hand motivations that it removes with the other.

This is one of the ways in which advertising becomes involved in the presentation of more and more elaborate uses of the commodities it advertises, sometimes getting to the point where it resembles the war-surplus store, where everything is good for something else than the purpose it was originally designed for! Right in the center of this marketing pattern stand all the devices by which the consumer is allowed to work his way as far as he wishes into the variant use of the product, the completion of the use of the product, the distribution of the product, and even the terminal manufacture of the product. For one of the genii that these advertising tendencies help to evoke is the self-sold, self-operating, in-the-act consumer. His pleasure, not merely as a discount-house refugee from the fair trade laws and brand-name fixed prices, is more fiendish than that of the old get-it-for-you-wholesale man. He is in the market to prove his talents not only as a trader but as a tinkerer and user and inventor of variable uses. As a self-sold consumer, he is the suburbanite (reported by William H. Whyte) who does group research on air-conditioning before a purchase is made. As self-operating, self-modifying consumer, he is, for example, the hot-rodder described in chapter vii.

As the group-researching advertiser has moved across the twilight zone that separates him from the consumer, the consumer has moved across to meet him. Advertisers need not say that he was uninvited. In one university town in the United States there is a soft-drink-dispensing machine that apologizes for itself in a way that invites the consumer to be as active and autonomous as he dares to. With the Coca-Cola, it provides a paper cup reading, "The machine can't think, but you can." This sort of provocation to the dormant independence of the consumer is as radical as the appearance in modern art of paintings that in 1880 avowed their incompleteness until the moment when the viewer marched away from them to a duelist's distance and then conquered them through half-lidded eyes—or paintings that in 1950 avow their incompleteness until the viewer has quite seriously considered, as he ought to, what it would be like to have his thalamus where his bile is.

The move on the part of the consumer to take over some of the final manufacturing and application of many products, especially those intended for semipermanent use in the home, is, to be sure, a partial reaction to high labor costs in the building and the associated trades. It will probably increase as the shortage of skilled labor grows in the next decade. At the same time, the desire of the consumer to have a more personalized part in consumption is reflected in some advertisements that speak of what the user can add to the product in more indefinable ways. Revlon cosmetics found it helpful to suggest that users might be women who had "danced with their shoes off," although the ads avoided an open assertion of this and tried not to limit the appeal of Revlon lipstick to women of that skill. In many of the products that are consumed in terms of intimacy, the rather scientific exhortations that followed the feminine-hygiene pattern of some years ago have given way to adjurations based on aesthetic criteria. Where science can be assumed, art is commanded. A prominent feature of cigarette, liquor, and related advertising is the ambiguity of appeal built into the advertisement: the decision to popularize a previously "class" product or the decision to attach class significance to a variation on a mass product almost always results in a sort of symbolist-surrealist advertisement with an ambiguous message. The do-it-yourself glamor and the "symbolist" advertisement are both responses to a market changing so rapidly that no one is sure of it and to a market troubled by the guilts associated with obsolescence by styling.

The externals of class status in the United States are closely linked to the pattern of discard of certain commodities before their wear-span is complete, and advertisers as well as designers are in the troublesome business of signaling stylistic obsolescence for these articles. One of the results is that they are always building a taste structure that is psychologically unstable. They can offer the sensitive consumer only two choices. One is that the consumer, if he chooses an item such as an automobile, of which wear-span is longer than use-span, can elect to buy a deviant commodity such as a Mercedes-Benz or a Volkswagen; and this will work only if merchandising lags so much that the consumer remains, for years, a pioneer. The other is that, having purchased his Cadillac, the consumer becomes a taste-leader by newness as well as by purchase; no matter how long its wear-span is, he will get a new one at the end of the use-span indicated by the styling of the advertiser. The former is self-defeating, for it depends on market limitation of a sort: the Volkswagen people dare not market a new model in the United States under the old name, because that would break its implicit contract with its buyers not to put into obsolescence a slowly changing model which gave as much prestige to the old-year owner as to the new. The latter is also self-defeating, not so much in the sales as in the sense that no Cadillac consumer can really rest his taste for many years in any year's model. The instability of taste commitment is one of the secret sores of advertising and design that resists disclosure and discussion because, if revealed, little could be done about it anyway.

One of the results in advertising imagery is that automobile advertising, above all, fluctuates between appeals to fantasy and to reality. Marketers of such soft goods as gin and lipstick can afford to—almost have to—explore their markets by a sustained use of ambiguity, the appeal through ads based on principles of "incomplete closure," letting the consumer finish part of the mysterious story by himself. Many home products, especially flooring materials, which might be taken as the archetype, can be made to appeal to the most fabricating instincts of the practical do-it-yourself man or woman. Automobile advertisements veer from one extreme to the other, now making the pitch to the imaginary engineer in every man, now making it to the imaginary dowager in every woman.

The guilt for the generation of an unstable taste structure is occasionally felt in the advertising profession, and one of the reasons is that the professionals have not asked what it would mean to develop an aesthetic for articles that have, in our economy, a longer wear-span than use-span. They should tackle this problem to the best of their ability. Hints as to the solution are only suggested in Ford's attempt to hypostatize an "above-obsolescence" model in the Lincoln Continental and the Big Three's general attempt to build a "classic" sports car which changes more slowly from year to year than anything else in their line. This "meta-language" of industrial design is not enough to meet the problem, but it should be explored further. More to the point would be a study of the degree to which do-it-yourself variation and commitment to products might win consumer loyalty not only to a given style but to family planning for usage by which a commodity might have a career in which wear-span equals use-span. A model is shown in the schemes that hi-fi merchants propose: partial replacement and modification of the commodity move with taste. Given the present state of the American economy, however, it would be dangerous to decrease the rate of obsolescence in goods without taking up the slack in the consequent rate of purchase.

There is no doubt that designers share with advertisers some sense of dismay at their contribution to the unstable taste commitment and that their part in examining the process is required. Meanwhile, the advertising men and their sponsors are committed by some of the newer salients of persuasion dealt with here, including obsolescence-through-fashion, to "meta-advertising functions," to saying, rightly or wrongly, a great many things about everything in the world except their product. In this sense they are not only confirmers (or deniers) of popular belief but also entertainers. It may be that along one line, with medical and hygienic commodities, they work toward long-run readjustments of the equilibrium between the public and the private, as in the instance of the Zonite ads of the 1920's; along other lines, the effect of their messages is to provide redefinitions of personality and culture in which are blended information, publicity, and entertainment.

We have emphasized the degree to which the meta-advertising message is built into the direct advertising rhetoric itself; but there is another dimension of American public relations in general that introduces entertainment—and the meta-advertising message—in a different way. The American marketers, including merchandisers, advertisers, and networks alike, create a pool of funds and a capital plant, in the form of the media organizations, which can and do entertain millions. The largest dollar expenditures in this field are, of course, the sponsored programs, programs in which the meta-advertising imagery, as in the case of Gillette sponsorship of fights, is closely connected with the product and its use, and other programs, such as Philip Morris' sponsorship of Lucille Ball and Desi Arnaz, in which the connection is remote. Over and above these advertising-sponsored entertainments, there are all the activities associated with "Culture" that are financed in part, directly or indirectly, by all the varying agencies of the publicity enterprise, including the networks as time-donors, acceptors of incidental tasks, and financiers of "sustaining" or non-billable items of media production. This spectrum should be examined for the degree to which it involves the advertiser, sometimes through the concept of the "indirect" or the "institutional" or the "soft sell" in meta-advertising functions. A pertinent case study involves the contrast and comparison of the social, cultural, and governmental setting of radio-TV here and abroad.

Advertisers as Entertainers

In Europe, the mass media are regarded as carrying out or modifying the work of the statesman, the journalist, the educator, and the serious artist; in the United States they are defined largely as carrying out the work of the businessman as advertiser, the theatrical entertainer, and the newspaper. The European mass media still reflect some institutional characteristics dating from the days when the literate were a privileged minority.

In this general tradition the European media are very largely the preserve of upper-middle-class talent and taste among those people who have received a university education or preserve an aristocracy of birth. The social layers that control the media antedate Gaetano Mosca's anxiety in *The Ruling Class* that general literacy would subvert liberalism. It might appear that the nationalization and "welfare-government" dominance of some of the media, especially the electronic media, in Scandinavia, Britain, Italy, as well as to some extent also in France and Germany, was inconsistent with this picture of the class control of the media. However, the experience of Britain might be cited as a case: under any government, Labor or Conservative, the British Broadcasting Corporation is the state corporation licensed under the Post Office to supply this public service. Its charter says that it is to be informative and entertaining and puts "informative" first. The apparently specific terminology of the enabling act is actually vague as to its possible applications, especially as to the selection of who will be responsible for programming. Indeed, the British Post Office would be in an impossible position (and so would Parliament) if it had to take anything like continuing direct responsibility for whatever is said to be good or bad about BBC.

In effect, the management of BBC has been the informal monopoly of the university-educated, with a considerable dominance by Oxford over all the other universities. The reason is that the government had a fairly well-structured set of expectations about what personnel of this sort would do; and they in turn had a well-structured set of expectations about what was expected of them. They accepted the responsibility of concretizing what was only a pious prayer of enactment on the part of the legislators. In general, they have pleased both Parliament and the public. If they have had their faults of fustiness, snobbery, and cultural inbreeding, they have also had their virtues of responsibility, magnanimity, and bureaucratic tact. This case can be generalized to say something about all European electronic media in the situation of state control.

This institutional setting of radio and TV is, in part, a consequence of the general rule that the older media in Europe, such as the newspapers, are still privately owned. The British and the Continentals tend to accept this as a historical fact without reminding Americans of its origin in policy. The press fought its way to freedom under radicals and liberals and has held on to it; the electronic media appeared at a time when concern over the control of the media as a "public preserve" made it inevitable that European consensus would hand them over to government rather than to the business classes. This distinction has had, in fact, some rather odd effects, at least from the American viewpoint. The newspapers, an older medium, have tended to retain their power over their readers as fractions of political-sentiment groups. This leads to some ironies. The policies of the *Express* may in fact be much more "lowbrow" than those of the BBC; but the *Express*, by identifying itself with the privately owned press of Fleet Street in general, likes to write and act as if it were superior to the BBC. In part, this is an attack on public as distinguished from private bureaucracy; in part, it is also an unconscious reference to a sense of belonging to an older order when the mass media were mainly print, when the media were "opposition voices," and when print itself was associated with literacy, with schooling, and with the upper social layers. Thus the question of the comparative social prestige of the older media and the new is as moot today in Europe as it is in the United States, though in a somewhat different way.

In Europe, the educated are the book-educated; the book is the sign of intellectual freedom and superiority. The French, for example, publish more than twice as many books for less than half as many people as we do and thus provide a greater plurality in the market for feelings and ideas. On the other hand, reverence for print in Europe still helps to give prestige to newspapers and magazines that would be left unread as partisan sensationalism in the United States. European venality and demagoguery in journalism, which tends to be organized around politicocultural splinter groups, is sustained in part because the electronic media are so dull and respectable and above the battle. We see, therefore, that in Europe print seems to pretend to older claims of prestige while at the same time taking over the lowest inflammatory functions, while in the United States the electronic media pretend to the prestige of novelty and, by taking over the more sensational functions, make the newspapers look fairly respectable. Again, the neutralization-by-nationalization of the electronic media in Europe means that they are handled with kid gloves by their educated managers. Advertising is forbidden in most national monopolies, and the parliamentary battle that preceded the act of toleration by which commercials were admitted to British TV is well known. Undeniably, European networks, especially BBC, have been more daring and more helpful than American networks on behalf of the less popular artistic and intellectual cadre of their national communities; but perhaps their communities, rather than being persuaded by the networks to accept this, allowed it from the beginning.

The net result is that advertising interests in the United States, under the general control of the Federal Communications Commission, not only are more responsible as entertainers and informants of the public than they are in Europe but are also more involved in the pitfalls of policy strewn in their way by their acceptance of these functions. On the one hand, they can truthfully claim to be better entertainers and more attention-getting informants over radio and TV than many a state ministry in Europe, and they can claim along with this that they prevented, as in the history of the BBC, the electronic media from becoming a bureaucracy which anonymizes and underpays talent to such a degree that it menaces its own creativity. On the other hand, the advertisers of the United States who use the electronic media can never hope to claim a perfect congruence between the commodities they advertise and the cultural gifts in the way of highbrow programs that they bestow on their audiences. Soaps, automobiles, foods, and the commodities of personal appearance are the major support of network radio and TV in terms of total advertising costs to the sponsors and of time-income to the networks. It may be that to reach markets for these products while at the same time assisting the networks to meet the mild demands of the FCC for broadcasts of public usefulness requires the advertiser to be interested, part of the time, in something more than direct selling. It may be that "institutional" types of advertising, which tend to meld and sometimes confuse the aims of advertising and of education, will increase. Yet their very increase, which may be reckoned as a short-term public good, is bound to make more salient the overwhelming question: Why should the networks advertisers have more to do than anyone else with the non-advertising content of the channels outside of the so-called educational stations? Do we really believe that the harm done to sexuality by the body-odor ads is counteracted by a give-away *Romeo and Juliet?* More pertinently, how many of the non-advertising functions can advertising sustain without losing its sense of identity and precipitating itself into cultural and ideological battles that are, as they say, "bad for business"?

The Hucksters' Temptation

The problem is a real one, even when it comes to the fore in connection with "campaigns" of selling. Once the campaign begins to make statements over and beyond statements for the market place, it is making statements that can culturally irritate a part of the market without inducing more sales from other parts of the market. Moreover, so much of the justification for advertising is based on the idea that advertised goods are better, and that advertising makes the competition between various goods more perfect and flexible, that advertising will always be forced to return to commodity emphasis in its messages no matter how much it wanders temporarily in the wilderness of popular education, uplift, the reinforcement of group snobberies, and so on. All these minor subjuncts of the advertising message appear and reappear but never say the same thing from year to year; the one thing that is constant, or almost so, is the mention of the product and its virtues. A motor company that recently undertook to educate the public as to safety principles in connection with the use of a safety belt in cars seems to have found that it was in effect educating people to be afraid of cars; it went back to advertising the product and has conspicuously soft-toned its ventures into insurance-type messages to the public.

The achievement of the cost-lowering wider market by means of all of the resources of the mass media nevertheless has some important non-market by-products and forces advertising personnel to face issues that are only marginal to the market at any time. It is not a direct market aim of the advertisers to increase a *general* aesthetic appreciation of all products in all lines, but advertising probably does do this. An interesting question involves the stages of this education, from decade to decade. Again, it is not the direct aim of advertising to upgrade the consumer's self-concept as well as his concept of the product; but in times of a rapidly gaining standard of living, market expansion tends to force this problem on the members of the profession. It is particularly during periods characterized by inflation and rapid social mobility that this tendency in advertising seems to increase the power of the media in bringing about a homogenization of the culture. However, this charge against advertisers and the media may be the result of a lag in perceptions. The deep homogenization of the market tends to occur in the deflationary segments of the merchandising cycle, when everyone is cost-minded, and few consumers will pay extra for individualization of products. The effects of this homogenizing marketing policy are not publicly observed and criticized as "standardizing" until the economic phase has changed; then, when marketing can advance only by intense application of the principle of the marginal differentiation of products (and when advertising actually does do some work against homogenization of taste), the criticism of advertising as a homogenizer comes pouring in. This is the lag that accounts in part for the harshly homogenistic thesis of Dwight MacDonald in his remarks on the advertising culture.

There is no doubt that within recent years advertising in the United States has been once more concerned with its reputation, particularly with regard to the charge that it standardizes. It is committed to the belief that this standardization is an appropriate aim to the degree that it rationalizes production costs and expands the market at diminishing unit-message costs. At the same time it feels uncomfortable about the matter. It is happy to be able to remind the public from time to time that it takes part of the responsibility of presenting a TV *Hamlet* or *Sleeping Princess*. It hopes it will not look professorial in arguing that the support of the agencies and the media system by advertising plays a part in producing a "surplus" which can then be programmed into the form, not of a commercial, but of something high-toned, like *Lucia di Lammermoor*. Advertising hopes, perhaps with good reason (considering the competition of one medium with another, each selecting variant audiences), to play the part of art patron as well as the part of the publicist. Only time can tell whether the profession will succeed in modeling itself on Lorenzo de Medici or on P. T. Barnum.

The Search for Standard Men

Margaret Mead has asked us to observe that when public messages serve the purpose of making almost everyone feel at home in the cultural and expenditure patterns of the middle-class core culture of the United States, some disconcerting things can happen. One is an increasing "reflexiveness" of the media culture and its audiences—an intensified mirroring of the actual, an intensified elaboration of the obvious. In a period of rising standards of economic welfare, this "reflexiveness," with its banal iteration of the symbols of welfare gain, becomes something like a subcase of the "materialism" that the Europeans used to be fond of charging Americans with.

The same climate of near-complacency may contain the origins of the generalized business and advertising belief that motives can be "found" by research. Of course they can be; but what is found depends very much on the questions with which one begins the investigation. There is a certain naïve realism in the belief among some advertisers that unambiguous patterns of motivation are sure to result from the application of methods developed originally in the psychology of Freud or the Gestaltists, say, or in the sociology of Durkheim or in the anthropology of a Warner or a Kroeber. Yet even when significant findings turn up, as they often do, the use of them may be problematic. As pointed out, it is commonly thought that great dangers can result from an unprincipled use by merchandisers and advertisers of the "secrets" of consumers' behavior that they like to hunt out. It seems an equally great danger that this search for a "mine of motives" in the consumer, to which the merchant and the advertiser can then respond as they see fit, has other difficulties built into it.

Indeed, it prompts one to think sometimes that manufactur-

ing, design, and merchandising leaders value motivation research quite as much because it proves the existence of *some*
rare form of human motivation as because it provides routine
specific market information. At this level, however, the very
notions of a personal motive and a cultural motive might be
said to have become confused. The invention of motives is one
of the highest responsibilities of leaders in any sphere of human
activity, and what they invent is the result of personal imagination and cultural experiment. Human motives do not emerge
or represent themselves simply to investigations that are given
over to sorting and reassorting a spectrum of social and cultural habits broadly distributed in majorities. They do not exist
before they are imagined. Therefore, the search for a series of
"standard men" in the market has some of the same will-o'-the-
wisp quality found in the medieval search for the angelic man,
the search by Adam Smith for the "economic man."

This is not an argument for an elitist theory of society; some
of the democratic experiments have enabled us to learn how
cultural minorities, such as women, children, and slaves, can
become crucial as "teachers" of the dominant. Democracy permits what we can call the socialization of the past, as when
children in the American culture, beginning at an early age,
are permitted to retrain their parents in ways that were banned
by older methods of child-rearing. What remains true, however, is that our society has leaders and that some of them are
merchants and advertising men and media men. It is quite impossible to allow them to discount their own motives (or their
own sense of a lack of motives) by permitting them to hint
that basic cultural motives can be discovered only by the min-
ing and sifting of statistical consensus or dissensus in the
United States. Leaders either have motives or they do not; and
their task is to express these in such a way that they are open
to public judgment. A sociopsychological naïve realism that
permits them to define themselves as the mere brokers of general motives is to call a tune for which the piper in the long
run may ask heavy pay.

. . . Someday we hope to come up with the
perfect tape—a fully recorded loop of
absolute quiet.—Edward Hermann

CHAPTER ELEVEN

The Suppliant Skyscrapers

Metropolis and Monument

Many of us agree with architect Richard Neutra that architecture should make allowances for the total human physique and that architecture's tributary arts ought to do their best for all the senses. Thus the sonic experiments of Edward Hermann (head of the Acoustics Branch, Wave Mechanics Laboratory, at the U.S. Naval Experiment Station, Annapolis) and others make us hope for an architecture in which sound, or anything that does the job best, will provide "walls" and "ceilings." Such hopefulness makes us eager, even granting the abatement of noise in American cities and industrial plants in recent years, for the coming of "sound perfume" in offices and public places. "Sound perfume" is (or will be) mechanically produced noise that, when broadcast into carefully acousticized rooms, serves as an invisible and "inaudible" wall between conversations not meant to intrude on one another.

Now that we are so close to solving such earlier industrial problems as big-city noise (one of the major barbarisms delaying the development of an urban civilization in the United

224

States) and now that we have a genuine contemporary movement in architecture, the stakes are high. They are high not only in terms of the industrial tenor of everyday factory, office, and domestic life but also in terms of monumental civic design. The resulting wider interest in the architecture of American urban areas generates a great deal of controversy and theoretical disagreement.

Fascinating as it is to imagine future interpenetrations of the solid and the wavelike, the tangible and the audible, in architectural composition, we must remember that changes in the use of the customary tangible materials of architecture have precipitated the great architectural debates of the age. A sound tape that is not silent, and dramatically so, recently recorded the remarks of Frank Lloyd Wright at a Chicago dinner in honor of an exhibition of photographs of Louis Sullivan's works. Irritated by some of the speeches of the evening, Wright punctuated with downward strokes of his cane, wonderfully audible on the tape, his charge against the banqueters that they were not truly honoring Sullivan; that they had defined the wrong Sullivan; that in general they were philistines compared to Wright himself. The old self-advertising Barnum of the architectural field, superb salesman at times of his own superb work, stalked out of the banquet room with the air of a genius just insulted by the mobocracy.

Perhaps Wright fumed because, in part, social changes in the United States during the past few years have undercut some of his antimetropolitan and anticentralist fervor. One might believe that his proposal to build a mile-high building in Chicago is an attempt to dominate some of the social and symbolic space that is developing in city centers as a result of demolition and suburban movements. Or one might interpret the proposal as an attempt to satirize, by a symbol of over-centralization, the very urbanism that angers him. The city should not be the powerful center in American life, argues Wright; but if it ceases to be so, perhaps he will be glad to use the emptied space for monuments in honor of himself. Meanwhile, however, the very nature of urbanism has been changing, and the city, some say, cannot produce a monument to itself, not to speak of a monument to a great architect.

It has always been a question whether a milieu that is changing rapidly can produce a monument or a symbol of itself. This question may be especially relevant in the period in which no great architectural or engineering work presents to the ordinary eye an easily readable picture of the man-hours it contains. Certainly the illiterate ancestor of the Egyptian fellahin, looking at the pyramids, could give himself a notion of the measurability—or the immeasurability—of the hand labor that went into them. Today, not even an experienced observer can make an image to himself of the individual labor that produces a dam; the mediation of mechanical power and indirect production makes such a picturization impossible. The ceremonial significance of ancient monuments was certainly enhanced, if not produced, by their appearance in societies of slow technical change and in production systems which made clear to everyone the sheer quantity of human labor that had been directed into a non-pragmatic use.

Today, the monumentality of the city is deferred. It might be helpful to think of this as resulting from a particularly American phenomenon of recent years—the leapfrogging of each other, in a variety of ways, by transportation and communication. Communication always leapfrogs transportation when it can use symbolic means of transporting information that originally had to be carried as slowly as one carried a brick. Largely as a result of the market-stimulated use of the mass-media system, American society has seen more of this leapfrogging of older systems of social contact by communication systems than any other country in the world. Today, an increasing number of social "bricks" are being moved over wire or air waves instead of being transported.

It also works the other way around. Transportation always

leapfrogs communications when it can afford to move in physical fact to a viewer or consumer or user something that had to travel symbolically before. Many of the identifications with the rural life that were achieved indirectly through the mass media by city people are now open to establishment by rapid transportation of artifacts between country and city; and the same is true for the urban identification of rural people.

In the arts and atmosphere of the media, the use of new symbolic means, such as the sociability of TV, for communicating rather than transporting realities induces the variety of effects noted in previous chapters. On the one hand, it subverts the symbolic medium to a new naïve realism; on the other hand, it may convert the listener to a new and higher realism. Thus, TV performers carrying canned sociability to social stay-at-homes offer them a product that could have been obtained in social life only by asking someone to drive over and be sociable. The result is that the TV performer employs art to act as a guest rather than as a fictional performer, and he tends to downgrade the fictional possibilities of his art. His receivers, on the other hand, are forced to recognize the presence of a fictional rather than actual guest; and this realization, at various levels of sensitivity, may well result in an upgrading of competence in the arts of sociability. As a further step, and particularly among the young, this may contribute to a sharpening of the sense of the various media forms themselves.

It is probable that in the long run the symbolization of the previously transported social fact leads to greater competence in the handling of symbols; this has been the history of the past, and it is likely to be true in the present and future as well. One reason is that the "vicarious transportation" of an image by communication from remote sources is not only a substitute for the similar thing in life but an addition to it. As such, it demands ultimately to be understood as a mirror rather than as a simulacrum. Young people, trained to media perception in ways that escape the older generation, can make distinctions between the documentary and the fictional in media presentations that involve differences some older groups remain quite unaware of.

Let us consider the opposite case: a commodity, service, or value that has been brought to the viewer or user largely by symbolic means is now transported to him—or he to it. The predicted weather arrives as a fact after it has been defined for the citizen-sufferer by the experts that watched it approach for three thousand miles; or, in a somewhat different case, the suburban life that was indirectly experienced through the media by urban masses now becomes their immediate experience as a result of their transportation to it by universal car-ownership, the superhighway, and all the things that have tended to shift the center of population in the United States first to the farms, then to cities, and finally to the suburbs and some towns. Even more dramatically, perhaps, similar effects are felt by the farmer. In 1900, many aspects of city life and its standard of living reached him only by the communications system—magazines, telephone, the radio. Today, most of the physical appurtenances of the urban standard of living are transported to him in actuality, and his style of life reflects the closing of a gap between communications and transportation contact with the urban style of life.

What are some of the cultural effects of this process? For one thing, "literalism" bulges, a good example being the determination of many American farmers of means to have a "city house" on their property, even if this implies a disrespect to more local methods and styles of construction. In this instance, a transportation system that serves centralized standardization of construction methods may work against him and his taste; he is saved only by receiving a media message to the effect that he would be better off to fix up the old house—the one that urbanites may value the most. Yet, in the United States, where so many people have transported themselves in recent years, one of the major effects is the reinforcement of local symbolic and architectural style. The easterners and the midwesterners, we can be sure, are the ones who conscientiously carry the good and the bad in what is called "California architecture" to farthest extremes. Generally, whenever the transportation system leapfrogs the communication system, there is a reinforcement of what is at the source of transportation and what is at its terminus. In the United States the gradients that separate regional and subregional styles in architecture are perhaps less impressive than their tendency to confirm what is most conventional in each other. The "ranch-house" style, spreading from the Southwest into California and then east, provided the perfect postwar rationalization for the "less-expensive," one-level houses that are really not less expensive per square foot of living space per wall-and-base measurements but which fill up the lot.

From this point of view it may be possible to redefine at least some of the areas of disagreement haunting those who admire the "functionalism" of modern industrial and metropolitanized scenes but are concerned about its lack of monumentality—its lack of deliberate and graciously realized visual symbols. They are not satisfied by the claims to functionality of a single office building or even a whole neighborhood development; nor are they satisfied that the display of gorgeous neon, seen at a distance from the superhighway or from the air, is enough. Without claiming that modern civic design, if there is such a thing, should be monumental, they would like to consider the ways in which it could be. One major criticism leveled at these hopes comes from John Burchard, who suggests that those who build may have nothing monumental to say or, alternatively, that society today has little that it wants to be said, by architects, monumentally.

If we could defer the discussion of symbolic reference, we might trouble ourselves also with another aspect of monumentality that seems difficult to achieve today—that of an architecturally determined viewpoint. Even if a monument had something to say, it is important, as Le Corbusier implies in some of his writing, that there should exist for it an audience more or less unambiguously located in space. The ancient and beautiful squares like the Piazza San Marco in Venice still say what they want to because they say it to pedestrians who have a limited choice of perspectives. But what of large structures left unsurrounded by perspectival space? What of structures that will be seen from fast-moving cars at points determined by the superhighway's curve? What of totalities that can be seen significantly only from the air—like some oil refineries—or of totalities that, when seen from the air, lose all effect because they were built to be seen in any other way?

This reference to a visual viewpoint, valuable as it is in reference to the visible sign or symbol of modern industrial life, is even more useful to us if we extend the notion to include non-visual and non-immediate viewpoints. To take the latter first, we may get a more symbolizing view of the city from a TV picture taken from an airplane than any other way. Two elements in this picture, however, are specifically modern experiences: the air-view and the vicarious reception of it from a remote source. Again, generalizing viewpoint to include the non-visual, we could speak of the presence of such a physically compacted thing as the city or the industrial plant as something constantly being transported symbolically by the communications media: old radio sound-effect files are full of cities and steel mills. The leapfrogging of transportation and of one-site assembly of symbolic materials and centers of remote communications clearly creates a multiplicity of new viewpoints. One of their major characteristics is that they do not, like Piazza San Marco or Versailles, provide the viewer with a rhythmically punctuated system of pedestrian viewpoints in space. On the other hand, with respect to the "object" viewed or sensed, they set up no convergence of linear directives toward an optical vanishing point. It is hard to see how monumentality can be monopolized by architecture or, even if so monopolized, then satisfactorily realized in the face of these conditions.

For most of us, when we bother to ask whether the city is monumental, the answer comes uneasily. We should like to claim that when we view it from our cars, traveling a nearby superhighway, we see it as a monument. But it sounds snobbish to claim this when we reflect on the experience of those who, say, once stood in the court of the Temple of the Sun and Moon in the Valley of Mexico. There, we could have been assured, in the festival time, that everyone was conscious of being in the presence of a deliberated monument and, what is more, conscious of being surrounded by many others who felt the same way. We are perhaps on better ground, then, when we consider the image of the city as it is "transported" to us by the mass media, even when we live in the city itself, as having monumental significance. This implies that we live in an age of the "communications" monument rather than any other kind. This partly composed and partly uncomposed monument is our equivalent to what ages that were conquering transportation rather than communications were able to achieve in the selective site-assembly of massive materials and symbolic form.

In that event, we could speak of a major principle of discovery in the exploration of what the city and the factory can be in the future: it would follow along the lines Henry Adams hinted at when he spoke of the progressive "etherialization" of certain aspects of social life in the modern age. This would be the progressive obsolescence of as many as possible of all space-occupying structures or structure-members that we use both for pragmatic purposes and for symbolic purposes. The withdrawal of imputations of efficiency from the more physically massive member (wall) and its transfer to the more attenuated physical member (the column) could be taken as the general model of a series of steps that could go even further in the same direction. The use of "sound perfume" instead of walls would be along the same line, and so would analogous "light perfume," or the optical conditioning of social visibility. Physicality in the signs and symbols of industrial life would serve its purpose by systematically demoting itself from attention. This challenge, unresponded to by British industrial design in the last two or so generations, has set a roadblock to British development in durable design. It could also ultimately do so in the United States.

The emphasis on regular architectural solids for their own "monumental" sake is, as one tradition in contemporary architecture, open to degradation and distortion. Such an emphasis leads many to feel that a badly built suburban imitation of a spare modern edifice is superior to the great open-air Bunsen burners that are our refineries and the massive smithies that are our steel mills. Yet it is in the form of such capital-goods construction that our architectural *élan* is most alive and most rewarding.

At this point, it may be asked whether the potential monumentality of the city is of interest to anyone but hypersensitives and thin-skinned critics of that congeries of subjects often called "urbanism." Does anyone care? Many, very much; and all of the ways in which the physique of the city is remodeled in advertising fantasy, in easel painting, in sculpture, and in the mass media tell us so. Yet there is an obligation to speak more specifically of the way in which urban monumentality, insofar as it pretends to exist already, registers this. It might be a good idea to recall the *Götterdämmerung* that overtook the invisible deities and demiurges that once inhabited the top floors of the city skyline.

A Change of Skyline

Working in an advertising office in New York, poet Hart Crane carried on the work of industrialism in such a characteristic form as institutional advertising for banks; living in the

streets, bars, and furnished rooms of Brooklyn, he tried to duplicate Whitman's feeling that there must be a bridge that
joins the older rural America with the new urban America.
Crane's picture of the city, as expressed in his address to the
Brooklyn Bridge, suggests the degree to which he was haunted
by change and how much he wished the architectural displays
of the city to offer the vision of a transcendent forgiveness.
Among other things, the "pardon" and the "reprieve" offered
to Crane by the sight of Brooklyn Bridge were the solace
offered to the separateness, smallness, and failures of the individual self in the big city: the presence of the great bridge
showed that the social organism is always lifting up some
symbol of creativity. The "fury" that was "fused" in the bridge,
according to Crane, was the fury of Time, which takes the
young, the innocent, and the deviant out of the hinterlands,
brings them to the anonymity of the city where they face
selves that could not have become manifest before, and then
forgives them for the faces that they show. The bridge, to
Crane, was a "harp" not only because it looked like one but
because it vibrated with sound and because it was an instru-
ment through which the city expressed itself. It was an "altar"
not only because its Gothic piers could be seen by Crane as
liturgical forms but because victims, he thought, were sacri-
ficed here, and because it monumentally stands for man's im-
manent intimacy with, and strangeness to, the universe.

Crane's early poetry moved his readers because he almost
self-consciously fell in love with the machine-made forms and
surfaces of the modern city. His first book was called *White
Buildings,* and his work abounds in evocations of the velocities,
complexities, artificialities, and plastic beauties of the urban
scene. It is instructive to compare the seriousness with which
Crane delights even in ugly architecture, display, and advertising with the nausea and scorn felt by the Spanish poet Gar-
cía Lorca at the physical presence of New York. Crane shared

and exploited that general attempt to make the city less
"opaque to the emotions" which is characteristic of one major
movement of taste in the United States after World War I. He
belonged to a generation that wished to accept as much as possible of contemporary industrial form as an iconography of
feelings. Assisted by the cubism of Picasso and his followers, it
went a long way along that road. Their apperceptions were assisted by technological change: in the 1920's the city became
a product of machinery and a machine itself—no longer a pile
of bricks thick-walled at the bottom and thin-walled at the top.
At the same time, it became the home of millions of lumens of
colored light. In Hart Crane's lines we hear the physical presence of the city with its tremendous new capacity for monumental significance accepted in a way that is new; and in this
recognition he speaks for his times.

Because Crane clearly saw the Brooklyn Bridge as instru-
ment, symbol, and rhetoric—as an "advertisement" for an age
announcing itself—we can take notice of how much all of us
feel the same way. In our everyday language we distinguish
constantly between "architecture" (the building) and "decora-
tion and advertisement" (the things that have been attached to
it by someone other than the architect). But in actual fact, we
sense all the time that we are dealing with a continuum—that
our feelings if not our vocabularies take in the building and its
signs in one perception.

To follow the theme requires, of course, a real relaxation of
some of the conventional definitions. In most recent discussions of Lever House in New York and of the Manufacturers'
Trust Company building, both buildings that make use of
large glass surfaces, the speakers overemphasize the structural
and functional qualities of glass. Architects praise both these
very good buildings because the huge window-walls "make
people feel as if they are close to the light, light being a physi-
ologically-based psychological need." If it is such a need, then
it is hard to explain why, as the *Architectural Forum* recently

showed, most skyscraper windows are bigger than most people want. By the use of shades through most of the day, occu-
pants on some levels reduce effective window size by more
than 30 per cent. Apparently, light is a physiologically based
psychological need only in relation to certain exposures of the
building surface, certain heights, and certain other elements
of context. In a central Manhattan building, who could doubt
that the photons that fall on this or that desk are significant in
terms of occupational status? The man nearer the light is the
man higher up. The truth of this observation about the business totem pole in New York certainly provides an inducement
to business builders to spread light farther and wider inside
their buildings as a boost to the status feelings of everyone
within. Could the proved increase in the employment stability
of Lever Brothers, after their move to the new building, be a
function of this generalization, as well as a generalization that
emphasizes the physiological value of light?

If it could be, then we must acknowledge the interdependence of quite understandable advertising and public relations
functions with architectural design. The subterranean connections are probably quite as interesting and important as the
ones that are fully realized on a conscious level in the planning
and design of the structure. Indeed, actual architectural practice suggests that these connections must be highly important;
most modern architects are only to a very limited degree practitioners of the functionalism they praise. Nor is it entirely
their fault. In many a building program, the architect never
receives from the client a truly comprehensive analysis of the
use that will be made of the structure; and without such an
analysis some aspects of the doctrine of functionalism cannot
be fulfilled. While we must be aware of the consciously symbolic and rhetorical elements of building, the "monumental"
aspects, we must also take notice of the aspects that provide
more or less unintentionally an "advertising" that reveals the
mood of the architect's clients.

Anyone who has looked out of the top storeys of a skyscraper is aware of that second city, the top-storey City of Monuments which was constructed far above street eye-level by the builders of the period roughly 1900 to 1925. The Bankers' Trust Company in New York is surmounted by a replica of a mausoleum of Asia Minor, and other skyscrapers sport temples and outsize urns. They are, no doubt, a response to the sort of taste that, in the commentary of a Britisher of the 1930's, found that most New York buildings of a later vintage looked "unfinished at the top." It was hard to draw a tall building in the the period 1900 to 1925 without adding something to the peak, simply because the whole building was taken in by the eye of the client as he viewed it on the drawing board. The result, however, of both this style and the styles that succeeded it, has some interest for us in terms of the actual storey levels at which decorative application occurred.

For one thing, we see that the careful contemplation of a top-storey monument on most city buildings has the effect, at a distance, of giving them an anthropomorphic look. The old skyline of New York and Chicago is a skyline of buildings which look in some way or another like the human trunk surmounted by a grotesquely human head. One can hardly doubt that their builders would have experienced a feeling of decapitation and dehumanization if they had permitted their draftsman to turn up the sort of flat-topped building which became the mode in the later twenties and is the standard today. It should be pointed out that in the early days of skyscraper construction— with due allowance for the purity of Sullivan's and Root's early buildings—there was a distinct taste for the projection of colossi in architecturally disguised form. As such, these buildings were advertisements for "big men."

Even more compelling, perhaps, is the realization that the storey-level concentration of décor has changed in the big-city building in the last sixty years or so. The Bankers' Trust Company building and others are examples of a period in which

most memorable decorative effects were lavished on the top
levels, as if to signify that they were truly available to only
those top-storey dwellers of executive offices, business clubs,
boardrooms, and such who were on the top of the social heap.
The history of tall-building architecture since then has been
a gradual reduction of the personalization of the top storeys,
as if in a post-Depression effort to minimize the existence of a
pantheon of powers invisibly inhabiting the Hellenistic pal-
aces, urns, and tombs of the earlier rooftops. While it is true
that Louis Sullivan offered grand solutions for the eye-level
view of the city walker by placing his in-scale decorative effects near sidewalk level in the Carson Pirie Scott and Company building in Chicago as early as 1905, he was plainly
ahead of the times. It took the architectural spirit of American
capitalism many years to acknowledge changes in the mood of
social politics in the United States by dragging the gods of
décor down from the topmost levels to the lowest levels of
visual accessibility.

This descending movement in the placement of decorative
and monumental icons, a change in the relation between high
and low points in structure, has been accompanied by a change
in the relations between the inside and the outside of urban
business buildings. The older, anthropomorphic, urn-topped
building emphasized remoteness and closure to the world; and
this was emphasized by the quality of its openings. Such
buildings, at street level, often possessed the small doors and
lobbies which followed, in some sense, the inevitable restrictions on non-load-bearing walls and volumes which controlled
the design of the lower floors of brick and masonry tall buildings. In the newer skyscraper design, it is interesting to see
that the lack of interest in roof-line decorative effects goes quite
often with an increased "opening-out" of the building at the
lower levels. This opening-out is made possible, in the first
place, by steel-frame construction; but it was exploited far less
in the earlier steel-frame buildings than in the later ones. Big

steel-frame buildings today, no matter what their use is, provide large open space at the floor levels. As "advertising" their effort is not to conquer by their roof-top magnificence the eye of a public standing far off and small but to enjoy the favor of a public that, walking nearby, might be tempted in to take a free guided tour, see a free movie, or simply enjoy the sensation of being seen on the inside by those who are still outside. In a sense, New York main-avenue architecture in particular is learning to let glass at street level be a showcase for the advertisement of anyone who stands inside.

This slow revolution in the "public and private" areas and uses of the big-business building has been induced, to be sure, by a variety of changes in public relations and advertising practices, not least of all the desire to make the public feel at home. Today, as walkers pass by any one of a number of glass windows and open spaces in Manhattan, they provide an audience for people standing within the buildings. The people within may be there "for business" or because they are on their lunch hour or because they have just lost a $20,000-a-year job and cannot quite decide what friend to see about another one; nobody on the outside can tell which. The result is that everyone on the inside is given that sense of self-importance which in the old days one had to pay a price for. Years ago in New York, a well-dressed man without a job built up his confidence between interviews by paying a manicurist for a half-hour of trying to make a date with her, and a well-dressed girl without a job spent her last dollar on a hair consultation. This buying of personal audiences is less necessary in an age in which architectural design makes it possible for anyone to look as if he had just emerged from a conference with a vice-president.

Business, by sharing the magnificence of its *mise en scène* with everyone, has undoubtedly increased the ambiguity as well as the opportunities of urban narcissism. In the new world of Radio Cities, the psychological penalties of being an actual "outsider" may be greater for the putative "insider" than they were in the old days when the guard came over and told him not to "loiter in the lobby." The day has not yet come when every large corporation building in an American city provides a traveler's aid, free movies, and a psychiatrist for every visitor; nor are vice-presidents yet detailed to lead the guided tour through the facilities. Until that day arrives, many of the public will not see that the skyscrapers, from being colossi, have become suppliants.

A Loop of Quiet

The city should speak to the muscles and to the ear as well as to the eye, and it is pleasant to imagine that the perfect city of the future could be found and identified by a blind man with an audiometer. Then, if he were able suddenly to see, he would open his eyes on a distribution of light and color perfectly suited to its purposes. What forms would he find? What massive communication and advertising and rhetoric would burst upon his vision? How would it look, and what would it say?

The city in the modern world that comes closest to being a materialization of the post-Impressionist and Cubist reordering of the world is Caracas, Venzuela. As a tribute to Picasso, Gris, and Léger, it is more than any school of painters ever was accorded before. Yet its most monumental expression of itself consists of two identical towers, in a dominating government office building, that straddle an underpass through which most of the traffic of the city still must flow. Whatever the history of this binary design, many viewers find the twin towers as unnerving as the legs of a giant without a trunk or head. For most of us, the essence of a monument is that it expresses itself once, not twice; that duplications of elements of design should not be reduced to the bare polarity of dual eminences that seem to rival each other in a mutual uneasiness. It is strange that a city in which the asymmetrical possibilities of modern architectural form, half prefabricated dimension and half sculpture (half North American and half European), should be surmounted by a symmetrical dualism that no modern painter would choose. Perhaps it speaks for the current duality of Venezuela, a nation balanced with a tremendous tension but balanced nevertheless between center and outlands, past and present, North America and South America, Europe and the New World.

We used to think that the single-mindedness of the American temper expressed itself well enough in the classically varied repetitions that make up the skyline where each corporate personality built one tower, and one alone, to add to the skyline. We hardly think so any more, now that we are less sure what the city as a whole advertises and now that the corporation moves some of its production functions from the industrial town to the suburb while at the same time it moves its overhead functions, to some degree, from the city to the suburb. What the city of the future will put forward as its massed visual message is not, we think, something that will be modeled exclusively on the present. Everything at the moment indicates that the physical surroundings of the city emphasize the escape from it more than the access to it and that very soon the pressure of industrial events will open up, near the center of cities and in the first loops surrounding them, open spaces that could not have been predicted before.

In Chicago, for example, the process is gradually leaving the Loop as a sort of free-standing hive in the center of a circular twilight zone. New uses of this zone tend to accentuate less intensive uses of the available area, both for population density and for building footage on sites. There is no doubt that open space will increase in this zone, but there is doubt about the uses than can be made of it. One thing is fairly certain: the blocks in this twilight area stand to be reorganized in the future in terms of units far greater than single-block size, as to both realty acquisition and development. It seems possible that this whole area or band may in the future become the "exposition" ground of Chicago as a merchant city, characterized by irregular large masses of development concentrating on exhibitors' showrooms, entertainment facilities, parks, and so on. The process is not an inevitable one, and it will be slow; but there is some indication that the maturity of the city as a physical object will come when this change makes itself felt as a pattern force.

It may be too optimistic to expect imaginative use of the emptied space near the city center. Possibly we shall see space that could have been monumental refilled piecemeal. Nevertheless, intelligent critics will continue to ask how urban life is related to urban appearance. Visitors to New York will continue to scorn the massive sordidness of its new East River apartments. Visitors to Chicago will continue to scorn the one-block façade along Lake Michigan, belied by what stands behind it. Frontality remains the poorest urban rhetoric in the world.

Imagination, not invention, is the supreme
master of art as of life.—Joseph Conrad

CHAPTER TWELVE

The Sirens' Song

Mechanical Manners

In the days when sport, art, and publicity were the long arms
of the theological and national policy of the Eastern Empire,
Justinian encouraged in Constantinople the growth of one cir-
cus faction at the expense of another; and on his frontier
against the Aryan Goths he erected at Ravenna the technicolor
mosaics that were the advance billing for the armies of Beli-
sarius. William Butler Yeats has celebrated the hieratic period
with a reference to a fabricated bird "set upon a golden bough
to sing / To lords and ladies of Byzantium," but he might have
found almost as good an icon in the charioteer bearing the
bets of Trinitarian partisans or in walls glinting with the tes-
serae of the Ravenna martyrs, fifth-column bishops, dollar
diplomats, and court ladies.

This period of summation and change, just before the Dark
Ages, reminds us that the rise of cities had created in classical
civilization some of the social forms we serve today. Rome gradually generalized the aristocratic play-force of the Greeks into
a coliseum mob, and Byzantium made the hippodrome political.

The development of free, skilled labor forces and machine production in places like Alexandria set up conditions for work and play which were to develop fully only later in the Italian free cities, especially Florence, where the urban rich fought and won a war of taste against the rural aristocracy. The escalation of whole social classes as groups in the ancient world helped to produce crises of production, leisure, and taste, the elements of which we recognize today. The conservative old oligarch in Athens could be heard arguing that imperial or counterimperial war was a condition of employment in the shipyards and a decent holiday for Athenians.

Although the classical world damned itself by a later phase in which it associated entertainment with martyrdom, it displayed a genius in forcing major questions upon us. The best discussion of activity and passivity in human personality may still be contained in Plato's *Phaedrus,* which, by raising the question of how one identifies with the active and passive in another, creates a test for all human relationships. In the same dialogue, the question is beautifully modulated into another question about the vicarious experience: What are some of the conditions by which another's experience comes to seem one's own? The dialogue answers this (as suggested in the discussion of Theuth and Thamus in chap. viii) by moving to consideration of the media and channels of communication. What is newly accepted by individuals and what is newly rejected when they move from one system (oral) to another (written)? This is a general statement of the specific problem of change in what is known, brought about by change in communication techniques and premises.

The life of the communication forms is such that changes in the form yield changes in the public-private equilibrium. For example, when alphabets appear, an old public passes and a new appears; and the individual, shocked by his objectification in a new system of signs and symbols, also reorganizes his orientation into something socially new.

Plato thinks of all this as having a bearing on manners, and (as argued throughout this book) shifts in the communication forms and in the public-private equilibrium are *always* felt to have an influence on manners. One modern formula is: "The more publicity, the less privacy." There seems to be some difficulty in defining the range of this question in relation to the media today. The media help to change the social scene by promoting both individual mobility and class escalations. Wars as well as transformations of etiquette are involved, and no one knows how much the media themselves are accountable for change. Between the changing notions of an etiquette or current sanctions of sociability and folkway or cultural pattern, there is an undefined area of social fact.

In this connection, for example, Henry James spoke of good wages as the only manners seen in his America, and this nice thrust entitles observers like himself to some consideration. With De Tocqueville, Gorer, and D. H. Lawrence, he shares a fascination with the ways in which American personality, folkway, and the media of publicity interact with each other. He repeatedly said that the American culture of his time was too derivative, too secondary, and most of all too young to have accumulated around the modes of social fact the overlay of repeated usage and multiple reference that comes with time. The multiplications of publicity were no sociopsychological substitute for the ivy-clad moment; quite the reverse.

Today, perhaps, he might weigh the judgment differently. The rapidity of social interchange induced by the mass media, extensive enough to make some believe that it induces a new conformity, may have helped to clothe the nakedness of the American social being. The repetitions of the mass media, especially the movie, have the effect of supplying an interim sense of density in the social scene. They enrich as well as stereotype the scenes and moments that Margaret Mead calls commonly symbolic. The media are a substitute for time, and, reversing the science-fiction teleporter that makes people young by changing their time-manifold, they make us all Rip Van Winkles, older than we are willing to admit. Where else do Europeans get their sense of age-in-youth and hardened precocity in American culture?

James had some notion of the possibility himself. Seeing a stiff and mawkish play in a Bowery theater in late 1905, with an audience much changed from that of his youth, he asked about the immigrants in the audience:

"Were they going to rise to it, or rather to fall to it, to *our* instinct, as distinguished from their own, for picturing life? Were they to take our lesson, submissively, in order to get with it our smarter traps and tricks, our superior Yankee machinery (illustrated in this case before them, for instance, by a wonderful folding bed in which the villain of the piece, pursuing the virtuous heroine round and round the room and trying to leap over it after her, is, at the young lady's touch of a hidden spring, engulfed as in the jaws of a crocodile)? Or would it be their dim intellectual resistance, a vague stir in them of some unwitting heritage—of the finer irony—that I should make out, on the contrary, as withstanding the effort to corrupt them, and thus perhaps really promising to react, over the head of our offered mechanic bribes, on our ingrained intellectual platitude?

"One had only to formulate that question to seem to see the issue hang there, for the excitement of the matter, quite as if the determination were to be taken on the spot. For the opposition over the chasm of the footlights, as I have called it, grew intense truly, as I took in on one side the hue of Galician cheek, the light of the Moldavian eye, the whole pervasive facial mystery, swaying, at the best, for the moment, over the gulf, on the vertiginous bridge of American confectionery— and took in on the other the perfect 'Yankee' quality of the challenge which stared back at them as in the white light of its hereditary thinness. . . ."

To raise that question, in the manner that James employs,

is to suggest, not only that the entertainment and media worlds can be enriched by new audience sensibilities, but also that new audiences and new media products together might hasten the accumulation of meanings in the whole social scene. In this passage, he seems almost to predict what happened when the movie appeared: a new medium, employed largely by new immigrants, changed not only the theater conventions but society itself. The movies socialized the immigrant; and the immigrant used the movies to enlarge the range of theatrical styles within the range of public acceptance. The total effect, even allowing for the stereotypy and mendacity of many movies, was to provide a new language of social intercourse in the democracy.

More Americans are familiar now than ever with a somewhat different approach to the social nakedness of Americans. A central theme of D. H. Lawrence's *Studies in Classic American Literature* is that Americans, lacking the restraints and sanctions provided by the older class societies of Europe, had to substitute for culturally predictable expectations of each other what Lawrence calls "blood knowledge." He partly blames but mostly praises us for our individualistic mystique, for our virtually sectarian pietism about a "contact with the other fellow." Could his "blood knowledge" be translated, not unfairly, into the more bloodless terminology of social psychology and be called "empathy"? Or was his point more likely a recognition that uncrystallized American manners themselves provided a justification for the non-empathic violence he appears to have valued? Either way, we find him portraying the American personality as an unprotected entity open to the pains as well as the gains of its democratic estate in history.

A related viewpoint is expressed by the British-born anthropologist Gregory Bateson, who speaks of a pressure in the United States toward the collectivization of the intimate and the private. We can attribute some of this collectivity to our uses of the mass media. Thus Bateson, Lawrence, and others force us to ask what is lost in terms of precious individual differences and mysteries when the mass media assist in providing coherence in the image of our society. The need for solidarity and the need for differentiation compete with each other, and the struggle is such that it involves far wider issues than those arising in the sphere of the mass media alone. Harold Nicolson, in his recent *Good Behavior*, hints tolerantly, if not condescendingly, that the industrial ethos of the United States will raise a new etiquette hero to be set beside the virtuous man of the Greeks, the British gentleman, and the *honnête homme* of the French. Nicolson says little about this emergent figure, but we may surmise that the new hero will look on his fellow men as beings in need of psychological support—every man his brother's analyst.

An exaggeration of this type, the man who thinks that he and other people need all the approval and glamor that publicity can give, irritates Louis Kronenberger in *Company Manners*, his recent study of American life. It is instructive to compare the hopes and fears of Kronenberger and Nicolson, the former deploring the destruction of old manners by Café Society, the latter assuming that the American system of manners is a triumph of informality.

Nicolson tends to overidentify etiquette with protocol, leaving us a bit confused about the social forms that are associated with power and the social forms that are associated with egalitarian contacts or genuine informalities. Surely, although most of what a Ponsonby can say about modern royal courts or cannibal entourages applies equally to the bridge club, it does not all apply. Again, Louis Kronenberger, who senses the danger of publicity, seems to assume too readily that the erosion of old manners is not replaced by the coral-like intrusions of the new. Thus, Nicolson's good word for American manners, modified by egalitarianism, industrialism, and the mass media, leaves us a little uncertain as to its drift; and Kronenberger's doubts about the tact of the new social and publicity leaders leave us too gloomy. Perhaps a perfect set of manners for an industrial and mass-mediated society would be, in the long run, nothing more or less than a flexible industrial folkway.

Ideals of personality enshrined in manners can, of course, be slanted toward preserving stratifications or encouraging mobility. The newer mass media sometimes seem to be working out definitions of mobility while at the same time denying the very existence of the higher levels to which one might move. Conversely, all judgments of the influence of the mass media on ideals of personal worth are in themselves based on notions of what our social structure is. Leslie Fiedler surely hits closer to the mark than anyone else when he notices that middlebrows are hardest on the mass culture because "they see, in the persistence of a high art and a low art on either side of their average own, symptoms of the re-emergence of classes in a quarter where no one troubled to stand guard." He refers to self-consciously "democratic" middle-class groups who cannot afford to recognize the existence of stratification because they believe that it *should* not exist.

Publicity and Privacy

Our world has long committed itself to the care of the general will of the people, and idealization of "consensus" has revolutionized relations between the public and the private spheres. In some senses, democracy has eroded the private. During the very decades of the nineteenth century in which the cult of individualism was developing, the interest of the national state lay in winning as completely as possible the emotional loyalties of all its members. Especially since the turn of the century, mass information, mass entertainment, and mass leisure have played an important part in this process. The mass media do as much as anything else to make the democratic experience a personal dilemma. In our world social solitude is both involuntary and suspect; yet the sense of belonging, when it occurs, is often tinged by a sense of counterfeit.

This is one of the prices we pay for the social consents engineered in part by the mass media as engines of social control. We are repaid in part by their real effectiveness as emotional policemen. The assertiveness of the "good" cowboy on TV today is in part a twentieth-century substitute for the sixteenth-century laws that hung a ten-year-old child for stealing a shilling.

We know that democracy would not have developed mass-media social controls and gratifications if the decline of the Old Regime had not been followed by the development of modern technology. Technological influences are felt intensely in the industries supplying new forms of communication and transportation; they are felt quite as directly in all the ways that a densified and high-tempo society forms new audiences in new ways. To speak of new audiences is to speak of new relations between what is public and what is private. Some think that no other culture in the world has gone as far as ours in employing the mass media to exact a consensus from the fantasy of the many; on the other hand, no one is certain that it is an "exaction." Few people in the world seem as happy as some Americans to give up privacy in order to convert themselves into exhibits of this or that in the publicity system.

Rather than ask whether the mass media are social manipulators of a sort, which we already know, we might ask whether we can afford to have them create an audience of so many people who have lost the sense of privacy. A new porosity of social character, emphasizing the folkways of consumption and the consumption of other people's personalities, appears on the scene. It disconcerts older American types accustomed to organizing their lives in terms of work and work-minded principles. The characteristic anxieties of the newer type lie in trying to control the leisure sphere of life, with its less visible and less tangible values as compared to the sphere of industrial work.

Romanticism gave us the idea that the folk might be an

unconscious genius in art; and this idea became important to Americans in the twentieth century. Europeans, criticizing American imitations of European forms and styles, asked Americans to revise their ambitions for a national culture and look at their folkish forms. Thus at the same time that reformers were scrutinizing the condition of the poor workingman in a land of riches, observers began to take note of popular art forms. As early as 1917 Gilbert Seldes began to make notes for his *Seven Lively Arts,* the pioneer study rightly taken to be the most influential statement of a sympathetic case for the popular arts in the United States in this century. By the mid-1920's the vanishing of the rural heritage inspired Henry Ford to invent what has become an industry—the preservation of the agrarian folk culture. Through this search for a usable past and an artistic present, the movie, jazz, and the American advertisement were entered in the annals of art history.

To many an appreciative observer of the mass media, especially such great and sympathetic reporters as Otis Ferguson and James Agee, the mass media appealed with their very superiority, in both the artistic and the moral sense, to much that once passed as genteel. The vaudeville and the movie and the sports arena of the twentieth century seem preferable to the favorite fiction and pastimes, the sentimental and prurient vaporings, of dominant middle-class culture in the nineteenth century. We might ask whether the miasma of American intellectual life in the nineteenth century, with its softening religion and hardening industrialism, would ever have been cleaned up without the emotional honesty, aesthetic dexterity, and plain clear-headed tolerance that grew up around the metropolitan city desk, the cartoonist's drawing board, and the movie lot. Far from thinking of the popular culture as degraded "class" art or refabricated "naïve" art, we might think of it mainly as a sophisticated transcendence of much that was naïve in our earlier cultural phases. The fine works of scholars like Matthiessen, Parrington, Mumford, and others makes us forget sometimes that a little Concord brightness in the nine-teenth century did not save the country from intellectual mal-feasance from 1870 to 1917. The 1920's, great blooming period of the popular arts in the United States, are certainly the great-est decade in our cultural history, notwithstanding recent at-tempts of post-Marxist and proto-Conservative pygmies to run it down. The Brown, Mauve, and Pea-green decades of the period 1870–1917 had to be ended by a cultural lynching party, it appears, and the trial was summarily conducted by Judge Nickelodeon.

It is possible to believe that the popular culture of the mass media replaces an elite culture that was better, that it stereo-types the imagination, and that it encourages a lazy middle class to forget its options and its responsibilities. Perhaps so. The conclusions of this book do not confirm these views. They do not confirm André Malraux's notion that the mass culture is a dangerous departure from the "universals" that upheld class culture in the Old World. They do not confirm Dwight MacDonald's irritation at "kitsch," nor do they confirm Denis Brogan's sometimes complacent defense of the present on the ground that it is no better or worse than the eighteenth cen-tury. They do not confirm George Orwell's surmise that mass cultural forms tend to transfer downward the vices of an aris-tocratic order but not its virtues. Something in all these charges is true; the task here has not been such prosecution.

Our culture does employ the media to encourage people to think of themselves as "machine-fodder" in the sense that it has become fashionable for people to justify their work or their consumption on the ground that "it keeps the machines going and others in jobs." Our culture does employ the media to aggressively segmentalize the audience, telling one group one thing and another group another. Our culture does permit the mass media to be "fair-traded" into a position of monop-oly in artistic pursuits and styles, as the movie industry well shows; it does permit intellectual tariffs in the media to oper-

ate. It does encourage the media to create in the mind of the
individual an Actuarial as contrasted with an Authentic self.
It does permit the media to swamp and destroy some aspects
of artistic, persuasive, and documentary form by exhibits of
conspicuous strain, expenditure, and redundance of human effort. Yet, as this book has shown, there are prominent counter-
vailing powers at work.

For the audiences developing today, a sense of media forms
and leisure forms is as important as a sense of content. The
forms must be studied from a variety of viewpoints cumula-
tively leading to a grasp of form as a cultural definition shared
(or not shared) with the audience. Members of the audience
must strive to reach a balance between the active and the passive, between participation and reception. Many accepted
definitions of "active" and "passive" today are not merely out
of date but are being recognized as such by members of the
audience.

A century ago we were accustomed to associate the concept
of activity with the external, the physical, the efficient, and
therefore with the processes of work and production. Our cultural history now forces us to learn that consumption demands
as much energy as does production. How, then, can this more
receptive process, as it is ordinarily defined, be a truly active
one? The Genteel Tradition solved the problem by requiring
the enjoyment of leisure to be as morally strenuous as work.
But art frustrates the type of social character and sensibility
that can never relax the will, never temporarily suspend the
ethical drive. The skills of relaxation and suspension are de-
layed in their development by our inherited American distrust
of any fictional experience that does not point to an unambiguous moral code of action. Otherwise, we think, the fictional
experience is too passive. This is the old problem—evaluation
of "make-believe" as contrasted to some assertedly "real" core
of experience which it "should" duplicate.

In general, custom and inertia seem to weigh heavily on our

new mass-communication industries. The media managers sometimes say that they use up fantasy faster than they can get the stuff. Yet they realize that in a densifying society their supply of fantasy is governor and buffer of the state and its parts. It seems unlikely that the literalism to be found in the media and leisure in the last two decades will be with us always. The skills of the audience are more evident than the lack of skills; and we do not have a truly complacent public.

It has been a pleasant risk to try to assign meanings to the plural myth of the popular culture of the moment. To suggest what the future holds, other than a decline of the naïvely realistic, would be difficult. It is easier to show what astonished the muses yesterday than to say what song the sirens will sing tomorrow.

Afterword
BY THE AUTHOR

My work with David Riesman on *The Lonely Crowd* in the late 1940's brought wholly new perspectives to my old interest in popular art-forms and I found myself writing new articles and making new notes on these matters. In the mid-50's Alexander Morin of the University of Chicago Press suggested to me that I should write a book dealing with popular culture, reverting to themes that I had broached in these articles and notes. With the considerable help of Robert Erwin, an editor of the Press, this suggestion, supported by time and some typing funds from the Ford Foundation, through the Center for the Study of Leisure of the University of Chicago, became *The Astonished Muse.*

One of my reviewers said that the book argues two main propositions. First, that the productions of popular culture including, for example, TV programs, but also including sports and popular fiction, cannot be discussed simply by reference to their producers, messages and audiences; they deserve also to be discussed in terms of the artistic or conventional forms

255

that make it possible or even probable that they will have this or that effect upon their audiences. Second, that almost every aspect of American popular culture suffers from attachment to a particular form or style, that is, a prevailing literalism. This is as clear an account of the book as I have come across. I myself would add that the book also tries to investigate themes of activity and passivity in the consumption of objects of leisure enjoyment ranging from fiction to the graphic and plastic arts.

The book as I re-read it reflects my still continued uneasiness at how frequently the sociological analyst of popular stuff, with an interest in audience effects and uses, ignores the forms in which that stuff presents itself and how much the humanistic analyst, with an eye to more approved literature, not only neglects to try out his theory of form on a wider range of popular stuff but also shies away from anything but a certain lip-service to the concept of the audience. It was first of all with the idea of balancing off the "content-analysis" bias of the sociologist with a "formal analysis" bias of my own that I tried to analyze what I loosely called the "forms" of science fiction, some TV programs, the hot-rod hobby, the football game and the city skyline. Toward the end of writing on the book, I realized that I was not only thanking the humanists for their suggestions about the constitution of artistic forms but also rebuking them for their disregard of concepts of the audience.

My own interest in audiences was of a partly historical turn of mind. When Thorstein Veblen published *The Theory of the Leisure Class* in 1899, he suggested political and psychological explanations for the appearance and employment of the new great post-bellum surplus in American life. The surplus could be used up, he suggested, in the conspicuous consumption of the exploiters who battened on the submissive habits of the exploited. Yet this conspicuous consumption habit, he suggested, was universal: under certain conditions it was

taken up, as in boom-time demands for silk shirts and vaudeville, by the exploited themselves. The interpretation of consumers and audiences offered by Veblen was ahead of its
time, and it had not been documented by detailed study of
the American market for consumer luxuries. Such a look at
how the American surplus created a huge market for public
entertainment began only when "Sime" Silverman, not long
after Veblen's book, started *Variety*. From that time on,
Veblen's systematic interpretation of American uses of the
surplus was matched by Silverman's colorful analysis of the
trades that waxed fat on the new demand for mass
entertainment.

Soon followed that period in American life when the presence of millions who possessed increasing purchasing power
but still had to learn English gave encouragement to those
media, such as the movie and the multicolored advertisement,
that emphasized non-verbal appeals. By the 1920's and the
1930's, following the suggestions made by Veblen, William
James, Walter Lippmann, and not a few Europeans who advised Americans to look as closely at their industrial "folk
culture" as at their budding high culture, Americans such as
Gilbert Seldes were ready to assess the new leisure forms
promoted by modern technology. Some argued that the unconscious genius of the folk had generated a vernacular which
would become classic; and theatrical dance styles did, later, in-
filtrate American ballet. A few argued that the new age of visual
and oral appeals in communication had returned us unexpectedly to earlier lyrical and epical ages of oral creation and
transmission.

Some of the Americans who tackled these questions from
World War I on were influenced by their increasing acquaintance with the generalizations of the cultural sciences: Freud's
suggestion that popular symbols are sources of identification;
Durkheim's suggestion that they are representations reinforcing the individual's anchorage in a group; and Redfield's sug-

gestion, drawn in part from Tönnies, that we would understand these things better if we saw them as existing on a continuum that displays at one end the older folk society and at another end the new urban society. The trail-breaking explorations of Lloyd Warner and his associates, especially William Henry, not only expanded my own sense of Durkheim's method but made me see American "collective representations" in a new way. Some of the most interesting critical works in this tradition, I suppose, are those in which the writer limits himself to one art form or social activity and tells us about it in a masterly way—an example is James Agee's piece on the "Golden Age" of American film comedy.

Because I myself was interested in whether I might hear related even though different sounds if I struck the notes of popular culture at widely different points on our keyboard of entertainment and consumption, I felt obliged to stretch my own scope and sample to the breaking point. To do what I wanted to do it seemed necessary to write sometimes as literary critic, sometimes as social historian, sometimes as social psychologist, and sometimes as art historian and architectural historian. I was much relieved to find that I was chaffed by a few for my overambitious pains. It was this that assured me I had really taken the risks that I had intended to take. On the other hand, my readers were not at all captious with respect to my treatment of two matters that bothered me some during the composition of the book. First, by looking for similar tendencies in different arts, was I in danger of assuming automatically, against so much evidence from history, that Art *A* and Art *B* must share characteristics with each other just because they are contemporaneous? Second, by taking an interest in situations in which one art form moves in the direction of doing the work traditionally associated with another art form (the cartoon's attempt at narration, for example), was I in danger of plunging into that confusion of the arts that Lessing criticized in *Laökoon* and that Pater fell victim to in the essay on "The School of Giorgione"?

The reader may notice that I rest heavily on certain notions that once might have been controversial but with which most educated people of today are familiar. The main one is that whereas a large number of individuals "do" art and expression, the possibility is that many of the works likely to survive from our time are works that are centrally and commercially-produced by groups or even mass-produced by groups. The generalization that fine design and workmanship are inheritances from individual and rural craftsmen and are destroyed by the cosmopolitan centers of mass production is still much overworked. In our own time it is easy to see all around us the provincial degeneration of urban classical American forms. To illustrate: many of the new suburban "community" newspapers which grew up after World War II from hand-out advertising sheets are parodies of journalism partly because of the very smallness and localism of which they claim to be proud.

We find the same thing in writing. In the 1950's the métier of prefabricating avant-garde literature moved into its post-World War II phase under the leadership of personalities such as Henry Miller. Since then, non-political revolt in a self-consciously "alienated literature" has become a virtual industry. Yet we do not have to look far in popular American fiction of the earlier twentieth century to find work conscientiously written for a market that makes some avant-garde writing look juvenile. In the 1920's a great variety of American writers were experimenting with vernacular styles, for the enjoyment of a public that had been trained to enjoy such writing by the newspaper and magazine writers after Mark Twain. The experiment yielded one best-seller which is also one of the best short works of farcical fiction written in the twentieth century, Anita Loos' *Gentlemen Prefer Blondes*. Original as Miss Loos' achievement was, I think it owed something to the current of popular vernacular journalism and fiction that preceded and accompanied it. How much better it still reads than much that claims attention as "anti-commercial" today.

Since writing the book I have struggled to verbalize more simply and clearly some of the general ideas that were in my mind, or were developing in my mind, as I worked upon it and I can now state some of these ideas in a more usefully positive and even polemic form than I could before. These ideas or prejudices all relate to the criticism of the arts and leisure in our time. The first is that concepts of the audience still need lively reexamination; the second that our concepts of artistic types need reconstruction; the third that "popularization" requires more fruitful definition and analysis; fourth that some of the familiar attacks on "impressionistic" criticism are unhistorical and fallacious; and fifth is that "symbolic" methods of analysis of the art work are clarified rather than endangered by their extension to popular art. The arguments that I now present for these five propositions lead into a sixth, over-arching proposition about the critical crisis of the 1960's, which I shall present toward the close of these remarks. First, then, the question of the audience.

Whereas the nineteenth century emphasized the artist and twentieth century criticism emphasizes the art work, both have pursued these emphases at the expense of a third variable, the audience. A good deal of American literary criticism since Irving Babbitt, for example, seems to be clouded by its assumption that serious consideration given to the concept of the audience is the same thing as sacrificing art in general to the demands of the audiences. Correction of this view comes from Queenie Leavis, Gilbert Seldes, Georg Lukács, F. R. Leavis, Raymond Williams, Kenneth Burke, Leo Lowenthal, Ian Watt, Richard Altick, Marshall McLuhan, Richard Hoggart, and Lennox Grey, but makes its way slowly. (Recent progress in the correction can be marked perhaps by the appearance of Wayne Booth's *The Rhetoric of Fiction*. This study does not by its nature obligate itself to provide any empirical study of audiences. Yet in the course of an examination of how a writer of fiction establishes "viewpoint," it at least begins to bring back to the study of artistic effects some of that respect toward the audience which, in spite of lip-service, has been lacking in much modern commentary and criticism.)

If my more learned readers should suspect that my attention to audiences betrays a sympathy for certain "rhetorical" approaches to art to be found in such Renaissance writers as Castelvetro and Piccolomini they will not be entirely wrong. The work of Bernard Weinberg *(A History of Literary Criticism in the Italian Renaissance)* seems to warrant the conclusion that even when such writers misinterpreted the *Poetics* of Aristotle and Horace's *Ars Poetica*—and even when they drew conclusions about the nature of art with which I myself would not agree—they raised new questions about the conceptualization of the audience that deserve continued attention today. I must add here my suspicion that one of the reasons for the indifference to audience-studies in some American humanists is that since they control a captive audience of graduate students they find it unnecessary to occupy themselves about the asperities of artists in search of audiences and audiences in search of artists.

Second, I feel more strongly than before that our thinking about the identification and classification of different types of art is muffled or clumsy in recent criticism. In literary criticism, Wellek and Warren *(The Theory of Literature)*, reviewing Brunetière's pseudo-biological treatment of artistic types (epic, tragedy, comedy, pastoral, satire, etc.) as analogues of natural species, reject this idea, but offer little in its place. What can be offered in its place is a concept of artistic types as comprising a culturally-defined division of labor—a division of labor dependent in part upon the *medium* in which the *artistic type* is embodied and the *channel* through which it moves to its audiences. If this be granted, then the most helpful suggestions toward a modern theory of artistic types seem to me to come from Leonard Doob,* Giorgio Braga,† and Joshua Whatmough.**

Doob's contribution permits us to see distinctions separating the basic media (speaking, for example), the extending media (writing, for example), and the media that are both extending and duplicating, or mass-media (print, for example). The use of such distinctions would naturally be very helpful in sketching the natural history of an artistic type, such as the pastoral, that seems to begin its existence in the oral or basic media tradition and then continues that existence, subject to alteration, in the channel of print; or in pursuing the transformations that occur when a work produced in one mass-medium (such as *Tom Jones*, in print) is re-produced in another (*Tom Jones* in film). To put it more generally, the classification of the channels through which works move is one major concern of a scheme of classification of artistic types.

Giorgio Braga's contribution consists of a distinction between the structural and the cultural aspects of a communication channel. He reminds us that it is possible for a communication to move successfully through a structural channel such as the air-wave and yet fail to be received at the end of that channel because the audience is culturally unprepared for the message. Such an event occurs when a popular song in English broadcast from Chicago accidentally homes in on the receiving set of a Japanese farmer who knows no English. It also occurs, in a subtler way, when a student who is not acquainted with the artistic convention of irony misreads a passage of satirical irony in Swift. Confusions—and of course, transmutations—of artistic type occur whenever the structural and the cultural aspects of a channel are "out of phase" with each other. Issues

---

Communication in Africa, New Haven and London, Yale University Press, 1960.

†"Toward a General Theory of Communication," *PROD*, Volume III, No. 9, May 1960.

**Poetic, Scientific and Other Forms of Discourse; A New Approach to Greek and Latin Literature*, Berkeley, University of California Press, 1956.

such as these seem to me to be called to mind by the possibility that the response of some present-day high-school students to the literary form of the traditional ballad may have been un-expectedly stimulated and enriched by the popularity of the folk singer on the air and on the disc. The examination of Braga's variables is another necessary concern of a theory of artistic types.

Whatmough's contribution would take too much time to discuss in the detail it deserves, but it consists essentially in the suggestion that the statistical study of style has by now probably become a precondition of classification in literature. Whatmough's approach seems especially valuable to me be-cause at a general level it defines the humanistic approach to learning as including respect for scientific methods of analysis and because at a more specific level it sees the study of litera-ture in the context of its media and its audiences. "However, anomalous it may seem," says Whatmough, "it is nevertheless true that this improved insight into the nature of literary form and appreciation should have been given so vividly by com-munication engineers, not by literary critics. . . ."

Investigations along the line of the three perspectives men-tioned here are scarcely to be found in the treatment of liter-ary types by literary critics even though something like them can be found at work, in highly intuitive fashion, in studies such as Ian Watt's remarkable *The Rise of the Novel*. Watt seems to me to prove conclusively that efforts to deal with such mat-ters as "viewpoint," "rendering," and "distance" in literary types classified as narrative fiction will falter until they follow Watt in studying the part played in such developments by the changes in the structure of communications since the mid-six-teenth century. I am suggesting, in sum, that the perspectives provided by Doob, Braga, and Whatmough can be helpful in dealing with a modern world of communication in which extremely varied and unanticipated adaptations of a work from one medium to another have been the order of the day.

Third, looking back at my own book has of course made me reconsider the whole question of the responsible relation of the fairly literate person to the mass-culture productions of his own time. Part of my present analysis of this runs along a line that resembles and may owe something to a remarkable 1956 essay by Harmon Grisewood, former director of the spoken word on BBC, in "The New Arts of the 20th Century."° Grisewood lists four characteristics that he finds prominent in the new media: anonymity, visual appeal, ephemerality, and a diffusionary impulse. He has much to say on all these points, but to me he is exceptionally interesting on the last, especially when he sees both the mass-media of today and the mosaics and portable icons of Byzantium as "diffusionary" or "distributive" inventions. This observation reminds us that we might go further than we now do in recognizing that any new channel or medium involves at least two distinct though overlapping purposes. One is the distributive purpose that Grisewood sees as being so prominent in the modern media. The other is the desire to standardize, prior to any distribution, a canonical text—this was a great historic motive for the adoption of the printed page as contrasted with the manuscript page, since the former is less prone to *variorum*.

The two distinct emphases of textual reliability and efficient distribution are not equally present in all traditions of literacy, the former being the major concern of the scholar, the latter being the major concern of the publisher and popularizer. Scholars, who concentrate on the recording-transmitting process and take older media for granted, are concerned chiefly with the preservation of the "text," in its older and more pristine medium; they are also concerned with those types of classification, analysis, interpretation, and evaluation which were developed around the text when it existed within that earlier "con-text." On the other hand, those who focus on the

---

°In *The New Outline of Modern Knowledge*, Alan Pryce-Jones, ed., New York, Simon and Schuster, 1956.

diffusion-process take the recording for granted as a means toward an end, taking the smallest allowable degree of interest in the methods by which the text has acquired canonical form.

The distinction that I have borrowed from Grisewood helps us to notice that the work of the diffusers proceeds only a little way before beginning to have its effect on what is considered to be canonical. For example: it is a good guess that the rise of audio-reproduction will tend to bring into balance again certain attitudes toward poetry that may have gone out of balance in the last hundred years. Emphasis on the printed text has induced a criticism of poetry that often obscures the object of the study because it assumes the primacy of the sight rather than the sound of the poem. Audio-recordings of poems, to be listened to, may create a context in which we have to take more seriously once again, and not in a Romantic sense, Coleridge's remark that "Poetry gives most pleasure when only generally and not perfectly understood."

Fourth, general reaction against so-called "Impressionistic" criticism led by Irving Babbitt and others has been much overdone and has become standardized in our own lifetime. Yet the prime criticism of a new form, at the time when it is appearing, is by definition impressionistic, and it is this impressionistic criticism that forms a base for all other kinds of criticism that follow later. While literary and art scholars and critics were mounting their attack on impressionistic modes of criticism between 1910 and 1940, the best criticism of the mass-media was being undertaken, as it had to be, in impressionistic terms. Think, for example, of the work of Otis Fergusson and James Agee. That such criticism can be as good as anything that follows is suggested by the fact that Hazlitt's impressionistic criticism of the Romantics is as good as anything that follows and far more convincing than most of it. The connected point is that journalistic criticism will always be superior in certain senses to academic criticism. As in Baudelaire's commentary on Constantin Guys, it is engaged in "discovering" its subject, whereas academic criticism is largely engaged in producing shades of judgment on objects already located by others and defined in advance as culturally relevant. Some of us now are beginning to see that the thirty-year American shift from energy represented in journalistic, applied, and impressionistic criticism to energy represented in academic and formal criticism has entailed some great losses (as well, needless to say, as some welcome gains) in American critical thought.

Fifth, it seems to me that criticism always reaches a standstill when it develops a vocabulary and method so neatly fitted to its object that you cannot separate the object from the method. As my teacher Larry Leighton used to say, the expositors are then taken for the artists and the exposition for the art. Modern symbolic and thematic analysis of art might be taken as an example. Some critical rejoinders to my own symbolic analysis of comic-strips seemed to make the objection that this mode of analysis is a serious matter that should be reserved for the most serious subjects. For if it can be applied to art works at all the various levels of quality, then how can it contribute to tests for that quality? But this is one of my main points. The capacity of a method as contributing to critical tests is itself tested by carrying out a variety of applications, not by *not* carrying them out. If it should be shown that some of the mythical features of a comic-strip are frivolous this raises the question whether the mythical features of, say, Pound may also be frivolous.

The five points I have presented make me think that the study of popular culture can make some few contributions to revitalization of the study of the art and the literature of the past, by shaking up and sharpening the "sense of relevance" in the practitioner of the discipline of arts and letters. The feeling of crisis being experienced by the more sensitive of those practitioners is perceptively summarized by Seymour Betsky in "Literature and General Culture": [*]

> We sense, without quite being able yet to demonstrate, that the discipline of letters, which means intellectual and emotional life and death to those of us who support them in profession or as vocation, is becoming so marginalized in our national life, or is now so tainted, that our very sense of having a function in communal or national life may be seriously questioned. We have the feeling that nobody cares whether the world of letters, as it answers to our demand for standards, lives or dies. We appear to have reached a point where there is only vestigial respect— a kind of cultural itch surviving from certain habits now in process of dying. In direct and in subtle ways this sense affects our personal lives and our commitments to scholarship, criticism and teaching.

A main reason for this state of affairs is of course the enormous growth of techniques for enabling people who have nothing to say, or lies to say, to command the ear of what used to be called, in more optimistic days, "the public." Congress in its wisdom encourages all this by two policies: one, making sure that all sorts of trivialities are supported by mail subsidy and by allocation of air channels; two, by silently sanctioning Post Office interference with the free flow of ideas into the United States by periodicals. This is reinforced by the prevailing "scientism" which perverts public educational grants policies in the direction of mechanical (and human) defense hardware. One protective response prescribed by Betsky for the humanist is that he should try, against the odds of specialization and status, to re-think the relations between literary art and "general culture." Betsky is impressed, as I am, by the contributions made to such a study not only by *Culture and Environment* (Leavis and Thompson), written in Britain thirty years ago, but also by more recent British attempts, notably those of Richard Hoggart (*The Uses of Literacy*), to carry out similar reorientations. I agree with Betsky's suggestion that we have much to learn from such explorations. However, it seems

---

[*]*Universities Quarterly,* Feb./April 1960.

to me that the study of "general and popular culture" displays
national strengths and national weaknesses on both sides of
the Atlantic.

Taking the admirable *The Uses of Literacy* as an example,
its great strength lies in its easygoing sense of the connection
between the power strata of social politics and the everyday
styles of life and leisure. It is much clearer, less labored, and
more down-to-earth than what Americans generally do with
such topics. On the other hand, British attempts to tackle broad
ranges of popular culture, even in George Orwell, seem to me
to have at least two noticeable failings. One, found in Hoggart's book, is a kind of sentimental overstatement of the
coziness and "belongingness" of the older working class life
and culture. The other is what I can only call a trained inatten-
tion to cultural clusters unfamiliar to the upper middle-class
and university set. For example, despite the educated Briton's
interest in regional planning he averts his gaze and curiosity
from the auto-and-freeway sub-culture that is developing in
Britain as a consequence of unexpectedly widespread car ownership. Again, some sort of unconscious repression of the critical faculties, perhaps based on class habits, must lie back of
British inability to come to terms with the popular culture of
its graphic and design arts. British university graduates still
chuckle at the "Pop" and postcard art of the sentimental taste
without apparently having noticed that such art has at least
some representatives in the Tate, in British pre-Raphaelite
painting.

If I am right in the points I have made so far, the study of
popular culture can restate old critical problems in a new and
revivifying way—but this leaves still unanswered the question
of how this might have practical effects on standards of judgment and taste. One answer is that such studies might ultimately come to have these effects in the most direct manner
of all—by helping to alter the prevailing *canon*, or list of works

of the past that occupy preferential ranking. One example will indicate what I mean. I think that most of my readers would agree that although Chaucer is widely taught, studied and read in the United States, his name rarely turns up in serious critical discussions. One reason for this may be that he has been weighed down by the gloss-makers who read him only too closely; another may be that he is inaccessible to many American college students who read him, in Middle English, only too incompetently. Still others may be that the rich and saucy confidence of Chaucer is alien to our age or that his particular sense of the comic has become inaccessible to us. Over and beyond this one cannot help feeling the negative force of Eliot, who leaves Chaucer almost entirely outside of his sense of our literary past.

One of the consequences of this silent but effective flanking of a reputation by Eliot is that Chaucer is mainly regarded as meat for the chalky textualist, or the "backgrounds" man, or the symbolic analyzer, but rarely as someone to read as a great artist. Strangely enough, on the other hand, the name of Dante turns up everywhere in the critical discussion; and American undergraduates bow their heads responsively at his name. In itself this is a good thing, especially since John Ciardi's use of plain-spoken American English rescued Dante from the Victorian manner in which he was previously translated and butchered. However, quite apart from whether Dante is as great an artist as Chaucer, he is not accessible to the American student, even in Ciardi's translation, for the reason that he can only be appreciated by at least some application to his Italian text. The net result, it seems to me, is an extraordinary inflation of the accessibility and relevance of the author of *The Divine Comedy* and a curious devaluation of the relevance and accessibility of the author of the *Canterbury Tales*.

This situation has been tolerated by the community of criticism in the United States for many years now, with little sign of effort to redress it. But the harbingers of correction may now be appearing in the popular culture. Folk song and ballad on discs seem to have reactivated the American student's interest in earlier English literary forms and their language. Chaucer himself has become available on the disc not only in modernized English but in Middle English. Difficult as his language may be for some young people it is at least more accessible than Tuscan. The time may come, not long from now, when the audio accessibility of Chaucer will help his reputation back to the heights where it belongs. My guess is that the climb might be speeded if readers keep early Walt Disney in mind when they read *The Parlement of Foules* and H. L. Mencken in mind when they read the *Canterbury Tales*. Indeed, now that our land is full of fat priests and well-financed churches, many of them "100 per cent American" and some of them racist, it seems as desirable to ask why Chaucer's satire of churchmen is not more generally enjoyed as it is to ask why men of the cloth are almost always such good guys in movies and on TV. Chaucer's re-ascent deserves to be assisted by a general review of the canon. It seems to me unlikely that the reconstruction of the canon—which is the ever-crucial task of criticism—will ever occur without the presence of energies released by re-thinking some of the problems in the light of the changing forms of our popular culture.

My greatest satisfaction in the risks taken by the book is that some of the themes I touched upon have been taken up again here and there by young critics, always in an entirely original way. One of my other gratifications is that certain of the arguments in the book seem to have been borne out by recent events. For a small example, the argument in the chapter on science and fantasy fiction seems to be born out by the experience of translating William Golding's *Lord of the Flies* into film. The Greek power of the novel, they say seems to have been lost when a camera was turned upon it. As for the sports chapter, it stands up today as well as any in the book and may be said to have gained a bit of relevance from developments in spectatorial sports since the 1957 publication of the book. Even though the bigger, better, harder-paced game of the professionals is exerting competitive economic force against university football, the latter continues to vitiate American educational policies, constituting a central factor in that degeneration of sports by mechanization and the market that John Tunis discusses so brilliantly in *The American Way in Sport*. Two by-effects of college football are especially morbid. One is that many a big-time college football player is pre-defined as a simple member of the jock-strap set whether he happens by intellectual character to be so or not. The other is that many an able young Negro who deserves his chance at college by some more everyday route is often made to feel that he can only attain it if he sacrifices himself to big-time collegiate football. I should add here that Robert Boyle, in his fine new *Sport, Mirror of American Life*, has much of value to say on race and racism in American sports.

I might add that since making my first notes on some TV programming back in the late 1940's I've become somewhat less interested in viewing and more interested in the political charades of the broadcasting industry. It was dispiriting to watch the struggles being conducted for a better broadcasting policy by Newton Minow in the face of a massive disinterest and lack of knowledge about his work by the mass of TV audiences. Only less so was the continuation by the Kennedy administration of the policies of previous administrations of failing to appoint to the FCC anyone with any accomplishments in artistic fields. Because of further reflection on policy problems in our radio and TV world, I have lately become more concerned with a question that I did not think it appropriate to deal with in the book: the question of public support for the various arts. Would it be a good idea to get further into such support than now exists? The positions have

been stated with some firmness on several sides of the issue
and many artists and critics in the U. S. seem to be hesitant
about big plans for such assistance. Their hesitancy seems
reasonable in view of the somewhat increased support they
have received recently from the free market and from the
foundations. Yet while we have something to fear we have a
great deal to gain, as August Heckscher says, from extended
public support for all the arts. To take any other position
seems to me to deny that American taste is being formed every
day by national, state, and local communications and fiscal
policies that have a massive effect on everything ranging from
the appearance of a through-way to the design of a car.

I want to mention briefly that I have always been sorry, as
an amateur iconographer, that my book did not contain one
whole chapter entitled "Beasts of the Machine," which would
have tried to sketch the directions to be taken in a study of
the symbolism of animals in advertising and trade-mark art.
The general idea of the chapter was to begin from the literature on heraldry, to follow this into the guild-crest and trade-
mark use of animal figures and then, from this vantage point,
to review the cast-iron bears who once dispensed soda-water
and the dairy cows, Smokey Bears, "Kool" Penguins, and other
animals who inhabit the mass-media world of today. It might
not be too difficult to show in such a study the degree to which
our lives are affected, through the clans and characteristics of
these various animals, by a covert culture of thought and feeling drawn from the world of zoology.

Finally, isn't it possible that today's vocabulary of criticism,
in almost every region extending from Berenson's "tactile form"
to Eliot's "objective correlative," is incapable of dealing with
the neo-aristocratic situation in which millions of Americans
have the money to fool with colors, make their own movies,
create their own exotic gardens, and do all the other things
that we see people doing around us every day? The artistic

activity of these Americans, as "doers" and as members of audiences, is not carried out upon the model of late nineteenth-century free-professional classes who got their culture in gift books and "Eight-Foot Shelves." It is carried out on the model of the British nobleman of Tudor times translating poetry from the Italian and trying his hand at something similar in English, himself. The truly gifted one among these amateurs is the usual one-out-of-fifty, but where he exists, his free-and-easy attitude makes the professionalization, specialization and machine-merchandising of much modern criticism look pretty grey by comparison.

In the longer run, such people are likely to be important forces in saving American criticism from the doldrums of a period which has taken the parson, the lawyer and the college professor, no matter what hacks they are, as the natural sources of a critical *elite*. A great advantage possessed by the amateurs is that since they don't have to make their living from the conventionally defined arts and criticism, they don't have to repeat mechanically the idea that art is more important than sport or food or any other enjoyment in life, an idea that has become so much an automatic response in American criticism that it sometimes perpetuates the alienations it claims to overcome.

What may be even more important, amateur privilege and privacy afford some shelter from the anti-intellectual, anti-creative pressures that strike with fuller strength, both from loyal vigilantes and from such a national misfortune as the House Committee on Un-American Activities, upon writers, teachers, actors and those of other callings whose work is more fully exposed to such forces. To the degree that the amateurs use this privacy and privilege well, as many do, they encourage the creativity and sustain the morale of their more professional and public fellows.

Honolulu, Hawaii
November, 1963

Acknowledgments

This book draws on an article, "More Trouble in Paradise," in *Fortune*, November, 1946; a memorandum prepared for the Corning Conference by the author and David Riesman (later published in *Creating an Industrial Civilization*, ed. Eugene Staley [Harper & Bros., 1952]); a review, "How Individuals Change Their Opinions," in the *Scientific American*, Vol. CXCII (January, 1955); an article, "The Plainest Plain Clothes Man," in the *New Republic*, January 31, 1956; and an article, "The Astonished Muse," in *Confluence*, Vol. II (1954).

Also on an article, "Football in America," with the collaboration of David Riesman, in the *American Quarterly*, Vol. III (Winter, 1951); an article, about sports in America, in the Italian magazine *Lo Spettacolo*, Anno IV (aprile–giugno, 1954); an article, "Pogo's Polity, Kelly's Genre," in the *Chicago Review*, July, 1954; an article, "Reactors of the Imagination," in the *Bulletin of the Atomic Scientists*, Vol. IX (July, 1953); a review, "The Dark Fantastic," in the *New Republic*, May 3, 1954; and an article, "The Cultural Context of Print in the Communications Revolution," in the *Library Quarterly*, Vol. XXV (October, 1955).

Also on pieces written for the *American Historical Review*, the *American Journal of Sociology*, *Poetry*, *City Lights*, the *Audio Visual Communications Quarterly*, and on notes prepared for lectures at the American Seminar at Salzburg and for lectures at Stephens College.

Also, and crucially, on the encouragement and criticism of David and Evelyn Riesman.

Index